The Moviegoing Experience, 1968–2001

ALSO BY RICHARD W. HAINES

*Technicolor Movies: The History of Dye Transfer Printing*
(McFarland, 1993)

# The Moviegoing Experience, 1968–2001

*by* Richard W. Haines

McFarland & Company, Inc., Publishers
*Jefferson, North Carolina, and London*

**Library of Congress Cataloguing-in-Publication Data**

Haines, Richard W., 1957–
    The moviegoing experience, 1968–2001 / by Richard W. Haines.
        p.    cm.
    Includes bibliographical references and index.

    ISBN 0-7864-1361-1 (softcover : 50# alkaline paper) ∞

    1. Motion pictures.   2. Motion picture theaters.   3. Motion
    pictures—Distribution.   4. Cinematography.   I. Title.
    PN1994.H246   2003
    791.43'09'045 — dc21                                    2002154978

British Library cataloguing data are available

Cover image: 2003 Digital Vision

Manufactured in the United States of America

*McFarland & Company, Inc., Publishers
    Box 611, Jefferson, North Carolina 28640
    www.mcfarlandpub.com*

This book is dedicated to Mary Beth Haines
and to my parents, who have shared my cinema
obsession for the last twenty-four years

# Acknowledgments

This book would not have been possible without the assistance of the following individuals:

Frank Angel, John Belton, Robert Bratcher, Jeff Brodrick and the Jerry Lewis website, Tom Cooper, Mitchell Cope, Tom Dugan, Mitchell Dvoskin, Fred Georges, Matt Gibbons, Richard Goldberg, Dave Harris, Robert A. Harris of The Film Preserve, Martin Hart of the Widescreen Museum website, Jeff Joseph of Sabucat Productions, Ed Jurich, Stephen LaMarca of the Bardavon, Terry Levine of Aquarius, Inc., Jim Markovic of Rainbow, Inc., Ross Melnick of the Cinema Treasures website, John Pommon, Aaron Sisemore, James Vernon. I'd also like to thank the following research assistants: Mary Beth Haines, Mitchell Dvoskin and Laura Gardner. A special thanks to Eric Levin for his editorial advice.

# Contents

# Preface

This book is the result of many years of research as well as firsthand experiences as a director. As a film buff, I felt that I had outgrown the type of movies being made. I also observed changes in the *moviegoing experience* in theaters over the decades. Simultaneously, new video formats and transmission systems improved home theatres.

Movies as an art form were in transition. The transformation in content, demographics, theatre design, projection systems, cinematography and release print technology since 1968 has had a tremendous impact on motion pictures. Digital cinema may re-define the very nature of the medium. This book will give a historical and analytical timeline of what happened to cinema over the last third of a century.

Richard W. Haines
*Fall 2002*

# Introduction

The experience of "going to the movies" equaled, and often surpassed, what was seen on screen. The theatre was central to the experience and, therefore, to the memory — which is, in fact, what movies were selling.[1]

The lights dimmed at the Beach Cinema in Peekskill, New York, in 1968. It was a first run house which opened in 1967, the latest edition of Ron Lesser Enterprise's family theatres in Westchester. The cinema contained a large 40 foot wide screen with curtains, a six hundred seat capacity and 70mm projection which was unusual for the area. Ticket prices were $1.25 for adults with a discount for children under 12. To encourage patronage, Lesser offered free coffee in the lobby. The seats were comfortable and aisles clean since the staff swept the floors between performances.

After the overture, the curtains opened on the MGM logo and *2001: A Space Odyssey* began. The 70mm copy was struck directly off the camera negative. Print quality was spectacular with razor sharp cinematography, vivid colors and impressive stereophonic sound which encompassed the auditorium. Kubrick's compositions of the wide 2.21 × 1 frame utilized the entire image area for dramatic effect. The reel to reel projection and screen luminance were topnotch. I sat a few rows away from the screen, which generated the illusion of peripheral vision.

While this 70mm venue was unique, competing cinemas and drive-ins ("ozoners") featured quality 35mm presentations with mono sound. All of the indoor theatres had large screens with curtains. The average size was approximately 35 feet wide in the smaller cinemas and a high end of 80 foot wide for the largest theaters. Ozoners offered a real bargain for families with subsequent run ("sub-run") double-bills with children under 12 admitted for free. Although I was only eleven years old when I attended the above screening, this "moviegoing experience" remains vivid in my memory as do other presentations throughout the sixties and early seventies.

Thirty-two years later, I attended a multiplex screening of *Space Cowboys* in upstate New York. This presentation was memorable too but for different reasons. The theatre had a typical 'bowling alley' architectural design with a small 20 foot wide screen masked off at the top for the 2.35 × 1 ratio without curtains.

As you entered the place, you noticed popcorn and other garbage cluttering the aisles. On screen were slides showing advertisements for local businesses. The lights dimmed slightly and the coming attraction trailers appeared on screen, out of focus. The slides played simultaneously. I complained to the manager but she told me insurance regulations didn't allow them to darken the theatre until the feature began. I had to return to the lobby again to remind her about the focus. This took some time since the operator had turned on the "platter" system and left the booth. He was one of the staff, not a qualified projectionist. Eventually, the slide projector was turned off and the lens focused.

After the four grainy trailers, the film began. It was in Panavision but there was a hot spot in the center of the screen due to a misaligned Xenon lamphouse that was set for the 1.85 "flat" ratio. The release print was murky and the color de-saturated as a result of the lighting design, under-exposed negative and generation loss of the release copy. This was exacerbated by dirt which had accumulated on the print because of the static charge of the estar stock and platter projection system. The stereo sound was not impressive because of the narrow speaker placement. None of this seemed to bother the teenage audience which talked throughout the screening as if they were watching a videotape at home. The movie was mildly entertaining but the presentation wasn't worth the nine dollar ticket price.

The art of cinema and the *moviegoing experience* are dependent on many factors. The screenplay content, acting and direction are integral to your enjoyment of the film. Equally important is the cinematography, release print quality, projection, screen size, theatre design and management. A chain is only as strong as its weakest link and beginning in 1968, they began to come apart.

# 1. Cinema in the Sixties

When film historians discuss significant years in the development of the motion picture industry, they usually cite the following: In 1927, *The Jazz Singer* was released in Vitaphone. The success of this picture and other early talkies made silent films obsolete. In 1935, the first three strip Technicolor film, *Becky Sharp*, was released. The process gained in popularity and by the mid-fifties color had replaced black and white for most productions. In 1948 the government issued a consent decree which separated distribution from exhibition which ultimately unraveled the studio system. In 1952, the television competition caused theatre attendance to decline. The industry responded by introducing new technology beginning with Cinerama and 3-D. In terms of economic and cultural impact, the year 1968 was equally significant, which is the subject of this book. Before discussing the changes that occurred in that year, let's look at the state of the art as it existed at the time.

## The State of the Art, January 1, 1967–October 31, 1968

By 1968, cinema was regarded as a unique art form as well as entertainment by audiences and critics. Even the Supreme Court acknowledged this after a controversial film was brought before it in the previous decade. The year 1951's *The Miracle* obscenity case inspired them to reverse a previous decision of 1919 which declared movies "a business, pure and simple." The ruling protected cinema as free speech within the boundaries of state laws regarding obscenity. Andrew Sarris' *The American Cinema* was published in 1968 which made his *auteur* theory popular among aspiring filmmakers who desired to be the "author" of their movies. For general audiences, the delicate balance between art and entertainment made going to the movies fascinating.

## Content

There were 477 feature films released during this time period. Of those, 446 were for general audiences and 31 were advertised as "recommended for adults." Most mainstream theatres would not play a motion picture unless it contained a Production Code Seal. The Code had become lenient by 1967 and most subject matters were allowed providing the producers handled controversial themes in good taste and adult movies be labeled as such. Among the notable features in this category were *Bonnie and Clyde, The Boston Strangler, The Detective* and *In the Heat of the Night.* Some independent distributors released product without a Seal or warning and booked them in urban theatres and drive-ins. Continental's *Night of the Living Dead* was an example. Since there was no enforcement mechanism in place, children often attended these films. The trend of adult content was not new. In the earlier part of the decade, a number of pictures had pushed the envelope including Stanley Kubrick's *Lolita* (1962) and Mike Nichols' *Who's Afraid of Virginia Woolf?* (1966). After some minor alterations they were given a Seal. Lolita's age was increased and the term "screw you" was changed to "damn you" in the Nichols film.

However, aside from the above films, most movies remained in the general audience category. This made good economic sense. While adult patronage might increase with controversial subjects, most exhibitors couldn't afford to restrict children from too many releases. Movies were big business and the same formula applied to them as it did to other products. The biggest profits were made by appealing to the broadest demographic range. This is not to suggest that general audience pictures couldn't have a perspective or edge but most avoided anything too graphic. Through 1968, the top grossing films were *The Sound of Music, Gone with the Wind, The Ten Commandments, Ben-Hur, Doctor Zhivago, Mary Poppins* and *My Fair Lady.* Among the popular releases of the period were *The Dirty Dozen, The Flim Flam Man, Hombre, How to Succeed in Business Without Really Trying, Jungle Book, The Lion in Winter, The Odd Couple, Planet of the Apes, You Only Live Twice* and *2001: A Space Odyssey.*

## Industry

The sixties was an era of mergers. Many of the production heads had died (Louis B. Meyer, Harry Cohn, Walt Disney) or retired (Samuel Goldwyn). Jack Warner sold out his controlling interest of Warner Brothers to Seven Arts. He remained the head of production but was no longer the

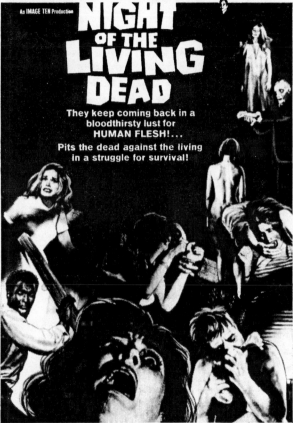

4 COLS. x 175 LINES..........700 LINES        **MAT 401**

1 SHEET

*Night of the Living Dead* (1968) was an independent film release without a Production Code Seal.

president. UA became a subsidiary of Transamerica and Paramount of Gulf and Western. The days of the movie moguls was over and directors were gaining a greater degree of creative freedom. Studios no longer represented the world view of their presidents as they had in the past under Meyer and Disney. The once mighty MGM was slowly dismantling and the quality of features coming out of Buena Vista lacked the imagination and charm they had while Disney was alive.

Theatre attendance continued its slow decline that began in the fifties. The moviegoing habit was no longer guaranteed and television competition increased as color broadcasts were standardized in 1966. NBC's peacock in "Living Color" became a symbol of the transition. My earliest memory of the new format was when Dick Van Dyke was hired to introduce *The Wizard of Oz* and inform viewers that the opening was in black and white and not to adjust their sets.

Another trend was studio involvement in television production. Universal began making two hour "movie of the week" specials for network airings and released them overseas in the theatrical market. Simultaneously, CBS and ABC set up subsidiary companies to produce motion pictures for cinemas. Theatre owners continued to campaign against cable television which they felt threatened their survival. Exhibitors suffered a setback when the Federal Communications Commission issued an ordered which authorized some "Pay TV."

## Exhibition

According to the 1968 *Film Daily Yearbook*[1] there were an estimated 13,600 indoor cinemas in the United States and 4,975 drive-ins. There were approximately 550 first run theatres in 95 cities with a population over 100,000. These were large screen cinemas that played new films prior to smaller houses which booked them sub-run. The average ticket price for adults was $1.30 with a discount for minors. Many drive-ins admitted children under 12 for free since a third of their income was derived from concessions. While ticket prices had increased from 1967 through 1968 by 11 cents, movies were still affordable entertainment for middle-class viewers. Screen sizes averaged between 30–40 foot wide for suburban cinemas and considerably larger for urban theatres, movie palaces and drive-ins. The biggest was the Indian Hills Theater in Omaha, Nebraska. It was a Cinerama house with a 105 foot wide deeply curved screen. New theatre construction began in the suburbs as companies made large screen single houses to patronize families.

Drive-in construction continued in the late sixties although at a slower rate than the previous decade. Ozoners represented approximately 25 percent of the U.S. theatres. Although they played sub-run double-bills, the screen towers were enormous and the atmosphere had a charm of its own. All included cartoons and animated intermission clocks as added attractions. As with indoor cinemas, families were the primary customers along with older teens on dates.

Most of the large cities had a few Roadshow houses among their first run cinemas which had screens that were above average in size. Some had a reserve seat ticket policy. While the admission price was more expensive, the quality of the presentation was worth the extra cost. As *Film Daily* reporter, James Morris, described them, "The roadshow theatre employs the biggest screen possible with the finest sound system available. It may enhance it's screen image through the use of wide-gauge Todd-AO film.... Overall, the equipment of the roadshow theatre and the behavior of its per-

**RADIO CITY MUSIC HALL**

SHOWPLACE OF THE NATION
IN THE HEART OF ROCKEFELLER CENTER

•

An institution known throughout the world for its presentation of outstanding motion pictures and stage shows notable for their fine quality, breathtaking beauty and perfection of execution.

*Radio City Music Hall* was one of the movie palaces of the sixties that exhibited mainstream films on enormous screens.

sonnel are expected to create an atmosphere that combines the dignity of the legitimate theatre with the spectacular impact and streamlined comfort now possible with the best modern theatre equipment."[2]

For example, New York's Rivoli had a huge Dimension 150 screen. The Cinerama also had a deeply curved one and both theaters offered state of the art 70mm which made viewers feel as if they were part of the action. The fifties and sixties Roadshow houses differed in design from surviving movie palaces. Rather than screen immersion as the goal, the surrounding architecture became part of the show. Atmospherics like Chicago's 850 seat Music Box Theater had moving clouds and twinkling stars on the ceiling. New York's Radio City Music Hall's ornate lobby was as spectacular as their cavernous theater. On the West Coast was Mann's Chinese Theater and The Egyptian which had unusual facades that enhanced their appeal. Both types of large screen cinemas offered unique moviegoing experiences. Among the Roadshow pictures of 1967–1968 exhibited in them were *Oliver, Camelot, Ice Station Zebra* and *2001: Space Odyssey* which were presented in 70mm. All Roadshow releases were made for general audiences.

Distributors and exhibitors utilized showmanship in their presentations. Aside from one sheet posters, there were banners, standees and stills to decorate the lobby. Store owners would display window cards advertising the film in return for free passes. Pressbooks were given to exhibitors with suggestions to promote the film like contests and newspaper articles. A typical promotional gimmick was created for the reissue of *Around the World in 80 Days* in 1968. Mike Todd Jr. held a press junket at his bank. A 70mm print was removed from the vault and brought to the theatre for the screening. He claimed that the print had been locked up since 1956 for safety and was being rereleased by special permission. This was obviously a stunt since an original print would have faded by then and the film was revised for reissue. These type of "carny" gimmicks made going to the movies more enjoyable.

Movie palaces and large screen cinemas were labor intensive. They had large staffs which included the manager, assistant manager, cashiers, ushers, security men and concession sellers. All of them worked under close supervision and were instructed to make each screening an event for patrons. Most theatres used the reel to reel projection method which required a qualified projectionist to operate the machines. Illumination was the carbon arc lamphouse which had been used since the silent days. It generated a bright screen image of 16 foot lamberts as required by the Society of Motion Picture and Television Engineers (SMPTE). Drive-ins used a special carbon unit to compensate for their screen size and distance. The 70mm projection systems used by Roadshow theatres offered spectacular image quality with directional stereophonic sound. Poor exhibition was rare and if problems arose the projectionist would have to answer to his union.

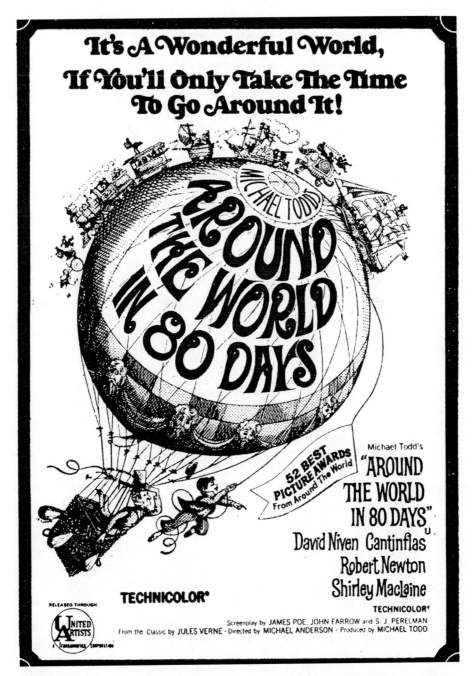

Ballyhoo continued to be used to promote films like *Around the World in 80 Days* (reissued in 1968).

## *Distribution*

Most films in the sixties were exhibited regionally which helped amortize distribution costs. The movie would open in either New York or Los Angeles and play those cities before being released in other major markets. Part of the revenue from New York could pay for advertising costs in Chicago and so on. Approximately 400 prints were made for "A" titles and 100 prints for "B" films. These prints would be sent to an exchange between engagements which inspected and repaired them before the next date. There were 330 exchanges in the US which included those of major companies like MGM (31) and smaller distributors like National General (14). The exchanges also supplied trailers, posters, pressbooks and publicity materials to the theatres. One of the largest was National Screen Service. Older prints were kept in storage for double bills, drive-ins, art houses and repertory cinemas so there was a huge selection of titles to book depending on the situation.

There was often a delay of six months from 70mm Roadshow presentations to general release in 35mm which enabled the larger theatres to retain an exclusive reserve seat "hard ticket" policy. There was also a window of a year or more before a first run feature would be sold for network broadcast, censored with commercial interruptions. Epic pictures like *Ben-Hur*, *Spartacus* and *My Fair Lady* were rereleased years after their first presentation and prior to the television premiere. The Disney company withheld their animated classics from TV and revived them in seven year cycles. The Bond films were reissued in double-bills throughout the era. Because of the television window and network cuts, it made sense to catch these movies in theatres.

The release pattern was to book the big titles "first run" in the largest theatres which had the greatest box-office potential. The terms varied but often incorporated a guarantee vs. a profit split between distributor and exhibitor depending on the location and theatre size. Some Roadshow houses were "four-walled" which meant that the distributor rented the theater from the exhibitor, covered its nut (operating expenses) and kept the revenue from the ticket sales.

Smaller theatres and suburban houses got the pictures on a "sub-run" basis at a later date. They had better terms and utilized the publicity generated by the first run bookings. Advertising and promotion costs were negotiable between theatre and distributor. In co-op deals, the exhibitor and distributor split the bill and profit sharing was pro-rated accordingly. After the film played out, the surviving prints were booked in double-bills, drive-ins or grind-houses which were rundown theaters in urban neighborhoods. These "clearance" dates were usually flat rentals. Prints were often in circulation for a year before being sent back to the exchange for storage and future bookings.

## Cinematography and Release Prints

Print quality remained excellent through 1968. Many copies were made directly off the camera negatives regardless of format (i.e. Technicolor, Eastmancolor, 70mm, B&W). This ensured a high resolution, fine grain image for most theatres including second run houses and drive-ins. Release prints were made in advance and sat in the exchange or lab until the opening. This enabled distributors to inspect them and correct any lab mistakes. Cinematography retained the standards of previous eras which featured saturated flesh-tones, vivid color, sharp depth of field and fine grain. Even exploitation films from AIP simulated this look within the limitations of their budget. Roger Corman's Poe adaptations all had good Panavision camerawork despite their meager production cost. Hollywood big budget features had superb photography necessary for large screen presentations. Freddie Young's camerawork on *Doctor Zhivago* (1965) and *You Only Live Twice* (1967) was typical of the quality of the era. Ted Moore's slick photography of the Bond films and the vibrant Technicolor of *The Graduate* and *The Good, the Bad and the Ugly* were notable examples.

There were exceptions, of course. Oswald Morris's photography of the Oscar winning *Oliver* (1968) intentionally diffused the lighting and desaturated the color to suggest the griminess of the London slum. *In Cold Blood* was shot in B&W by Conrad Hall in a documentary style on the actual locations of the crime. Burnett Guffey's photography on *Bonnie and Clyde* used a warm color design to simulate a period feel with some diffused sequences for effect. These photographic experiments, while stylish, were not considered appropriate for other subject matters which adhered to the classic "studio" look.

To summarize, despite storm clouds on the horizon of dwindling attendance, color broadcasts and cable television, the state of the art in 1968 was excellent. Exhibition was universally good with some Roadshow presentations of big budget spectaculars. Cinematography was standardized in terms of quality with a few notable experiments that broke the rules. The majority of studio features were made for general audiences with a limited number of titles recommended for adults. The balance and diversity of product kept both large and small cinemas in business and motion pictures a mainstream entertainment medium. For select audiences that liked risqué foreign product or exploitation there were alternate venues like Art theatres and urban grind-houses. Both played pictures that did not contain the Production Code Seal. All of this was to change in November of 1968.

# 2. Demise of the Production Code

Striving to balance freedom and control, Breen veered more toward the latter than the former ... he helped secure a reasonably uniform product for conservative American exhibitors, and he hindered the quick-buck producers and bandwagon jumpers whose pictures could whet the censor's knives for all releases.[1]

From 1934 through 1968, the motion picture industry operated under a Production Code. As previously mentioned, studio films were required to have a Seal of Approval before they could exhibit their product in large theaters. It was entertainment business standards and practices. While there were some smaller independent houses that booked non–Seal approved pictures (i.e. foreign films, domestic exploitation), most opted to adhere to the code for the reasons detailed below. Before discussing the significance of its demise, I'll give a brief history of Hollywood self-regulation.

## The Production Code Under Will Hays, 1922–1933

After a series of scandals including the Fatty Arbuckle rape trial,[2] William Desmond Taylor murder and the death of Wallace Reid from drug abuse, Hollywood tried to improve its image as the West Coast "Sodom and Gomorrah" by adopting a self-regulatory code. It was initially referred to as "Thirteen Points" or "Thirteen Standards" and implemented in 1922 with Postmaster General Will Hays as head. An ex–Republican national chairman with White House connections, he acted as an agent for the studios to keep local censors and government at bay. In general, producers

were advised restraint when handling controversial plays and subject matter. The code was expanded in 1927 and the restrictions included profanity, nudity, drug use, sexual perversion, venereal disease, white slavery,
scenes of childbirth, childrens' sexual organs, miscegenation and ridicule
of religion, race or nation. Some of it was contradictory, specifically the
ban on interracial sex and ridicule of race. Hays' enforcement tended to
be lenient at first, based on the economic needs of the industry . When
box-office revenue decreased, sex and violence increased to attract adult
customers. It was obvious the "Thirteen Points," were not written in stone.

The danger was that public relations between Hollywood and religious groups were strained. A number of organizations worried that children were seeing inappropriate films. Since the studios owned the movie
palaces their pictures played in, they had to accommodate local restrictions and community standards. Hays mediated these concerns. In 1930,
the guidelines were known as The Production Code. Historians often refer
to movies made in the early thirties as "Pre-Code," which is inaccurate.
They were still subject to restrictions detailed by Hays which were not rig-
orously enforced. Among the controversial productions of 1932–1933 were
Mae West's *Night After Night* and *She Done Him Wrong*, MGM's *Red Dust*,
Sam Goldwyn's *Nana* and RKO's *Of Human Bondage*. These films were
risqué for their era.

## The Production Code
## Under Joseph L. Breen, 1934–1955

After threats of government censorship and local censor cuts, the
Production Code was enforced to a greater degree than in past. In contrast to the "roaring twenties," the thirties was a decade of big government.
During the Depression, industry operated at the discretion of the Fed
which began with The National Recovery Act[3] (NRA) and continued
through Roosevelt's Proclamation of Unlimited National Emergency of
May 27, 1941, and World War II. Meanwhile, religious organizations continued to complain about film content. Eleanor Roosevelt was among those
that threatened federal censorship if Hollywood didn't clean up its product. Hays persuaded them to let Hollywood police itself.

The end result was a new Production Code. Additional restrictions
included vulgarity, obscenity, lewd costume and repellent subjects. The flag
had to be respected along with the sanctity of marriage. Adultery and
scenes of passion had to be discreet and crime and violence could not show
sympathy to the criminal. This still permitted a broad range of subject

matters. In December of 1933, Hays conferred to his associate, Joseph L. Breen, the powers over motion picture content. It was a position he would hold through 1954 despite a brief absence in 1953. His staff included Geoffrey Shurlock, who later succeeded him. Breen's job was to moderate the concerns of the Catholic Legion of Decency and other religious organizations with the creative factions of the business. While he often fought it out with producers, Breen was considered an insider serving the best interests of the industry.

There were pragmatic issues he dealt with. As previously mentioned, a limited number of prints were made on each feature and booked regionally throughout the country. Prior to 1934, they were subject to local censor cuts. This practice dated back to the silent era. As author Eric Schaefer notes, "By 1920, existing state and municipal censorship bodies could ravage prints of movies with demands for cuts, which seldom coincided from area to area, or they could reject films completely."[4] Breen persuaded the state censor boards to comply with the rulings of his office which meant that the same copies could be shown throughout the country. While local censors still occasionally deleted footage, most prints played intact. This standardization of product was necessary for the distribution system of the time. General audiences were required to fill the seats of the large screen cinemas and movie palaces. Restricting children due to content would've put them out of business.

Many historians have objected to the barriers imposed on writers and directors in the thirties and forties. A closer examination reveals they had a degree of creative freedom within the system. Content was negotiable depending on budget and clout. David O. Selznick had to argue his case about using the word "damn" in *Gone with the Wind* but the Hays office allowed him to include prostitution, sexual innuendo and some graphic on-screen violence including a gunshot wound to the face. Selznick's prestige and the popularity of the novel persuaded them to accommodate the producer.

In 1941, Hays retired, leaving Breen in charge although it was still referred to as the Hays Office. He continued the principles set down by his predecessor and allowed adult stories to be filmed providing they stayed within the bounds of what was accepted as good taste. While toned down, *Kings Row* and *The Postman Always Rings Twice* were still effective adaptations of the novels they were based on with the latter a steamy "film noir" for its time. Preston Sturges' sex farce, *The Miracle of Morgan's Creek*, used double-entendres to amuse adults. The Code forced screenwriters and directors to be disciplined when handling sensitive material and creative in circumventing restrictions. Considering the fact that 57 of the

American Film Institute's list of America's 100 Greatest Movies were made within Production Code guidelines suggests it couldn't have been as onerous as its opponents claimed. Many of my favorite movies were made within the 1934–1955 era.

Of course there were some producers who wouldn't cooperate. Howard Hughes ignored Breen when he made *The Outlaw* in 1941. Although he submitted the script to the board, he shot it without their input. Hughes booked the film in independent theaters without a Seal. The picture was amusing as camp but did not serve the interests of those who wanted to reform the Code since the eccentric millionaire made it solely to titillate audiences. Breen worried that giving Hughes a Seal would inspire a glut of exploitative sex that would bring on the wrath of local censors or government.

Other exemptions from Code restrictions were foreign films booked in Art houses. Breen denied a Seal for *The Bicycle Thief* when the distributor refused to trim two scenes which depicted a boy urinating and a brothel sequence. It was released uncut and won a special Oscar in 1947. Overseas product often played uncensored in these venues but profit was limited outside of the large theater chains.

A trend of the late forties and early fifties was a series of "message" movies like *Gentlemen's Agreement* (1947), *Crossfire* (1947), *Pinky* (1949) and *Storm Warning* (1951). While the filmmaker's intentions were good, these stories over-simplified the problems they addressed. Their approach was rarely subtle and entertainment value limited. These were the type of pictures that ran into problems with Breen and associates who objected to stories with overt propaganda. The exception was war time productions where the government requested this type of picture be made to rally public support for the cause.

The majority of releases did not contain censurable material. Classics like *Babes in Toyland, David Copperfield, The Prisoner of Zenda, A Night at the Opera, Snow White and the Seven Dwarfs, The Wizard of Oz, Pinocchio, Fantasia, Miracle on 34th Street* and *Abbott and Costello Meet Frankenstein* were popular entertainment and works of art. Code restrictions had little bearing on their subject matter. A movie did not have to be controversial to be worthy nor should cinematic quality be defined in those terms. Films with political or social content dated rapidly as attitudes changed and artistry took a secondary position to the message. They did not hold up as well as dramas and comedies that depicted the foibles of human nature or thrillers, mysteries and musicals of the era. The MGM logo summarized the studio system's ideal, "Ars Gratia Artis" or "Art for Art's Sake."

# The Production Code and the Blacklist, 1948–1959

> The subversive apparatus of the Soviet Union grew exponentially in the postwar period, as Stalin ordered the creation of a huge web of international front organizations[5]

> Communists infiltrated trade unions, slipped jabs at capitalism into scripts and schooled young screenwriters on how to inject pro–Soviet doctrine into scenes[6]

The postwar era was "Pax Americana" for most citizens. There was tremendous upward mobility and most in the middle class believed a degree of conformity was necessary for economic stability and a civil society. The country put the Depression behind them and moved forward. Unfortunately, poverty remained a lingering problem as did discrimination, although racism was not confined to the white European majority. Politically, the pendulum swung to the right which caused a clash between conservative and leftist factions in society.

During World War II, the Communist Party of the USA (CPUSA) cooperated with American industry until the Nazis were defeated. The exception was the brief period of the Hitler/Stalin pact when they considered the German Chancellor a strategic ally. After the war, this popular front collapsed. The CPUSA commenced labor agitation, espionage and in some cases treason.

Many idealists adopted communism in the early days of the Depression because they believed our system had failed. In the mid-thirties, the New Deal safety net, social security and other market reforms took the edge off of free market capitalism. The postwar economic boom made most people drift away from socialism. Simultaneously, information leaked out from various sources that Russia was not the worker's utopia Party members claimed but a totalitarian disaster. Humorists noted that the only difference between Hitler and Stalin was the size of their mustache. Unfortunately, this had no impact on Marxist ideologues. American communists continued to pose as progressives who championed the noble causes of racial equality and improved working conditions. Behind the scenes they worked for Stalin who exploited the disenfranchised and acted as spoilers in unions and civil rights organizations. Some liberals were unable to distinguish their rhetoric from reality. Others saw through the facade and formed a coalition with conservatives to combat their influence.

In 1938 Congress formed a committee to investigate fascist, extremist and other subversive groups in the U.S. which was known as "The House Un–American Activities Committee" or HUAC. It was run by Texas representative Martin Dies. Prior to the war, HUAC uncovered Nazi front groups. It expanded its investigation to communists afterwards. It was a bipartisan effort until Wisconsin Senator Joseph McCarthy demagoged the issue for his own political gain and undermined the proceedings. McCarthy was a despicable politician but the hysteria he created about the "Red menace" was not without foundation.

Many contemporary film journalists have framed the HUAC hearings as a first amendment issue. In *Naming Names,* author Victor S. Navasky wrote, "it remains true that the Communists in Hollywood (actually most of them were ex–Communists by the time of the mass naming of names in 1951) and the entertainment industry in general posed the smallest threat to the security of the Republic."[7] The motion picture industry has rewritten its past into the over-simplified depiction of Communists as "good guys" and anti–Communists as "bad guys." In this scenario, Moscow hard-liners like Paul Robeson were heroes and conservatives like Walt Disney villains. Elia Kazan and others who testified against Party members were categorized as informers. What actually occurred from 1947–1959 was more complicated.

According to Kenneth Lloyd Billingsley's recent book, *Hollywood Party* and other sources, CPUSA members burrowed into trade unions and guilds and instigated a never-ending series of strikes accompanied by intimidation and violence while the studio system was dismantling. Attendance was down due to the usurping television medium and the government forced Paramount, MGM and others to sell their theater chains. Party members saw it as an opportunity to try and dominate the industry. There is documentation that communist agitators were behind a vicious strike outside the Warner's lot in October of 1945. Cars were overturned and people were beaten. James Balash, an employee at the studio, was hit with brass knuckles and his jaw broken. Several people from an alternate union had their houses firebombed. During a rally at MGM, strikers torched a car. Similar rioting occurred at Technicolor in September of 1946. Any damage to the negatives stored there would've been an archival catastrophe. These CPUSA-orchestrated incidents did not fall within the boundaries of protected free speech or political discourse.

The Soviets controlled a series of fronts like the Conference of Studio Unions (CSU) which was run by Herb Sorrell, whose Party cell name was "Herb Stuart." In some cases they did extract concessions from management, often with strong-arm tactics. A wartime front was *The Hollywood Anti-Nazi League* which disclosed Hitler's atrocities but covered up Stalin's crimes and anti–Semitism. For example, as part of the Hitler-Stalin pact, the dictator turned over Jews that had escaped into Moscow to the Gestapo. Many of the people involved in these organizations were unaware of who was pulling the strings. Stalin referred to these well intentioned liberals as "useful idiots" and they were generally known as "dupes." Writer Jack Moffit testified that the Screen Writer's Guild was heavily infiltrated and Party member John Howard Lawson advised him to incorporate five minutes of Marxist doctrine into every script. Non-communist screenwriters were ostracized and found it difficult to get work. The CSU also discriminated against those who didn't support their agenda.

A number of conservatives created the Motion Picture Alliance for the Preservation of American Ideals (MPA) in response. Members included writers Morrie Ryskind, Robert Hughes and Jim McGuinness. Among the stars were John Wayne and Clark Gable. The spokeswoman was objectivist philosopher Ayn Rand, who championed individual rights and liberty over collectivism. There were also labor leaders who opposed the Party like International Alliance of Theatrical Stage Employees (IA), Roy Brewer and Screen Actors Guild (SAG) president, Ronald Reagan. Both were New Deal Democrats who believed the CPUSA undermined management/labor relations. A magazine called *Counterattack* published "Red Channels" which listed Party members and front groups. The CPUSA used their papers, *Studio Voice* and *The Screen Writer* to discredit anti–Communists and spread Russian "dezinformatsiya" (misinformation).

By the mid-forties, Hollywood had divided into two hostile camps, pro–Communist and anti–Communist. Everyone else was caught in the middle. The infighting caused HUAC to investigate the film industry in 1947 and 1951. Joseph McCarthy was not in charge of these investigations nor was he a public figure during the first round. The committee chairman in 1947 was New Jersey Republican, J. Parnell Thomas. The 1951 hearings were run by Georgia Democrat, John S. Wood. While their tactics were unethical, opponents on the Left behaved no better. The emphasis was on screenplay content rather than labor violence which was a misguided choice. Some of the movies listed as pro–Soviet were made while they were our allies (e.g. *Mission to Moscow, Song of Russia*, 1943). In both cases, the government requested these pictures be produced as part of the war effort. It enabled the communists to claim First Amendment violation which they used as propaganda fodder for the media.

"Friendly witnesses" who testified against communist party infiltration included Louis B. Meyer and Jack Warner who represented the studio heads, actor Adolph Menjou and writer Ayn Rand who was the only one who had first hand experience of living under socialism since she was born in Russia. The hearings were a sham and became a circus when everyone used them as a forum to make speeches. The end result was a motion picture and television blacklist of real and alleged subversives.

The most controversial figures of the time were Alvah Bessie, Herbert Biberman, Lester Cole, Edward Dmytryk, Ring Lardner Jr., John Howard Lawson, Albert Maltz, Samuel Ornitz, Dalton Trumbo and Adrian Scott known collectively as "The Hollywood Ten." Other than one director, Dmytryk, all were screenwriters. They refused to answer questions about their CPUSA affiliations or activities when questioned by House investigators and were sent to jail for contempt of Congress. They attempted to make a constitutional issue out of it but the fact remained, all ten were communists with an agenda.

While the moguls knowingly hired Reds in the thirties, the Production Code, Seal of Approval and studio system kept them in line. They probably did not take the hypocritical rhetoric espoused by wealthy Marxists like Dalton Trumbo seriously. As the system began to unravel, they lost control of them. Trumbo advocated using "art as a weapon" while others organized crippling strikes and riots. They misrepresented their intentions to defenders like Humphrey Bogart and Edward G. Robinson who later withdrew their support. Both told the press they had been duped by them. Actress Francis Farmer visited Russia and disclosed actual conditions upon her return. The CPUSA hounded and harassed her and was partly responsible for her mental breakdown.

It's important to place the investigations within the context of their times. America was at war, even though it was a cold one. The outcome was uncertain and many on the Left wanted Stalin to prevail. Prior the hearings, Winston Churchill gave his famous "Iron Curtain" speech in 1946. In 1948 the Berlin crisis and Alger Hiss case hit the news. In 1949, China fell to Mao and the Russians detonated their first nuclear bomb which they acquired from domestic espionage. In 1950 the Korean war broke out and the Cold War turned hot. In 1951 the Rosenbergs went on trial for treason. Opponents referred to it as a "Red scare" and "witch hunt" but recent declassified documents and decoded Venona cables prove conclusively there were communist agents in our government and industry. Hiss, the Rosenbergs, Sorrell, The Hollywood Ten and other Party members were working on behalf of the Soviets. This is not a defense of HUAC procedures but an acknowledgment that the problem was real and had to be addressed.

The actual blacklisting of communists began under President Truman when he instituted his loyalty oath for government employees following the Alger Hiss case. Republicans and most Democrats supported this action as well as his containment policy to prevent Soviet expansion and Marshall Plan to rebuild Europe in the Western mold. Obviously, the CPUSA opposed this agenda. Neither the studio heads nor public at large were inclined to associate with those who espoused the Party line. While one can empathize with idealists of the thirties, many Leftists in the postwar era were Stalinists who posed a threat to those who hired them. Actors like Paul Robeson became Kremlin apologists which rendered them unemployable. Breen and the Production Code board did not want the medium to become a political forum for activists like Dalton Trumbo. The studios also lost a great deal of money due to production and laboratory delays during the CPUSA-backed labor disputes of 1946. The moguls were very lenient about ideology and trendy causes but drew the line at those who interfered with the production and distribution system.

Edward Dmytryck, disillusioned with his comrades, switched alliances and became a friendly witness. He stated publicly that Hollywood communists took their orders directly or indirectly from the Comintern[8] (Communist International) in Moscow. For example, they told their handlers to accuse anyone who disagreed with them of being fascists and anti–Semites. This strategy was used by many Party members. It was ludicrous considering the fact that anti–Communists like Clark Gable and James Stewart served in the armed forces during the war and conservative moguls like Meyer and Warner were Jewish. Ex–Party member Elia Kazan also testified against them. His film, *On the Waterfront* (1954), depicted the moral dilemma with the corrupt longshoreman's union standing in symbolically for the CPUSA.

From a legal standpoint, the studios were not obligated to hire communists if they felt there was a conflict of interest. Most contracts had a morals clause which The Hollywood Ten violated when they went to prison. While film producers used the labor unrest as rationale for firing Party members, there was less justification for blacklisting ex-communists and sympathizers especially if they were no longer serving the regime. Actors Larry Parks and John Garfield could be considered legitimate victims of this. Unfortunately, HUAC and the moguls made no distinction between the two groups and lost some of their moral foundation and legitimacy. Non-communist liberals and union advocates were implicated when the CPUSA entangled them in their web while committee chairman Parnel Thomas was indicted for corruption and went to jail.

Three hundred twenty-four production personnel were blacklisted out of an industry total of approximately 17,500 which was less than 2 percent. Most had Communist Party affiliations but they did not all represent a financial risk to their employers. According to Scott McConnell of the Ayn Rand Archives, friendly witnesses like screenwriters Jack Moffitt, Morrie Ryskind, Fred Niblo Jr. and Albert Mannheimer also found it difficult to get work after testifying which proved there were still fellow travelers working against them behind the scenes. Adolphe Menjou lost work when Party members spread false rumors about him being a fascist. Before and after the investigations, the Left was involved in blacklisting too.

If the studios painted too broad a stroke in identifying the Red menace then the CPUSA's violence and fanatic devotion to a brutal dictator hurt the progressive cause. Both sides engaged in discrimination against their ideological opponents. The practice of blacklisting people through guilt by association should be condemned but actual Party members do not deserve the accolades given them by revisionist historians. The studios had little choice but to remove them from their rank and file or suffer major financial loss. The conservatives won this round of the culture war but their victory was reversed in the late sixties. The political stakes at the time were complex and both sides behaved poorly.

The blacklist had an impact on the Production Code throughout the fifties. There were a handful of anti–Communist movies like *My Son John* (1952) and *Pickup on South Street* (1953). Like other propaganda films, most were badly made with the exception of *Silk Stockings* (1957), a musical remake of *Ninotchka* (1939). The studios probably made them to take the heat off the industry.

In 1953, a group of blacklisted communists formed a company called Independent Production Corporation (IPC) to make a feature entitled *Salt of the Earth*. It was directed by Herbert Biberman, produced by Paul Jarrico and written by Michael Wilson. A number of unions boycotted the film including the UAW and IATSE. As a result, few theaters were willing to book the movie and it bombed. If organized labor wanted to derail Biberman, a boycott was unnecessary.

The box-office hits that year were *This Is Cinerama*, *House of Wax* in 3-D and *The Robe* in CinemaScope. Few viewers would've been interested in IPC's Marxist polemics. Charlie Chaplin also made a controversial picture in 1957 entitled, *A King in New York*. The screenplay was a poorly written satire of American culture and HUAC. Chaplin's real-life son played a young revolutionary who shouted Party slogans in the film. It was not given a U.S. theatrical release until 1973. 23 blacklisted communists took their case to the Supreme Court which responded as follows: "The writ is dismissed improvidently granted because the original judgment was on adequate state grounds."

Detailed below is a list of anti–Communist movies made between 1948 and 1959 along with Cold War dramas that were open to multiple interpretations.

## Anti-Communist Features

Behind the Iron Curtain (Canadian) 1948
Sofia 1948
Bells of Coronado 1949
Conspirator 1949
Guilty of Treason 1949
I Married a Communist 1949
The Red Danube 1949
The Red Menace 1949
Walk a Crooked Mile 1949
The Flying Saucer 1950
I Was a Communist for the FBI 1951
The Whip Hand 1951
Arctic Flight 1952
Assignment-Paris 1952
Atomic City 1952
Big Jim McLain 1952
Diplomatic Courier 1952

Invasion U.S.A. 1952
Red Planet Mars 1952
Red Snow 1952
The Steel Fist 1952
The Thief 1952
Walk East on Beacon Street 1952
My Son John 1953
Man on a Tightrope 1953
Never Let Me Go 1953
Runaway Daughter 1953
Savage Drums 1953
Savage Mutiny 1953
Prisoner of War 1954
Trial 1957
The Commies Are Coming 1957
Jet Pilot 1957
Silk Stockings 1957

## Cold War Dramas

High Noon 1952
Invaders from Mars 1953
Hell and High Water 1954
Night People 1954
On the Waterfront 1954

Invasion of the Body Snatchers 1956
Time Limit 1957
North by Northwest 1959
On the Beach 1959

Other than these pictures, most directors avoided overt political content and messages, although a few producers like Stanley Kramer incorporated them into his films. The de-politicization of cinema combined with the television competition forced them to refocus their attention on spectacular new technology to improve declining attendance. It resulted in a decade of showmanship unrivaled in the history of the medium. In quick succession, audiences were treated to Cinerama, 3-D, CinemaScope, VistaVision, Todd-AO, Technirama and MGM Camera 65. Appropriately, "Cinerama" was an anagram for "American." The climax of *This Is Cinerama* was a tour of the U.S. with patriotic narration by Lowell Thomas.

Some blacklisted writers continued to work under fronts or aliases. Dalton Trumbo wrote the screenplays for *Roman Holiday* (1953) and *The Brothers Rico* (1957) while Carl Forman and Michael Wilson co-authored the script for *The Bridge on the River Kwai* (1957) using these devices. All three writers were talented but seemed to be more successful within restrictions that prevented them from using it to promote their political agenda. After 1960, these restrictions were incrementally abandoned.

Regardless of where one stands on this thorny subject, the exclusion of prominent Leftists did not result in a decline in quality. The moviegoing experience reached its zenith from 1951–1959. Among the notable titles made during the blacklist era were John Ford's *The Quiet Man* (1952) and *The Searchers* (1956); Alfred Hitchcock's *Strangers on a Train* (1951), *Rear Window* (1954), *The Trouble with Harry* (1955), *The Man Who Knew Too Much* (1956), *Vertigo* (1958) and *North by Northwest* (1959); 3-D classics *House of Wax* (1953), *It Came from Outer Space* (1953), *Creature from the Black Lagoon* (1954) *Kiss Me Kate* (1954) and *Dial M for Murder* (1954); Sci-fi thrillers *The Thing* (1951), *Invasion of the Body Snatchers* (1956), *The Incredible Shrinking Man* (1957) and *The Fly* (1958); William Castle's audience participation films, *The House on Haunted Hill* (1958) and *The Tingler* (1959); comedies *Gentlemen Prefer Blondes* (1953), *How to Marry a Millionaire* (1953) and *Some Like It Hot* (1959); dramas *Shane* (1953), *East of Eden* (1955) and *Giant* (1956); musicals *Singin' in the Rain* (1952), *The Band Wagon* (1953), *It's Always Fair Weather* (1955), *Guys and Dolls* (1955) and *The King and I* (1956) along with the widescreen epics *This Is Cinerama* (1952), *20,000 Leagues Under the Sea* (1954), *Oklahoma!* (1955), *Around the World in 80 Days* (1956), *The Ten Commandments* (1956), *The Big Country* (1958) and *Ben-Hur* (1959). It's my favorite decade of cinema.

## Fifties Counterculture Influence

After being driven underground, some Leftists began to reemerge as the counterculture. Among them were "Beat Movement" writers Jack Kerouac, Neal Cassady, Allen Ginsberg, William S. Burroughs and others. Judging from their writings, one could conclude that Beats were alienated individuals who rejected the nuclear family, work ethic and capitalist system. What they proposed as an alternative was somewhat vague other than hedonism and substance abuse.

Beatniks were often in trouble with the law and other authorities, which enhanced their rogue status. An intoxicated Burroughs accidentally killed his wife while trying to shoot a shot glass off her head in a display of his marksmanship. Allen Ginsberg's controversial poem "Howl" was written while he was confined in a mental institution. With the exception of Keruoac, many Beatniks were sympathetic to the Soviet Union or at least did not consider them a serious threat. They had no political power and few people took them seriously outside of intellectual circles and academia. Beatniks appeared in movies like *Bell, Book and Candle* (1958) but were usually depicted as comical characters.

Other icons of the era were Hugh Hefner, Alfred C. Kinsey and Wilhelm Reich. Hefner legitimized skin magazines with his classy *Playboy*. Since books and magazines were not considered obscene if they contained "redeeming social value," he secured mainstream writers and celebrity interviews to take the heat off his centerfolds. The premiere issue featured 20th Century–Fox star, Marilyn Monroe. By 1956 *Playboy* was a publishing phenomenon. In 1948 Kinsey released his study, *Sexual Behavior in the Human Male* and in 1953, *Sexual Behavior in the Human Female*. While much of the data in these Kinsey Reports has been questioned in the interim, the public began discussing the topic in the open rather than in private. Reich was an Austrian-born psychiatrist who combined Freud with Marx and claimed that increased sexual freedom would result in socialist equality. He linked sexual repression with fascism although his fellow German communists were no less tolerant and threw him out of the party. The writings of these men contributed to the sexual revolution in the following decade.

All of these influences had a tendency to chip away at the Production Code. As the studios sold their theater chains, they let their long term contracts lapse which increased independent production. These producers were not signatories of the Hays Office nor did they want it dictating content. Breen had to expand the Code to allow formerly prohibited scenes like rape in *A Streetcar Named Desire* and the murder of a cop in *Detective Story* which were both released in 1951. Otto Preminger bypassed the Code as Hughes had in the previous decade when he released *The Moon Is Blue* (1953) and *The Man with the Golden Arm* (1955) without the Seal. The Code was being stretched to the limit but most distributors thought it wise to retain some semblance of self-regulation to keep local and government censors at bay. It was a tumultuous relationship between the producers and Breen but the industry awarded him a special Oscar in 1954. He retired that year and his associate, Geoffrey M. Shurlock, replaced him.

## The Production Code Under Geoffrey M. Shurlock, 1955–1959

Shurlock was less dogmatic than Breen about content and pragmatic about the cultural changes society was going through. During his term, movies became more risqué and violent. The Code was modified again in 1956 by rewording some of its restrictions which were open to interpretation. The outright ban on drug addiction was removed and the subject matter was allowed as long as the portrayal did not "encourage, stimulate or justify the use of such drugs." This was an accommodation to UA's *Man with the Golden Arm* (1955). The same standard applied to formerly forbidden subjects like abortion and white slavery. Both were later depicted in films like *Alfie* (1966) and *Thoroughly Modern Millie* (1967). Frank Tashlin's zany comedy, *Will Success Spoil Rock Hunter?* (1957) and the Doris Day/Rock Hudson farce, *Pillow Talk* (1959) were examples of the new leniency regarding sexual themes. Billy Wilder's *The Apartment* (1960) contained innuendo which went over the heads of young children. *Suddenly Last Summer* (1959) dealt with homosexuality in a restrained manner which was a topic in the Kinsey Reports a few years earlier. *Ben-Hur* (1959) had a great deal of violence within a religious framework. The sea battle depicted amputees with bloody limbs and the death of Messala was graphic and disturbing.

The counterculture influence was expanded in the mid-fifties by a new kind of music popularized by Elvis Presley. Labeled "Rock and Roll" by disc jockey Alan Freed, it was a combination of black Rhythm and Blues and forties Boogie Woogie. The term itself was black slang for sex. Stars like Chuck Berry and Little Richard had multi-racial appeal to teenagers. Compared to sixties protest songs, early Rock was pop music without a distinct political agenda. Elvis made four hit movies before getting drafted and gave a worthy performance in *King Creole* (1958). Aside from Presley's features, there were a number of B movie productions that featured the music as a subject matter including *Don't Knock the Rock*, *Rock Around the Clock*, and *Rock, Rock, Rock*, all from 1956. The best Rock movie of the era was Frank Tashlin's satire, *The Girl Can't Help It!* released the same year. John Lennon cited it as one of his favorites.

Confronting these trends could not have been easy for Shurlock, who was faced with the competing ideologies of the era. Conservatives were in charge of government and believed the counterculture was a corrupting influence that inspired juvenile delinquency and undermined America's resolve to combat communism. At the other end of the spectrum liberal producers, directors and actors were more tolerant of the new forms of music and changing sexual mores. They also wanted to patronize the youth audience. Overall, Shurlock found a balance through the sixties.

## The Production Code Under Shurlock, 1960–1968

The blacklist officially ended when Kirk Douglas gave Dalton Trumbo screen credit for his work on *Spartacus* in 1960. *Spartacus* was an entertaining sword and sandal epic but suffered from Trumbo's decision to portray the lead character as a mythical Soviet hero rather than depict actual events. According to novelist and historian, Colleen McCullough, Spartacus was not born a slave. He was a Thracian who served in the Roman army under Sulla. His rebellious behavior lead to a charge of insurrection. He was sentenced to become a Gladiator in the school of Lentulus Batiatus. Spartacus lead a revolt with fellow Gladiators, then incorporated slaves into his ranks. His army was eventually defeated by Marcus Licinius Crassus and he died in the final battle. This could've been the basis for an interesting drama but the facts didn't suit Trumbo's agenda. He made Spartacus a slave liberator who set up a socialist society on Mt. Vesuvius and died Christ-like on the cross as a martyr. It illustrated how ideology took precedence over other considerations for screenwriters like Trumbo.

Stanley Kubrick's direction undermined Trumbo's intent when he made the Romans more appealing than the slaves. Sequences featuring the political scheming of Laurence Olivier, Charles Laughton and Peter Ustinov were entertaining and droll. Scenes of Tony Curtis reciting poetry and Douglas giving speeches in their fictional commune were pretentious and dull. The film's main appeal was the gladiator training school, battle scenes and vivid Technirama photography. Trumbo's name in the credits created controversy and newly elected President Kennedy and his brother, Robert, crossed the American Legion picket lines to attend a screening. This endorsement opened the door to future "New Left" ideologues who would dominate the medium by the end of the decade.

John Wayne released *The Alamo* the same year. It featured a spectacular climax with vivid Todd-AO photography and competed for 70mm theater space which made its Roadshow bookings limited. Wayne directed and starred in the film which was a pet project of his for years. The script was by the right wing screenwriter, James Edward Grant. Like *Spartacus*, it was historically inaccurate and contained heavy-handed speeches by lead characters. In contrast, Robert Bolt's screenplay for David Lean's *Doctor Zhivago* (1965) was an example of superior craftsmanship regarding this type of film. Rather than depicting everything in black and white terms like Trumbo and Grant, characterization was complex and events were illustrated in shades of gray as in real life. *Spartacus* and *The Alamo* were entertaining spectacles but represented a new direction as earlier restrictions on overt political content eroded away.

Controversial subjects continued to be allowed in films like Stanley Kubrick's *Lolita* (1962) with the proviso that they be restricted to mature audiences. Some theaters admitted children anyway. Other adult pictures included *Elmer Gantry* (1960), and Billy Wilder's *Irma La Douce* (1963).

Wilder's comedies were considered racy for their time. Theater owners faced potential problems booking these pictures. All fifty states had some type of obscenity laws which were not universally applied. Most were vague but contained fines, prison sentences or both. For example, in Pennsylvania "obscene" was defined as "that which, to the average person, applying contemporary community standards, has as its dominant theme, taken as a whole, an appeal to prurient interest." As entertaining as *Irma La Douce* was, it could fit that description in religious communities. Penalties included fines not exceeding $2,000 and prison terms of not more than two years for exhibiting, distributing or advertising obscene matter. North Dakota fines were less at $1,000 and one year in prison. Nevada was less specific with their fines of $500 and 11 months in jail for "Giving any obscene or impure show." At least in Ohio the person had to "knowingly" exhibit an obscene motion picture.

Shurlock remained lenient regarding sexual themes. The Sean Connery Bond films contained numerous references like the name "Pussy Galore" and threatened laser castration in *Goldfinger* (1964). The spy craze was one of the more entertaining cycles of the era that would've had a difficult time under Breen but passed under his successor. I was a big fan of the series and Ian Fleming's novels.

The mid-sixties counterculture influence climaxed with the release of cinema's best Rock movie, *A Hard Day's Night* in 1964. Even those who objected to Beatlemania had to admire Richard Lester's unique combination of catchy tunes and wacky comedy. It was followed by *Help!* which was a funny spoof of 007 films. The Vietnam war and other influences changed the nature of Rock movies shortly afterwards. Beginning with the Beatles' *Rubber Soul* album in 1965, hints of activism and drug references began to be incorporated into songs. Rock changed from pop music to a form of social protest. Other groups like Jerry Garcia's Grateful Dead, the Rolling Stones, Jefferson Airplane, the Lovin' Spoonful and folk singer Bob Dylan contributed to the cause. Many were participants in the "Acid Test" which was a combination of hard rock and LSD as promoted by Timothy Leary and Ken Kesey, author of *One Flew Over the Cuckoo's Nest*. Kesey and his group known as the "Merry Pranksters" toured the country trying to indoctrinate young people into his alternate lifestyle. Other than a few low budget exploitation films, this aspect of the sixties' counterculture would not be depicted on screen until the demise of the Code a few years later.

David Lean's epic, *Doctor Zhivago* (1965), became the most successful anti–Communist film of all time. An element of satire was introduced into the subject with Billy Wilder's *One, Two, Three* (1961), Stanley Kubrick's

*Dr. Strangelove* (1964) and *The Russians Are Coming, the Russians Are Coming* (1966). *Fail-Safe* (1964) and *The Bedford Incident* (1965) also dealt with nuclear war and the Soviets from a liberal perspective. Party membership was a plot devise in Otto Preminger's *Advise and Consent* (1962) and Franklin Schaffner's *The Best Man* (1964). The political blood sport of the stories made both Republicans and Democrats look bad.

By 1965, the industry petitioned for some kind of classification system combined with a reformed Production Code which Shurlock endorsed. This would allow additional screen freedom while restricting minors from unsuitable material and give theaters cover in the event they were charged with obscenity. Most restrictions were ignored anyway. While the Code remained in place, filmmakers did not submit a script for pre-approval which had been the formula under Breen. They shot them independently and negotiated for the Seal after completion. In many cases, only minor cuts were required. *The Pawnbroker* (1965) contained brief nudity which was allowed because it was artistically important to the theme.

In 1966, Jack Valenti left the Lyndon Johnson administration and became the new president of the MPAA with an impressive salary of $170,000 per year. Among his first changes was to scrap the 1956 Production Code. The "Standards for Production" were enacted with eleven statues which could be summarized as follows: The value of human life had to be respected; evil, sin and crime could not be justified; graphic brutality was not allowed; exploitative nudity was forbidden; illicit sex relations could not be justified; restraint regarding sexual aberrations was required; neither obscene speech nor racial slurs was allowed; religion could not be demeaned and there could not be excessive cruelty to animals. The Seal would be granted based on how these controversial subjects were depicted within the film. This was an important distinction. The aforementioned *Alfie* (1966) contained an abortion sequence but did not advocate the then illegal operation. Some studios set up subsidiary companies to distribute movies without the Seal while remaining signatories of the MPAA for other pictures. MGM distributed *Blow Up* (1966) in this manner with the nudity intact.

A simple classification system was adopted. Movies were either categorized as suitable for general audiences, suggested for adults or denied a Seal entirely. *The Sand Pebbles* (1966) and *Bonnie and Clyde* (1967) were Seal approved films with graphic violence. As long as the new Code and Seal remained in place, it kept movies within a mainstream context and prevented the medium from sliding down that slippery slope into exploitation, pornography and propaganda. Most theaters played general audience pictures with an occasional adult-oriented feature. While there were some controversial pictures from 1966–1968 (e.g. *In the Heat of the Night, Guess Who's Coming to Dinner*), they had not yet crossed the line nor was there a major product shift. Urban theaters, grind-houses and drive-ins continued to book low budget exploitation pictures without a Seal like AIP's drug film, *MaryJane* (1967).

Finally in November of 1968, Valenti made a momentous decision. To Shurlock's surprise, he scrapped the remnants of the Code and Seal. He took the position that any form of industry self-regulation was censorship. Shurlock stepped down accordingly although he remained a special consultant in his retirement. Valenti announced that there would be no restrictions on content but films had to be classified. He created the Code and Rating Administration for these purposes. "CARA" was later known as the Classification and Rating Administration and finally the MPAA of which it was part of. Motion pictures would no longer carry a Seal of Approval nor stay within a mainstream context politically or culturally. This turned out to be one of the most significant changes in film history.

## The Ratings System Under Jack Valenti, 1968–2001

Valenti was an experienced political operative, a skill he learned from his mentor. As the spokesman for the industry, he informed the media that his classification system would act as a guide for parents. At the time, most exhibitors supported it. The National Association of Theater Owners (NATO) thought it would ward off censorship in parts of the country where explicit sex and violence in movies was forbidden by local ordinances to protect minors. Many would have second thoughts about the system and its long term effect on exhibition a few years later. The ratings were subject to revisions over the years. Detailed below is a summary:

### 1968–1970

G   General Audiences, all ages admitted
M   Mature audiences — parental guidance suggested
R   Restricted, children under 16 not admitted without parent or adult guardian
X   No one under 16 admitted — Age limit may vary in certain areas

Parents found the M rating confusing so the board changed the classification to GP in 1970. The age restriction in R and X were increased. The XXX category was not authorized by the Administration and self-applied by distributors of hard-core pornography to distinguish it from soft-core product.

## 1970–1972

G   All Ages Admitted, General Audiences

GP   All Ages Admitted, Parental Guidance Suggested

R   Restricted, Under 17 requires accompanying Parent or Adult Guardian

X   No One Under 17 Admitted — Age limit may vary in certain areas (soft-core)

XXX   No One Under 21 Admitted (hard-core). Not authorized by CARA

In February, 1972, the board changed GP to PG. The age restriction on X was increased again.

## 1972–1983

G   General Audiences, all ages admitted

PG   Parental Guidance Suggested

R   Restricted, under 17 not admitted without parent or adult guardian

X   No one under 18 admitted — Age limit may vary in certain areas (soft-core)

XXX   No one under 21 admitted (hard-core). Not authorized by CARA

The PG-13 classification was added in 1984 to allow some R rated content in PG films, rendering the PG rating somewhat meaningless.

## 1984–1990

G   All Ages admitted

PG   Parent Guidance Suggested, some material may not be suitable for children

PG-13   Under 13 requires an adult guardian

R   Restricted, no one under 17 admitted without a parent or adult guardian

X   No one under 18 admitted (soft-core)

XXX   No one under 21 admitted (hard-core). Not authorized by CARA

The X classification was changed to NC-17 in September of 1990. Most pornography was distributed on video rather than cinemas.

## 1990–2000

G   All Ages admitted

PG   Parental Guidance suggested

PG-13  Under 13 requires an adult guardian
R       Restricted, no one under 17 admitted without a parent or adult
        guardian
NC-17 No one 17 and under admitted

Valenti stated that the ratings system was implemented "To encourage artistic expression by expanding creative freedom and to insure that the freedom which encourages the artist remain responsible and sensitive to the standards of the larger society."[9] It became apparent that while the first goal was put into effect, the second was to be completely ignored.

## The Ratings Game

From its beginnings, the classification system had problems. By what criteria were the films being rated? What content constituted an R instead of an M? Producers and parents requested details of what was permissible in each category but Valenti declined. He stated that CARA would base their ratings not only on the amount of sex, violence and profanity but how it was depicted within the story. While this sounded reasonable, it gave them tremendous power. The difference between an M, R and X was substantial in terms of box-office potential. Some newspapers refused to accept advertising for X rated films. Critics of the system claimed that Valenti ran his Administration like a fiefdom with a great deal of secrecy and without accountability to the public.

Like the abandoned Production Code Seal, ratings were negotiable depending on industry clout. For example, *A Clockwork Orange* was originally released with an X rating due to its "ultra-violence." After a few minor trims, CARA reclassified it R. It's unlikely the impact of the subject matter was reduced by the removal of a few shots. Warner Bros. wanted a wider release of the film and CARA cooperated with them. *Midnight Cowboy* was originally distributed by UA with a self-imposed X rating. This was one of the first X rated releases by a major company. After generating good reviews and box-office, UA submitted the film to the board in 1971 and received an R. Simultaneously, low budget independent films received harsher ratings. Brian De Palma's *Greetings* (1969) was X rated even though it was less graphic than the above films.

In 1976, the National Church Council denounced the X rating and stated that the MPAA system was unsatisfactory as an indication of screen content. They complained about the proliferation of sex shops surrounding theaters that played X product and the incursion of pornography into

Before the X rating became associated with pornography, a number of studios released major titles with this classification, like *Midnight Cowboy* (1969).

previously respectable theaters. The Council did have a point about inconsistent standards. *The Secret of Santa Vittoria* (1969) was rated M for mild profanity. *Popi* (1969) was rated G but had similar strong language. Irregularities continued in subsequent years. *The Gypsy Moths* (1969) and *Naked Witch* (1969) were originally rated M but reclassified R. Allied Artists' *Last Summer* was released in 1968 with an X rating. It was reclassified R in 1969, then PG in 1972 but R again in 1974. Many of the early X rated features were reclassified R including *Medium Cool* (1970) and *Myra Breckinridge* (1970). *The Wild Bunch* was released with an R rating in 1969 and a 144 minute running time. Warner Bros. later trimmed the release prints to 134 minutes but left the violence intact. In the nineties, they planned a theatrical revival of the complete version. Warners submitted it for classification and it was rated NC-17. The MPAA later restored the original rating. Reissues of classics made within the Production Code were inexplicably classified PG including *Citizen Kane* (1941) and *Casablanca* (1941). It's conceivable that the distributors requested the PG instead of the G so the films wouldn't be categorized as children's product. This muddle of changing classifications confused parents trying to determine what was suitable for family viewing.

In 1984 there were complaints about the violence in PG rated films like *Gremlins* and *Indiana Jones and the Temple of Doom*. Both were entertaining pictures but contained gore that previously fell into the R category. The latter film had a heart plucking sequence. Since these were big budget features, Valenti accommodated the studios by creating a new category, PG-13, to allow some R rated content in PG films. For example, *Titanic* (1997) had topless nudity.

Over the decades the Administration became more lenient, especially for big budget studio releases. The recent film, *Hannibal*, had a grisly brain eating sequence that would've received an X years ago but got an R. In the eighties and nineties, the X rating remained the last barrier to the majors. Simultaneously, sexually explicit material increased in many studio releases. *Crimes of Passion* (1984), *9½ Weeks* (1986) and *Basic Instinct* (1992) all contained graphic sex scenes and had to be trimmed to receive an R which the directors resented. Valenti created the "NC-17" classification in the nineties so that the MPAA could trademark it and films like MGM/UA's *Showgirls* (1995) could avoid the "X" stigma.

Many of the above mentioned features were quality productions and in the case of *Midnight Cowboy*, *A Clockwork Orange* and *The Wild Bunch*, classics. However, in my opinion it appeared that CARA was politically motivated in many of their classifications which did not serve the interests of the filmmakers, exhibitors or parents.

## The Post-Code Era

The demise of the Production Code and Seal altered the content of motion pictures permanently. It changed the very nature of cinema and had a long term effect on the moviegoing experience. Trends and genres evolved in the late sixties and early seventies that took advantage of the new screen freedom.

## Counterculture Cinema

Prior to 1968, there was a movement in the industry generally referred to as "New Hollywood." These were filmmakers who had no alliance to the old order regarding content or production methods. Among them were John G. Avildsen, Brian De Palma, Robert Downey Sr., Tom Laughlin, Dennis Hopper, Leonard Horn, William Klein, Jim McBride, Melvin Van Peebles, Paul Morrissey, Richard Rush, Michael Wadleigh and Haskell Wexler. Most of these directors were young and part of the sixties counterculture which was a radical variation of fifties beatniks. This was not a grassroots movement with mainstream support but loosely affiliated activist groups which included hippies, yippies, campus revolutionaries and black militants. While the CPUSA was no longer a significant political party, much of their rhetoric was adopted by them. Although small in numbers, their opposition to the Vietnam war united them into a powerful social influence. Unlike the beatniks, some were willing to resort to violence to advance their cause. Riots and civil unrest erupted in major cities and universities. Borrowing tactics from the Old Left, those who objected were labeled as "racist," "reactionary" and "fascist," which encompassed the bulk of the American middle-class. Conservatives called them the silent majority. Organizations like the Weather Underground (Weathermen), and Symbionese Liberation Army (SLA) crossed the line from activism to terrorism. The SLA kidnapped heiress Patty Hearst and indoctrinated her into their group.

The ideology espoused by the New Left was a combination of sexual liberation, socialism and ethnocentrism. The problems Marxists faced was that none of their predictions had come to pass. Capitalism, with all of its flaws, resulted in material abundance throughout the Western world. There would be no proletariat revolution because the safety net enabled the poorest citizen to live in better conditions than most people in communist countries. Author Herbert Marcuse maneuvered around these facts by stating that affluent societies oppressed their people which resulted in alienation and sexual repression. In his 1964 book, *One Dimensional Man*, his remedy was to put the "pleasure principle" before the "performance principle" which had obvious appeal to young people and was the philosophical basis of the sexual revolution.

Hippies went the next step which was to drop out of society completely. They originated in San Francisco's Haight-Ashbury and New York City's East Village in 1966. They advocated sex, drugs and rock n' roll, lived in squalid communes, were partial to Eastern philosophy and guerrilla theater where the audience was a participant in the performance. Yippies were activist hippies with Abbie Hoffman the prime example. Campus revolutionaries included Greg Calvert and Carl Davidson. The origins of their movement began with Students for a Democratic Society or SDS. One of its founders was Tom Hayden, who later married Jane Fonda. He was the principal author of the 1962 Port Huron Statement which advocated participatory democracy instead of our representative republic. The SDS was among those responsible for the rallies, protests and student uprisings at colleges like Columbia, San Francisco State College and Berkeley. Although they framed their activities as "The Free Speech Movement" there was little opportunity for political discourse when students occupied buildings and insisted that administrators give in to their demands.

Blacks had legitimate grievances which included discrimination in hiring practices and Jim Crow laws down south. Mainstream liberals and conservatives attempted to remedy these problems with social legislation. Black militants rejected these efforts and called for a separatist nation within the United States. Leaders of this "Black Power" movement included Malcolm X and Stokely Carmichael. Black Panther founders Huey Newton and Bobby Seale called for armed revolt against whites. They also espoused African Nationalism and condemned blacks who participated in American society.

Other participants included drop-out radical Jerry Rubin, Peter Berg with his anarchist "Diggers" and Andy Warhol who mass marketed pop art in his "Factory." Beat poet Allen Ginsberg was the bridge between fifties and sixties countercultures.

New Hollywood filmmakers who subscribed to these views used motion pictures for agitation-propaganda (agit-prop), similar to Dalton Trumbo's art as a weapon. Depending on where you stood on the political spectrum, sixties counterculture movies either reflected the changing values of a new generation or were trying to de-construct every cherished tenet of American society. The foreword to the original Production Code stated, "Hence, though regarding motion pictures primarily as entertainment without any explicit purpose of teaching or propaganda, they know that the motion picture within its own field of entertainment may be directly responsible for spiritual or moral progress, for higher types of social life, and for much correct thinking." The first provision of the general principles emphasized that "No picture shall be produced which will lower the moral standards of those who see it." Counterculture filmmakers flaunted their rejection of these abandoned guidelines combined with a moral and artistic relativism.

Other notable directors who are often labeled as New Hollywood included Martin Scorsese, Peter Bogdanovich, George Lucas and Francis Ford Coppola. They were of this generation but less overtly ideological although Coppola produced the anti-war epic, *Apocalypse Now* in 1979. In general, their films didn't fit into this category. While Scorsese and Coppola's features had a liberal perspective, they did not contain the blatant propaganda of these pictures. At the very least, their films contained fully rounded characters and complex narratives rather than the stereotypes and over-simplified plots of movies like *Billy Jack* (1971). Some filmmakers adopted more of an attitude than a story in titles like *Alice's Restaurant* (1969) and *Steelyard Blues* (1973).

Counterculture movies had heavier doses of sex, violence and profanity than typical studio product of the time. As with previous sociopolitical pictures, artistry took a secondary position to the director's statement. They were different than earlier message films in that they were not only critical about some aspect of America but condemned society as a whole. Titles included *The Activist, American Revolution 2, Glen and Randa, Greetings, Groupies, Heat, Hi Mom!, Joe, The Landlord, The Magic Garden of Stanley Sweetheart, Mister Freedom, The Revolutionary, Trash* and *200 Motels*. These pictures depicted the "turn on, tune in, drop out" hippies in *Woodstock*, campus revolutionaries in *Getting Straight* and black militants in *Sweet Sweetback's Baadasssss Song*. Others fell into the "radical chic" category like *Medium Cool* and *Putney Swope*. The sexual philosophy of Wilhelm Reich was examined in *WR: Mysteries of the Organism* (1971). Even writer Norman Mailer got into the act with his movies, *Wild 90* (1967), *Beyond the Law* (1968) and *Maidstone* (1969). He obviously exempted film stock from his diatribes against plastic.

The counterculture director's experience in the business was often limited. Some were film school graduates like Martin Scorsese who paid their dues with exploitation producer and distributor Roger Corman. Coppola and Bogdanovich also started with Corman before moving up to studio work. Paul Morrissey was the principal filmmaker at Warhol's Factory. Since they didn't work their way up the ranks of the studio system, they didn't adhere to classic narrative structure. In Stuart Hagmann's *The Strawberry Statement* (1970), the jittery camera zoomed in and out, photographed action upside down and shot directly into the camera lights. The pressbook of this picture noted that the film had a hippie director. Dennis Hopper's *Easy Rider* (1969) featured bizarre editing with flash cuts and drug-oriented montages. Hopper had industry experience as a character actor in the fifties and was one of the older rebels. Co-Producer Peter Fonda was an up-and-coming leading man and registered Republican when he decided to drop out and become one the hippie icons of the era. Prior to this film, he had made two similar pictures, *The Wild Angels* (1966) and *The Trip* (1967).

Counterculture films had an improvisational quality that appealed to the youth of the time. They were certainly different than studio product like *Airport* (1970) with its slick Todd-AO photography, star performers

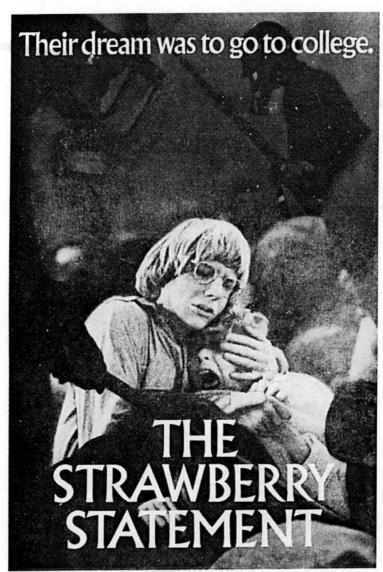

Counter-culture films like *The Strawberry Statement* (1970) were made for a
targeted youth crowd rather than general audience.

and polished editing technique. De Palma's *Greetings* and *Hi Mom!* resembled student films. Most of these movies would've been refused a Production Code Seal a few years earlier. For example, drug use was permissible as a subject matter under the modified Code providing it wasn't endorsed (e.g. *Bigger Than Life*, 1956). Post-Code movies like *Easy Rider* advocated their use along with free love and bad hygiene. The film had a profound impact in its time and was quite a change from Columbia's product of the previous year. Jack Nicholson's role as an alcoholic lawyer stole the show and gave the picture its philosophical basis. Laszlo Kovac's cinematography was stylish and better than expected considering the low budget. The lifestyle depicted in this picture was enticing to young people facing the draft, urban riots and a culture war.

Animation was incorporated into the genre with George Dunning's *Yellow Submarine* in 1968 which was rated G. Ralph Bakshi's *Fritz the Cat* in 1973 was the first adults only cartoon which was marketed with the tagline, "He's X rated and Animated." It was loosely based on Robert Crumb's underground comic although it did not utilize his unique style of shading in the art work. It was followed by a sequel, *The Nine Lives of Fritz the Cat* in 1974 directed by Robert Taylor. The success of Bakshi's picture enabled him to produce additional adult cartoons like *Heavy Traffic* (1973) and *Coonskin* (1974).

Films in this genre had inconsistent box-office returns. Hopper's *Easy Rider* ($16,200,000 U.S./Canada gross[10]), Wadleigh's *Woodstock* ($14,500,000), Advilsen's *Joe* ($9,500,000) and Rush's *Getting Straight* ($6,000,000) were hits. There were sleepers like Van Peebles' *Sweet Sweetback's Baadasssss Song* ($4,100,000) and Laughlin's *Billy Jack* ($4,000,000). Others performed poorly like *Pound, Prologue* and *The Revolutionary*. The high grosses of the former were no guarantee that similar product would do as well. Van Peebles' *Don't Play Us Cheap* (1973) and Hopper's *The Last Movie* (1971) were not successful. Some of these films were "four-walled" which meant that the distributor rented the theater outright and covered its nut (operating expenses) but made all of the profit. *Billy Jack* was released this way and continued to play around the country which increased its long term gross to over $20,000,000 by 1975. In these cases the exhibitor did not reap the benefits of the booking but didn't lose money either.

The grosses of G rated pictures like *Airport* ($37,650,796) in the same era should be noted since there appeared to be a generation gap regarding viewer preference. General audiences tended to be more predictable since many subsequent disaster films were also profitable. Perhaps the gap was most apparent in the Academy Awards presentation of the era. *Oliver*, a general audience feature, won the Oscar in 1968. *Midnight Cowboy*, an X rated movie, won it in 1969.

# AIRPORT

## ADVERTISING
## PUBLICITY
## PROMOTION

**BURT LANCASTER**
as MEL BAKERSFELD

**DEAN MARTIN**
as VERNON DEMEREST

THE #**1** NOVEL
OF THE YEAR—NOW
A MOTION PICTURE!

**JEAN SEBERG**
as TANYA LIVINGSTON

**JACQUELINE BISSET**
as GWEN MEIGHEN

**GEORGE KENNEDY**
as JOE PATRONI

"★★★★ **HIGHEST RATING!**
A thriller of human interest,
humor and suspense galore!"
— Wanda Hale, N.Y. Daily News

"**BLOCK-BUSTING...A SURE-FIRE HIT!**"
— Dorothy Manners, L.A. Herald-Examiner

"**Better than the novel...completely
engrossing...completely captivating!**"
— John B. Tucker, ABC-TV

A ROSS HUNTER Production

# AIRPORT

STARRING

## BURT LANCASTER · DEAN MARTIN
## JEAN SEBERG · JACQUELINE BISSET
## GEORGE KENNEDY · HELEN HAYES
## VAN HEFLIN · MAUREEN STAPLETON
## BARRY NELSON · LLOYD NOLAN
## DANA WYNTER · BARBARA HALE

| MUSIC COMPOSED & CONDUCTED BY | FROM THE NOVEL BY | WRITTEN FOR THE SCREEN & DIRECTED BY | PRODUCED BY |
| --- | --- | --- | --- |
| ALFRED NEWMAN | ARTHUR HAILEY | GEORGE SEATON | ROSS HUNTER |

A UNIVERSAL PICTURE · TECHNICOLOR® · Produced in 70MM TODD-AO®

Sound Track Album exclusively on **DECCA RECORDS**
also available on 8-Track and Cassette Tape!

**HELEN HAYES**
as ADA QUONSETT

**MAUREEN STAPLETON**
as MRS. GUERRERO

**VAN HEFLIN**
as D. O. GUERRERO

**BARRY NELSON**
as ANSON HARRIS

**LLOYD NOLAN**
as HARRY STANDISH

*Airport* (1970) was made for general audiences and competed with counterculture films in the marketplace.

The studios jumped on the bandwagon and made some bigger budget features with a counterculture perspective. The most successful was Robert Altman's *MASH* (1970) which grossed approximately $30,000,000 during its first run. The screenplay was by Hollywood Ten writer Ring Lardner Jr., whose intention was to discredit any war where America fought communist aggression including Korea and Vietnam. Altman's unique style and outrageous humor did not make this immediately apparent to viewers which expanded its appeal to a broader demographic. Other blacklisted Party members and fellow travelers emerged. Their films were very critical of American society. Herbert Biberman made *Slaves* (1969) which was rated X. This was his first feature since *Salt of the Earth* (1953) but it fared no better and was a critically panned dud. Waldo Scott wrote the screenplay for *Midnight Cowboy*. After 1969, there were few anti–Communist films and some that depicted Marxists in a positive light like *The Front* (1976) and *Reds* (1981).

Not all counterculture films were controversial. Some were off-beat and quirky like Hal Ashby's *Harold and Maude* (1972), Joseph McGrath's British import, *The Magic Christian* (1969) or surreal like David Lynch's *Eraserhead* (1978) which was a late entry. All three were cult favorites in repertory houses and have held up better than the more obvious agit-prop titles. Aging studio directors like Stanley Kramer contributed to the genre with *R.P.M.* (1970) but failed to capture the targeted audience illustrating how fickle they were. Roger Corman's *Gas-s-s-s* (1970) was another disappointment. Distributors lost a great deal of money trying to replicate the success of early youth oriented pictures.

There was also a reaction against them. Conservatives and moderates were disturbed by the violence associated with sixties radicalism. In the previous decade, the crime rate had declined but beginning in 1964 it began to soar which coincided with the civil rights movement and campus activism. As Irwin and Debi Unger noted in their book, *Turning Point: 1968*, "It was not necessary to be personally mugged or burglarized to feel the effects of the crime surge. By 1968 the air was charged with stories of the worsening plague.... In December the FBI announced that violent crime for the first nine months of the year was 19 percent higher than for the same prior the year before, with homicide up 21 percent."[11] One of the first movies to deal with this was Don Siegal's *Dirty Harry* (1972). Clint Eastwood played a tough detective who tracked down a psychotic hippie while confronting liberal bureaucracy in the criminal justice system. Charles Bronson played a businessman who became an urban vigilante to lower the crime rate in *Death Wish* (1974). Both pictures dealt with middle-class anxiety although movies with a right wing perspective were fewer in number in the post–Code era.

Whatever attributes or liabilities counterculture pictures had was short-lived. After America's withdrawal from Vietnam in 1973, the movement gradually fizzled out. The only thing that unified such disparate groups as campus radicals, hippies, yippies and black militants was their opposition to the war. This united front collapsed and separated into hostile factions without a unifying cause. By the time Milos Forman's *Hair* was released in 1979, it was considered a period piece and did not do as well as anticipated even though it was a good musical. It's one of the few pictures in this category that has withstood the test of time.

The sixties counterculture directors who survived had to mainstream their pictures and tone down the radicalism. Some like John G. Avildsen and Brian De Palma adapted and had successful Hollywood careers. De Palma's production values improved although he often pushed the envelope with explicit sex and violence. The MPAA made him cut films like *Scarface* (1982) to receive an R. Other filmmakers like Downey and Van Peebles were unable to adapt to the changing political landscape and faded from view. While Leftist references continued to appear in later releases, the obvious propaganda of movies like *Sweet Sweetback's Baad Asssss Song* was rare throughout the late seventies and eighties. In summary, these filmmakers and their pictures redefined cinema as a medium for political activism.

Detailed below is a list of notable counterculture films. I've included both independent and studio made product. Since the distributors and labs that processed many of these films folded long ago, many of these title may be lost outside of private film collections.

**1968**
The Acid Eaters
Alice in Acidland
The Animal
Blast Off Girls
Candy
Head
Hooked Generation
I Love You, Alice B. Toklas!
MaryJane
Psych-Out
The Queen
Revolution
Three in the Attic
Wild in the Streets
Yellow Submarine

**1969**
The Activist
Alice's Restaurant
American Revolution 2
Bob & Carol & Ted & Alice
Changes
Easy Rider
Futz!
Gay Deceivers
Generation
If
John and Mary
Last Summer
Macunaima (aka Jungle Freaks)
Medium Cool
More
Out of It
Putney Swope

Salesman
The Sex of the Angels

**1970**
Adam at 6 AM
The Baby Maker
The Boys in the Band
Brand Xs in the Band
Brewster McCloud
Can Heironymous Merkin Every Forget Mercy Humppe and Find True Happiness
Carry It On
Coming Apart
Cover Me Babe (aka Run Shadow Run)
Cowards
Crescendo
The Christine Jorgenson Story
Dionysus in '69
Dirty Mouth
Explosion
Five Easy Pieces
Fortune and Men's Eyes
Free Grass (aka Scream Free)
Gas-s-s-s
Gimme Shelter
Getting Straight
Glenn and Randa
Greetings
Groupies
Halls of Anger
Hi Mom!
I Am a Groupie
It's a Revolution, Mother
Joe
The Landlord
The Last Movie
Let It Be
Little Murders
Lonesome Cowboys
The Losers
Love Commune (aka Ghetto Freaks)
The Magic Christian
The Magic Garden of Stanley Sweetheart
Making It
A Married Couple
MASH
Meat Rack

Midnight Cowboy
Move
No Blade of Grass
Panic in Needle Park
People Next Door
Performance
Potpourri
Pound
Prologue
The Revolutionary
Right On
R.P.M.
The Strawberry Statement
Up the Cellar
Trash
Vanishing Point
The Wife Swappers
Witchcraft 70
Woodstock
W.U.S.A.
The Young Graduates
Zabriskie Point

**1971**
Alex in Wonderland
The American Dreamer
Been Down so Long It Looks Like Up to Me
Believe in Me (aka Speed Is of the Essence)
Billy Jack
Born to Win
B.S. I Love You
Cactus in the Snow
Celebration at Big Sur
Chrome and Hot Leather
Cisco Pike
Dealing
Drive, He Said
Dusty and Sweets McGee
El Topo
Everyone Should Have One
Eroticon
Friends
Getting Straight
The Gladiators
Glory Boy
Guess What We Learned in School Today?

Harold and Maude
Hoa Bin
Is There Sex After Death?
I Want What I Want
J.C.
Jennifer on My Mind
Mad Dogs and Englishmen
Maidstone
Medicine Ball Caravan
Millhouse: A White Comedy
Pacific Vibrations
Percy
Pigeons
Pink Angels
Pink Narcissus
Punishment Park
Pursuit of Happiness
Raga
Red, White and Blue
Some of My Best Friends Are
The Ski Bum
Taking Off
Thumb Tripping
A Ton of Grass Goes to Pot
200 Motels
Welcome Home, Soldier Boy
WR: Mysteries of the Organism
You've Got to Walk It Like You Talk
   It or You'll Lose That Beat
Zachariah
Z.P.G.

### 1972

Bummer!
Clay Pigeon
Concert for Bangladesh
The Deathmaster
Dynamite Chicken
Emitai
A Fan's Notes
The Female Bunch
Fillmore
Flesh
Fritz the Cat
F.T.A.
Gay Liberation
Georgia, Georgia
Greaser's Palace
Group Marriage

Hail
Heat
The Hitchhikers
Homo Eroticus
Journey Through Rosebud
Limbo
Meat Rack
Medicine Ball Caravan
Our Latin Thing
Outside In
Parades
Pickup on 101
A Place Called Today
Private Parts
Red Psalm
Richard
Rip-off
Savages
Scarecrew in a Garden of Cucumbers
Pete Seeger ... a Song and a Stone
Stand Up and Be Counted
Stigma
Summer Soldiers
Teenage Mother
There's Always Vanilla
To Find a Man
Wild Rebels
Wintersoldiers
Women in Revolt

### 1973

Black Moses of Soul — Issac Hayes
Challenges (Spanish)
Cia Manhattan
David Holzman Diary
Dealing
The Female Response
Godspell
The Harrad Experiment
Heavy Traffic (animated)
History Lessons
I.F. Stone's Weekly
Jesus Christ, Superstar
Jimi Hendrix (documentary)
The Jimi Hendrix Story
Manson
Oh Calcutta!
Point of Order
The P.O.W.

Rejeanne Padovani (Canadian)
Siddhartha
Steelyard Blues
Two People
You're Three Minutes Are Up

**1974**
Captain Kronos, Vampire Hunter
Good to See You Again, Alice Cooper
The Groove Tube
Harrad Summer
The Holy Mountain
Janis
Jimi Plays Berkeley (documentary)
Lenny
Mixed Company
The Nine Lives of Fritz the Cat (animated)
Open Season
Pink Flamingos
Pink Floyd
Rock City (documentary)
Sex Madness/Cocaine Fiends
The Trial of Billy Jack
A Very Natural Thing

**1975**
Female Trouble
Guitar Picks and Roach Clips

Ladies and Gentlemen, the Rolling Stones
The Rocky Horror Picture Show
Rock N' Roll Your Eyes
Steppenwolf

**1976**
Salsa
The Slap
The Song Remains the Same
Tunnel Vision
Underground

**1977**
Between the Lines
Joyride
The Kentucky Fried Movie
Some American Feminists (aka Quelques Feministes Americaines)

**1978**
Eraserhead
The Last Waltz
The Rubber Gun
Up in Smoke
Word Is Out

**1979**
Hair

## Sexploitation

Another genre that took advantage of screen freedom was the porno film. There had been "nudie" pictures in previous decades that played grind houses and burlesque theaters. They included sex hygiene films (*Mom and Dad*, 1948), nudist-camp movies (*Garden of Eden*, 1955) and striptease pictures like Irving Klaw's *Teaserama* (1954) featuring pin-up Bettie Page. Some of them were shot in 16mm Kodachrome and blown up to 35mm. No major theater would play this product and those that did faced legal problems. Both Klaw and Page were investigated by the government. In 1959, Russ Meyer released one of the first nudie films with a semblance of a plot, *The Immoral Mr. Teas*. It was a hit in theaters that risked booking it. Frontal nudity was avoided in these pictures and props were used on the set to cover these areas. Admission was restricted to adults. Meyer and others continued to make this product in the sixties. Among the titles were *Lorna* (1964), *The Smut Peddler* (1965) and *Mondo*

*Topless* (1966). The ratings system changed sexploitation's status within the industry for a few years.

The X classification was not always associated with pornography. From 1968 through 1972, a number of major studio films were rated X. It was the only category that CARA hadn't registered a trademark. Among the titles were MGM's *The Best House in London* (1969), UA's *The Damned* (1969), Paramount's *Tropic of Cancer* (1970) and Allied Artists' *End of the Road* (1970). Some counterculture films were also released with this rating including Paramount's *Medium Cool* (1969), Regional's *The Activist* (1969) and Andy Warhol's *Trash* (1970). Although the subject matter, nudity and violence put these pictures in the "adults only" category, they were not pornographic. Fox's *Myra Breckinridge* (1970) and *Beyond the Valley of the Dolls* (1970) walked a thin line between adult content and porn. Warner Bros. *The Devils* (1971), *A Clockwork Orange* (1972) and New Line Cinema's *The Street Fighter* (1975) were X rated due to violence.

Detailed below is a list of non-pornographic X rated films released by major distributors and independents. Many were reclassified R.

### 1968/1969

The Activist (Regional)
Adealen '31 (Paramount)
Benjamin (French import-Paramount)
Best House in London (British-MGM)
Birds in Peru (French-Universal)
Can Heironymus Merkin Every Forget Mercy Humppe and Find True Happiness (Universal)
De Sade (AIP)
Greetings (Sigma III)
The Killing of Sister George (Cinerama)
Last of the Mobile Hot Shots (Warner Bros.)
Last Summer (Allied Artists)
Laughter in the Dark (French/English-UA)
Lonesome Cowboys (Sherpix)
Medium Cool (Paramount)
Paranoia (Netherlands-CUC)
Putney Swope (Cinema V)
Sex of the Angels (Italian/West German-UA)
Slaves (Continental)

### 1970

Beyond the Valley of the Dolls (Fox)
The Damned (UA)
Dionysus '69 (Sigma III)
End of the Road (Allied Artists)
Glenn and Randa (UMC)
Hi Mom! (Sigma III)
Myra Breckinridge (Fox)
Naked Under Leather (French–Warner Bros.)
Performance (Warner Bros.)
Pound (UA)
Stop! (Warner Bros.)
Trash (Cinema V)
Tropic of Cancer (Paramount)
What Do You Say to a Naked Lady? (UA)
Witchcraft '70 (AIP)
Zabriskie Point (MGM)

### 1971

The Body (British-MGM)
The Devils (Warner Bros.)
A Place Called Today (Avco-Embassy)
Portraits of Woman (Finnish-Allied Artists)

Sweet Sweetback's Badassss Song
(Cinemation)

**1972**
A Clockwork Orange (Warner Bros.)
Decamaron (Italian-UA)
Farewell, Uncle Tom (Euro International)
Fritz the Cat (Cinemation)
Heat (Levitt-Pickman)
Last Tango in Paris (UA)
A Place Called Today (Avco-Embassy)
WR-Mysteries of the Organism (Cinema V)

**1973**
Blood for Dracula (Bryanston)
Deathline (AIP)

Flesh for Frankenstein (Bryanston)
Flesh Gordon (Graffiti Productions)
Heavy Traffic (AIP)
Le Sex Shop (Peppercorn-Wormser)
What? (Avco-Embassy)

**1975**
Blood of Dracula (Cinerama)
Female Trouble (New Line Cinema)
The Street Fighter (New Line Cinema)

**1976**
The Last Woman (French-Columbia)
Maitresse (Tinc Productions)

**1977**
Andy Warhol's Bad (New World)
Salo (Zebra/Peppercorn-Wormser)

CARA also allowed distributors to give their productions a self-applied "X" rather than submit them for classification. This inspired a glut of sexploitation which the rating was ultimately associated with. There were two categories within the genre. The X rating from 1968–1971 referred to "soft-core" pictures like *Fanny Hill* (1969) which contained nudity and simulated sex. XXX from 1972 onwards was a category distributors created for "hard-core" movies like *Behind the Green Door* (1972) which had on-screen sex and penetration.

For the first few years, sexploitation continued to be soft-core. The difference was that mainstream theaters occasionally played this product. Exhibiting this formerly forbidden material increased revenues in some places. While the bulk of the pictures were marketed by independents, some mini-majors like Avco Embassy released a few X titles like *Monique* (1970). When Cinemation's *Female Animal* (1970) played New York City, the *Independent Booking and Buying Guide* noted, "The progress of sexploitation film in America from back room moviola to 42nd Street grind house to Broadway first run ... is reaching a new audience because of its more respectable bookings at New York's Victoria and Avco Embassy East Theatres...."[12]

Soft-core productions often attempted a veneer of legitimacy. The Swedish B&W import, *I Am Curious, Yellow,* incorporated political references amidst the simulated sex. This redeeming social value categorized it as an art house film which grossed $8,500,000 domestically. Radley Metzger's *Camille 2000* was listed as "art-sexploitation" and had Mod production design. It was photographed in widescreen and was one of the few pictures in this genre to be printed in Technicolor. I screened a film collector's copy a few years ago and it looked good.

These movies were tame compared to what followed. In 1970, *Mona* negated the limited respectability X product had when on screen sex was shown. For some audiences, this was the difference between adult entertainment and cinematic prostitution. Couples that attended art films like *I Am Curious, Yellow* would be less likely to patronize theaters that played *Inside Georgina Spelvin*. Despite the high grosses of soft-core pictures like *I, a Woman* and *Fanny Hill* (both $4,500,000), hard-core began to dominate the market. The most controversial picture of the era was *Deep Throat* (1972) starring Linda Lovelace. It was subject to extensive litigation and co-star Harry Reems was brought up on charges. For a while it was banned as obscene in New York. I traveled with some high school friends to see it in New Jersey and even though we were minors, they let us in. Needless to say, we were disappointed. It was a typical boring porn, not withstanding Lovelace's ability to control her gag reflex.

By 1971, XXX had established itself as a profitable venue in many urban areas. San Francisco and New York City were considered the porn capitals of the country. Times Square was known for its multitude of hard-core theaters. As *Variety* noted, "What has happened over the past year is the emergence of a porno elite, a number of directors and/or producers whose names in pic advertising for hard-core locations ring a libidinous bell with porno aficionados...."[13] Gerard Damiano, the Mitchell Brothers and Alex De Renzy were among them. Stars included Marilyn Chambers and Jaimie Gillis. Before appearing in pornos, Chambers modeled for the Ivory Snow company which removed boxes containing her image from shelves.

Porn stars often used aliases. Dorothy May was known as Georgina Spelvin which was the traditional theatrical pseudonym of actresses who wanted to remain anonymous. John Curtis Estes was called Johnny "Wadd" Holmes. Nora Louise Kuzma took the name Traci Lords. Among the hard-core films of the era were *The Devil in Miss Jones* (1973) and *Resurrection of Eve* (1973). Cambist's *1001 Danish Delights* and *Bordello* (both 1973) were available in hard and soft-core versions to expand their bookings.

I worked briefly in the adult industry in 1983. While I was an editor at Troma, Inc., they were still distributing porn and I met some of the producers of the era including Vernon Becker (Constellation Films) and Lee Hessel (Cambist Films). I was hired to recut *The Love-in Arrangement*, *The Secret Dreams of Mona Q* and others from hard-core to soft-core. Jaimie Gillis appeared in the footage. I later hired him for a gag cameo in my 1989 feature, *Space Avenger*. In a homage to his career, Gillis played a

In the early seventies hard-core porn dominated the adult industry.

businessman who made love to an alien. She got so hot during the encounter, she literally burned him to a crisp.

After the initial excitement and notoriety wore off, hard-core became predictable and dull. Screen sensuality was both psychological as well as physical. An effective erotic sequence required seduction and foreplay as well as intercourse. This required some acting ability and technical finesse and was even attempted in early soft-core pictures. In contrast, XXX product usually had poor production value and only depicted the mechanical aspects of sex. Acting ability was often limited to faking orgasms. Producers resorted to grotesque or violent subjects to attract new customers bored with the formula. *Long Jeanne Silver* (1977) starred a nude amputee. Like most teens, I attended some of these pictures at the time but my friends and I walked out of this one. It was revolting when the lead actress inserted her stump into various orifices. *Ilsa, She Wolf of the SS* (1974) bridged the gap between sexploitation and horror. Neither picture could be described as erotic.

In 1970, Chris Condon produced the first 3-D porn to achieve widespread success entitled *The Stewardesses*.[14] It inspired a limited sub-genre of dimensional sexploitation in both hard-core and soft-core categories which included gay product. Others titles were *The Chamber Maids* (1972), *Three Dimensions of Greta* (1973), *The Groove Room* (1973), *Prison Girls* (1973), *Ramrod* (1973), *International Stewardesses* (1974), *Love in 3-D* (1974), *Wild Cat Women* (1976), *Experiments in Love* (1976), *Funk in 3-D* (1976), *The Lollipop Girls in Hard Candy* (1976), *The Playmates in Deep Vision 3-D* (1976), *The Starlets* (1976), *The Capitol Hill Girls* (1977), *Heavy Equipment* (1977), *Manhole* (1977), *Disco Dolls in Hot Skin* (1978), *The Surfer Girls* (1978), *Wild Cherry* (1981), *Menage a Trois* (1982), *Beauty Girls for Love* (1983), *Sexcalibur* (1983), *Blonde Emmanuelle* (1984), *Scoring* (1984) and *Venus* (1984). Although the classics *Creature of the Black Lagoon, House of Wax* and *It Came from Outer Space* were reissued simultaneously, 3-D became associated with porn for most of the seventies and did not lose that label until the early eighties with the release of *Comin' at Ya* (1981) and *Jaws 3-D* (1983).

The year 1972 was the end of the line for the X classification as far as studios were concerned. UA released Bertolucci's *Last Tango in Paris* starring Marlon Brando. It was the first time a major star of the past appeared in such graphic material although the sex scenes were soft-core. It was also the last time Brando appeared in good physical shape. Critic Pauline Kael lobbied on behalf of the film but despite the critical acclaim, it did not inspire a trend of legitimate adult dramas. X had become so associated with hard-core, the major distributors avoided releasing films with that rating after 1973 and usually cut them to get the desired R. Despite Valenti's anti-censorship stance, forcing distributors to recut a film for classification was comparable to censoring a film for the Production Code Seal under Breen and Sherlock.

After 1972, there were occasional X pictures that surpassed expectations. Paul Morrissey's *Flesh for Frankenstein* (1973) and *Blood for Dracula* (1973) were outrageously funny satires with excellent production value and off-beat performances. They were photographed back to back at

*Opposite:* Typical 3-D porn (*The Groove Room*, 1973) from the era.

# The Funniest Ⓧ—Rated Flick to come down the Tube this year—

**Only a Boob would take a girl into**

IN **3 D** **DEEP THROW** PROJECTION

**RATED Ⓧ**

"THE GROOVE ROOM"  starring
SUE LONGHURST • OLLIE SOLTOFT • MALOU CARTWRIGHT  and DIANA DORS
Produced and Directed by VERNON P. BECKER
in EASTMAN COLOR
a CONSTELLATION FILMS INC. release

Cinecitta by Luigi Kuvieller. The special effects were by Carlo Rambaldi and atmospheric musical scores by Claudio Gizzi. Warhol Factory regular Joe Dellasandro starred in both along with androgynous German actor, Udo Kier. *Flesh for Frankenstein* was filmed in SpaceVision 3-D. Some of it was quite effective except for close-ups which had extreme convergence. *Blood for Dracula* had funny cameos by Roman Polanski and Vittorio De Sica. *Flesh Gordon* (1973) was another campy comedy and had innovative stop motion animation by Dave Allen, Rob Maine and Jim Danforth. Unfortunately, this level of professionalism was rare as hard-core overwhelmed the industry.

Sexploitation reached its nadir in 1976 with Monarch's *Snuff*. It barely fit into the porno category but its notoriety called attention to the genre. Advertised as an illegal "snuff" film with an on-screen torture and murder of a woman, it was booked into mainstream theaters on a regional basis.

When it played Times Square in New York City, it attracted media attention and protests. Feminists formed a group in opposition to it called "The Organization of Women Against Pornography" which still exists. Vincent Miranda and David F. Friedman of the Adult Film Association of America launched a picketing campaign against the film. They also proposed a ratings change to qualify X with an "Adults Only/E" for erotic films and an "Adults Only/V" for violence but nothing came of it. As it turned out, the picture was a fraud. The climax was derived from another feature which depicted a staged murder with unconvincing special effects. It did illustrate the depths to which some post–1968 exhibitors were willing to descend to increase short term box-office revenue. This was not what the advocates of screen freedom intended but it was too late to roll back the clock.

The herpes outbreak in the seventies and HIV crisis in the eighties further degraded the adult industry and ended the sexual revolution. Traci Lords disclosed that she was only 15 when she made her early films, which put them in the category of child pornography. Johnny "Wadd" Holmes died of AIDS in 1988. The genre eventually shifted to home video formats and most of the porn theaters closed.

Sexploitation had a long term impact on exhibition. Theaters that played hard-core product became run-down and disreputable. It was tragic to see former movie palaces in Times Square (e.g. *The Selwyn*) become grind-house dumps. Prostitutes, drug dealers, pimps and other unsavory characters patronized the areas which made them crime-ridden and dangerous. Martin Scorsese's *Taxi Driver* (1976) depicted the decay of urban porn houses.

# Blaxploitation

The riots of 1967 ruined b.o. even in the ghetto districts because the decent elements feared braving the trip to the nabe cinemas.[15]

The 1960s was a decade of black activism. In the movie business, actors like Sidney Poitier and Bill Cosby petitioned for expanded participation in production. Both played mainstream roles in dramas and comedies with the latter a major television star. Their appeal was multi-racial. Poitier directed a number of features for black audiences including *Buck and the Preacher* (1972), *Uptown Saturday Night* (1974) and *Let's Do It Again* (1975). There were also dramas like *Black Girl* (1972), *Sounder* (1972) and *Lady Sings the Blues* (1973) which received good reviews.

There was a gradual acculturation of blacks that began in the fifties. Nat King Cole had his own variety show in 1957 and Sammy Davis Jr. was a popular entertainer and member of Frank Sinatra's Rat Pack. Many early Rock musicians crossed the color barrier like Chuck Berry and Little Richard. By the sixties, Sidney Poitier was a major box-office attraction in films like *Lilies in the Field* (1963) and *A Patch of Blue* (1965). He won an Oscar for his performance in the former. A new trend was started when Poitier's role in *The Bedford Incident* (1965) was unrelated to race. Duane Jones' character in Romero's *Night of the Living Dead* (1968) and Cosby's lead in the television show, *I Spy* (1965–1968) also had little to do with ethnicity.

Although inroads were made by these and other performers, exploitation producers saw an opportunity to capitalize on the "black power" movement while targeting the 16–26 year old demographic. The genre that catered to this world view was referred to as "blaxploitation." Rather than depict educated, upwardly mobile professionals like Cosby and Poitier, they concentrated on those segregated in the urban ghetto. The heroes of blaxploitation films were often drug dealers (*Super Fly*, 1972), pimps (*The Mack*, 1973) or other criminals (*Black Godfather*, 1975). The fact that these pictures played upon white fear and black racism was part of their popularity for the intended audience. Most were rated R or X. The paradox was that "whites" of European ancestry who were vilified in these films were not politically monolithic nor were most opposed to black progress.

There were blaxploitation pictures that took a different perspective. In movies like *Hit!* (1973), Billy Dee Williams combated drug dealers although those that took this tact fell short of actually criticizing the counterculture which glorified substance abuse. I saw some of these films at the Paramount in Peekskill, New York. It was originally a movie palace but

**Never a dude like this one!**
**He's got a plan to stick it to The Man!**

Repro poster for *Super Fly* (1972).

had become an urban grind-house in the seventies. Attending these screenings was somewhat dangerous since the audience interacted with the screen characters and shouted racist expletives at them.

While a few blaxploitation movies like Ossie Davis's *Cotton Comes to Harlem* (1970) and Gordon Park's *Shaft* (1971) had crossover appeal, the majority were limited to those who subscribed to the militant agenda. Among them were *Black Is Beautiful (African Sexualis)* (1970), *Slaughter* (1972), *Dolemite* (1975) and *The Monkey Hustle* (1977). A number of these pictures were directed by blacks like Davis, Parks and Van Peebles. Others were made by Caucasian low budget filmmakers like Larry Cohen (e.g. *Hell Up in Harlem*, 1973). *Blacula* (1972) and *Black Belt Jones* (1973) merged exploitation genres.

The ethnic stereotypes depicted in most of these movies undermined race relations. Since some were made or distributed by the majors, their production value was somewhat better than the counterculture and sexploitation films although they were not top quality pictures. Few, if any, would've received a Seal had the Production Code remained in place. It's ironic that opponents of the Code often claimed it was racist, ignoring the changes that had been implemented by 1966. It could be argued that post–Code blaxploitation films were more damaging than sixties Seal approved movies which contained black characters like *The Professionals* (1966) or *To Sir, with Love* (1967). Since the filmmakers were associated with the counterculture movement, they fizzled out with it by the late seventies. Blaxploitation also politicized the medium.

Detailed below is a list of notable blaxploitation features which includes both studio and independent releases. A large percentage of these films are racist as are the titles.

**1968**
If He Hollers Let Him Go

**1969**
Up Tight!

**1970**
Black Is Beautiful (African Sexualis)
Cotton Comes to Harlem
Five the Hard Way
It Won't Rub Off, Baby (aka Sweet
　Love, Bitter)
Walk the Walk
The Watermelon Man

**1971**
Black Angels

Black Jesus
Honky
Murder of Fred Hampton
Shaft
Soul to Soul
Sweet Sweetback's Badasssss Song

**1972**
Black Mama, White Mama
Blacula
Bone
Born Black
The Bus Is Coming
Comeback Charleston Blue
Cool Breeze
Farewell, Uncle Tom

The Final Comedown
Hammer
Legend of Nigger Charley
The Limit
Malcolm X
Quadroon
Rainbow Bridge
Shaft's Big Score
Slaughter
Soul Soldier
Soul to Soul
Stigma
Super Fly
Top of the Heap
Trouble Man

### 1973
Black Belt Jones
Black Caesar
Blakenstein
Black Gunn
Black Vampire (aka Ganja and Hess)
Brother on the Run
Charley One-eye
Cleopatra Jones
Coffy
Detroit 9000
Dynamite Brothers
Five on the Black Hand Side
Gordon's War
Greaser's Palace
The Harder They Come
Hell Up in Harlem
Hit!
Hit Man
I Escaped from Devil's Island
The Mack
Mister Freedom
Sambizanga
Savae!
Save the Children
Scream, Blacula, Scream
Shaft in Africa
The Slams
Slaughter's Big Rip-off
The Soul of Nigger Charley
The Spook Who Sat by the Door
Sugar Hill
Super Fly TNT

Sweet Jesus, Preacher Man
That Man Bolt
Trick Baby
Wattstax

### 1974
Angela Davis: Portrait of a Revolutionary
The Arena
The Big Bird Cage
Black Bunch (aka Supersisters)
Black Eye
Black Jesus
Black Samson
Black Six
Black Starlet
Brother John
Change of Mind
Don't Play Us Cheap
Dr. Black and Mr. White
The Education of Sonny Carson
Eldridge Cleaver
Final Comedown
Foxy Brown
Honey Baby, Honey Baby
Melinda
Run, Nigger, Run (aka The Black Connection)
Savage Sisters (aka Ebony, Ivory and Jade)
The Take
Tough
Three the Hard Way
Three Tough Guys
Thomasine and Bushrod
Together Brothers
Truck Turner
Voodoo Black Exorcist
Willie Dynamite

### 1975
Abby
The Black Gestapo (aka Ghetto Warriors)
Black Godfather
Black Lolita (3-D aka Wildcat Women)
Black Shampoo
Bogard
Boss Nigger

Bucktown
Cleopatra Jones and the Casino of
    Gold
Cleopatra Jones Meets the Dragon
    Princess
Coonskin (animated)
Dolemite
Friday Foster
Sheba, Baby
Soul Vengeance (aka Welcome Home
    Brother Charles)
Stud Brown
Super Dude
TNT Jackson

**1976**
Avenging Disco Godfather
Black Fist (aka Black Streetfighter)
Black Heat

Dr. Black and Mr. Hyde
Dolemite 2: Human Tornado
Crackers
Hot Potato
J.D.'s Revenge
Lady Cocoa
Lord Shango
Meet Johnny Barrows
No Way Back

**1977**
Brothers
The Guy from Harlem
The Monkey Hustle

**1978**
Mr. Mean
Young Blood

## Exploitation

Like sexploitation, exploitation films had been around for decades as a shadow cinema. They encompassed various genres including the sex hygiene film (*Mom and Dad*, 1948); narcotics addition (*Reefer Madness*, 1936) and horror (*Maniac*, 1934). The production values were poor in these pictures and their sole appeal was circumventing Production Code restrictions. Dwain Esper and Kroger Babb were among the "Roadshow" men who promoted and released these pictures on a state by state, hit and run basis. In the post–Code era, the first two categories were phased out and the latter expanded upon.

Horror films were a staple of Hollywood product since Universal released *Frankenstein* and *Dracula* in 1931. Their cycle of gothic pictures inspired others to contribute to the genre, most notably Val Lewton. Early horror films were suspenseful and macabre but not graphic since the Production Code didn't allow explicit violence. In the fifties, Hammer Studios released a series of remakes that had brief instances of mild gore combined with good production value and color. They passed Code scrutiny and were expanded upon in the sixties. Indie directors Herschell Gordon Lewis' *2000 Maniacs* (1964) and George Romero's *Night of the Living Dead* (1968) introduced new levels of blood and guts.

The post–Code era allowed producers to incorporate an unlimited amount of graphic on-screen violence. A new genre was created which is referred to under numerous names but I'll go with "Splatter" films. The distinction between this and a horror film is that the former is scary and the latter merely disgusting. In specific instances, gore can add to the impact of a horror film. Romero's classic utilized cannibalism with a Freudian twist. The image of the daughter eating her father and brother eating his sister was disturbing. I saw it at the Las Vegas Cinerama theater in a double-bill with *Ben* in 1972 at age fifteen. It actually gave me reoccurring nightmares for many years.

Unlike the best horror movies, splatter films were not character driven. Their main purpose was to display as much graphic gore as the desired rating allowed. Early exploitation promoters referred to it as the "spectacle" element of the product. Most splatter pictures were cut to receive an R although some were released un-rated like *Mother's Day* (1980). I was the sound editor on that picture, which was my first industry job. Although it was profitable, the reviews were brutal which was typical for this type of film. Critic Tom Buckley of the *Village Voice* called the director "anti-talent." A sub-genre was the "shockumentary." Sixties titles like *Mondo Cane* were reissued during the era. They were designed to disgust audiences with graphic footage of slaughterhouses and other bloody events.

In general, movies in this category were low budget ventures with poor production value, acting and cheap special effects. Among the early titles were *I Drink Your Blood* (1971) and *Last House on the Left* (1972). As with X product, there were a few that surpassed expectations. *Mondo Cane* contained an interesting sequence on Bikini Beach and a haunting theme song. *The Conqueror Worm* (1968) had a good performance by Vincent Price and *Night of the Living Dead* (1968) became a cult classic. *The Texas Chainsaw Massacre* (1973) was stylish and contained a few scares. It was also less graphic than the average picture in this category. John Carpenter's *Halloween* (1978) was a later entry that had good acting and camerawork despite the formula plot.

Most splatter films faced the same problem as sexploitation. They became predictable and boring. Each picture had to surpass the last one to make an impact. Even the advertising followed a formula. The Hallmark Releasing company distributed a number of movies with the same tag, "keep telling yourself it's only a movie." Producers tried gimmicks to generate interest. *Mark of the Devil* (1972) was a German import with bad dubbing but some fairly convincing torture scenes including a tongue pulled out of a woman's mouth. As a stunt, the distributor gave out vomit bags to patrons with their own classification, "Rated V for Violence." This bit of low budget showmanship was more memorable than the picture itself.

Splatter films often played drive-ins and urban grind-houses. As they

# This VOMIT BAG and the PRICE of one ADMISSION will enable YOU to SEE...

the first film
rated V
for violence

Guaranteed
to upset
your stomach

**mark of the devil**

## POSITIVELY THE MOST HORRIFYING FILM EVER MADE

© Copyrighted by Hallmark Releasing Corp. Patent Pending

## SEE IT SOON AT A THEATRE NEAR YOU

An outrageous marketing gimmick for a 1972 splatter genre film.

gained in popularity, they were exhibited in mainstream theaters. Their appeal to the targeted youth audience inspired Hollywood to increase the level of gore in studio films. Warner Bros.' *The Exorcist* (1973) was one of the first big budget features to have explicit and gross special effects.[16] It was far more convincing than low budget efforts. The film was well produced and scary. It received an R rating. As Pauline Kael noted, "If *The Exorcist* had cost under a million, or had been made abroad, it would almost certainly be an X film, but when a movie is as expensive as this one, the M.P.A.A. rating board doesn't dare to give it an X."[17]

As subsequent Splatter movies continued to increase the amount of blood and guts, Hollywood followed suit. Titles in the former category included *The Hills Have Eyes* (1978) and *I Spit on Your Grave* (1978). Fox's *Alien* (1979) and Universal's *The Thing* (1982) were grislier than previous studio releases. The latter two would fall into the category of horror rather than Splatter and were suspenseful pictures.

Splatter movies came in cycles. The first was in the early seventies which encompassed both domestic product and foreign imports from Italy, Germany and Spain. Like other exploitation films, producers merged genres. *Northville Cemetery Massacre* (1976) was a biker movie that included graphic violence as did *Grimm's Fairy Tales for Adults* (1970) which was a sexploitation picture.

The next wave of splatter films was in the early eighties beginning with the low budget hit, *Friday the 13th* (1980) which revitalized the slasher formula. My contribution to this nefarious genre was *Splatter University* in 1983 which was my first feature although I no longer make exploitation films. When producers ran out of ways to mutilate the human body, the genre fizzled out although it's made a recent comeback with *Scream* (1996) and the spoof, *Scary Movie* (2000). In both cases, these films were mild compared to the ones made in the past and had better production value. Whether graphic gore is more frightening than psychological terror (e.g. *Carnival of Souls*, 1961, *Repulsion*, 1965, *Silence of the Lambs*, 1991) is a matter of taste. There are critics and fans of both types of horror films. Splatter exploitation did increase the level of cinema violence in general.

Another genre in the exploitation category that appeared after 1968 was the Martial Arts film. The cycle began with the import of Bruce Lee Chinese features in the early seventies. Among them were *Fists of Fury*, 1971 and *The Chinese Connection*, 1972. Lee was a former television star (*The Green Hornet*) whose Hollywood career had fizzled out. He went to Asia to make low budget action pictures that featured his unique style of martial arts combat. Although he was an excellent athlete, the movies were badly made, had atrocious dubbing and incoherent plots. They became popular in urban cinemas and Hollywood took notice. Warner Bros.' *Enter the Dragon* (1973) starred Lee and had better production value than the imports. It was the best picture he had appeared in when he died of a brain edema the same year.

The genre didn't disappear after his untimely death and other indies imported additional Asian product with stars named "Bruce Li" and titles like *Bruce Li, Super Dragon* (1977). Martial Arts was integrated into other categories including blaxpoitation (*Black Belt Jones*, 1974), horror (*Legend of the Seven Golden Vampires*, 1971), and 3-D (*Revenge of the Shogun Women*, 1977). It continued into the eighties and nineties with new martial arts stars Steven Seagal (*Above the Law*, 1988), Jean-Claude Van Damme (*Bloodsport*, 1988) and Jackie Chan (*Rush Hour*, 1998).

While martial arts films were very violent, the action was so outlandish they couldn't be taken seriously. Combatants would get kicked in the groin then jump up and start fighting again. The sound effects were similar to those used in Three Stooges comedies. It was not uncommon to hear the same slap effect for a face kick and stomach punch, especially in the Chinese imports. The US made product was somewhat better and there were at least two memorable productions in the genre, *Enter the Dragon* (1973) and *Under Siege* (1992). Most of these pictures were rated R but had little impact on exhibition and I mention them only for the historical record.

Detailed below is a list of notable splatter features from the first cycle. Most of these films were grind-house product although there were a few gems as previously mentioned.

**1968**
The Conqueror Worm
Night of the Living Dead

**1969**
Bloodthirsty Butchers
Night of Bloody Horror
Torture Garden

**1970**
Africa, Blood and Guts (1966 reissue
 aka Africa Addio)
Beast of Blood
Flesh Feast
Grimm's Fairy Tales for Adults
I Drink Your Blood

I Eat Your Skin
Mondo Cane I (1962 reissue)
Mondo Cane II (1964 reissue)
Next Victim! (Italy/Spain)

**1971**
Blood Freak
Carnival of Blood
Corpse Grinders
From Ear to Ear
Next!
The Peace Killers
Secret Rites
Sweet Savior (aka The Love-Thrill
 Murders)

**1972**
Bloodsuckers (aka Incense for the
   Damned)
Feast of Flesh
Mark of the Devil
Scream Bloody Murder
Twitch of Death Nerve

**1973**
Andy Warhol's Dracula
Andy Warhol's Frankenstein
The Body Shop (aka Dr. Gore)
Cannibal Girls
Caldron of Death
House of Psychotic Women
Last House on the Left
Silent Night, Bloody Night
Slaughter Hotel

**1974**
Blood Splattered Bride
Deranged
Kwaheri (reissue made in 1964)
Mark of the Devil II
Shriek of the Mutilated
Texas Chainsaw Massacre
They Call Her One Eye
Torso
Vampires

**1975**
Behind the Door
Ilsa, Harem Keeper for the Oil Sheiks
Ilsa, She Wolf of the SS
Mary, Mary, Bloody Mary
Street Fighter

**1976**
Blood Bath
Eaten Alive
The House by the Lake
Horror Rises from the Tomb
Northville Cemetery Massacre
Scum of the Earth
Snuff
Survive
Switchblade Sisters

**1977**
Autopsy
Eyes (aka Mansion of the Doomed)
The Last Cannibal World
Rabid Ruby

**1978**
Eyeball
Halloween
The Hills Have Eyes
Incredible Torture Show
I Spit on Your Grave
Legacy of Blood

# *Indies*

In the late sixties, there were seven major distributors: Columbia, MGM, Paramount, 20th Century–Fox, United Artists, Universal and Warner Bros./Seven Arts. There were also five mini-majors including Allied Artists, Avco-Embassy, Disney's Buena Vista, Cinerama Releasing and National General.

The years 1969–1979 also saw the greatest increase of independent distributors in the history of the medium. Most existed solely to take advantage of the new screen freedom. However, within their ranks there were some legitimate companies that booked foreign films, art house pictures, children's product and filled a niche in the marketplace. Some distributed films in various categories which accounts for the multiple listings below although most focused on one type of product.

## Art House Distributors

Foreign films were very popular at the time and a number of independents catered to this market. Some of these companies also booked domestic art house pictures. Among the notable ones was Continental, which was a subsidiary of Walter Reed theaters. They secured the rights to the Sovscope 70 Russian epic, *War and Peace* (1968) and released it in two parts with a U.S. running time of 373 minutes. The company also marketed exploitation fare like Romero's *Night of the Living Dead*. Kino International was founded in 1977 as the theatrical distributor of the Janus library which contained the works of notable foreign directors like Fellini and Kurowawa. The American Film Theatre and Theatre Television Corporation released photographed versions of plays. Classic Festival Corporation reissued Chaplin's films. Detailed below is a list of companies.

Ajay
The American Film Theatre
Anglo-Amalgamated EMI
ArtKino
Associated British EMI
Bauer International
British Lion
Carnival Films
Carolyn Films
Cine-III Distributors
Cinema V
Classic Festival Corporation
Clover/Liberty Studios
Cohen, Shlomi
Continental
EDP Films
Empresa Cinema Internacional
Exxel Film Group
Fania Releasing
Filmtri Continental
First Artists
Golden Films
Julio Tanjeloff Productions

Kino International
Libra
Macmillan Audio Brandon Films
Magna Distributing
Maysles Brothers
Merchant-Ivory
Midwest Film Productions
Monument Films
New Yorker Films
Nu-Image Film
Opera Presentations
Pathé
Peppercorn-Wormser
PRO International
P.W.E. Inc.
Quartet
Rank
Royal Films International
Sovexport Film-Kino
Specialty Films
Surrogate Releasing
Theatre Television Corporation
VIP Distributors

## General Audience and Children's Films Distributors

The number of R and X rated films inspired some companies to cater to general audiences and the juvenile trade by booking G and GP (PG) rated fare. While there were a few hits in this category like Pacific International's *Adventures of the Wilderness Family* (1976) and Mulberry Square's *Benji* (1974), most were minor pictures with little adult interest so they probably did not increase family attendance in the long run. Many were released via saturation bookings. Sun International (Sun Classics) marketed implausible documentaries like *In Search of Noah's Ark* (1976) and *The Outer Space Connection* (1975) which were popular for a while as were nature films like their *The Life & Times of Grizzly Adams* (1975). Opera Presentations released titles like *The Live, Love and Music of Giuseppi Verdi*.

Others included K. Gordon Murray and his competitor, Barry Yellen of Childhood Productions. They had cornered the "Children's Matinee" market in the sixties by importing poorly dubbed and grotesque Mexican and German fairy tale features. Murray's releases included *Little Red Riding Hood*, *Puss 'N' Boots* and *The Golden Goose*. Among Yellen's pictures were *Snow White*, *The 7 Dwarfs to the Rescue* and *Sleeping Beauty*. I saw these movies in theaters as an adolescent and found them quite bizarre. Murray and Yellen also had subsidiary companies that released R and X grind-house product. Murray's Trans-International Pictures offered titles like *Shanty Tramp* and *Savages from Hell*. Yellen's Chevron released *I, A Woman Part II* and *How to Seduce a Playboy* which was quite an unusual line. American Films, Ltd. CPA Investors IV, Ellman Film Entertainments, K-Tel International, Scotia American and Turtle Releasing also booked both G and R rated titles.

Detailed below is a list of companies that catered to the general audience and juvenile market.

AFC Distribution
Ambassador Releasing
American Cinema
American Films, Ltd.
American National
April Fool's Films
Artists Creation
Atlantis Productions
Big Horn Productions
Borden Films
Brock, Stan
Brut Productions
Capital Productions, Inc.
Cardinal Films
Centrum International
C.F.F. Inc.
Childhood Productions
Cinamco, Inc.

Cinamerica
Clamil Productions
Commodore Releasing
Concord
Cornsweet, Harold
Costeau Group
CPA Investors IV
Dana Don
Dandrea Releasing
Dingletone-Dabema
Dottie-Dayton Productions
Downtown Distribution
E.D.P. Films
Eicoff, Alvin
Ellman Film Entertainments
Epoc Releasing
Film Gems
Films-A-Life

Indie distributors Barry Yellen and K. Gordon Murray dealt with both G rated children's matinee features (like *The 7 Dwarfs to the Rescue*, 1965) and R and X rated exploitation, which was an unusual pairing.

4-Wall Distributors
G.G. Productions Releasing Company
Golden Circle
Hans Domnick Films
Happy Trails
Hauge, Alan
Heritage Enterprises
HNT Corporation
Howco International
Inter Planetary
K. Gordon Murray
K-Tel International
Key Whole
Lighthouse Productions
Maragill
McMiddigen, John
Menora
Mulberry Square
North American Film
Opera Presentations
Pacific International
Palladium

Pan-American
PHA Films
Prentiss Productions
P.W.E. Inc.
Raylin Productions/Creative Enter-
   prises
Reader's Digest Productions
Renalda Films
Roja Corporations
Rumson Films Distributors, Inc.
Sanrio Film Release
Scorpio International
Scotia American
Sierra Associates
Specialty Films
Sun International (Sun Classics)
Surrogate Releasing
TBS Film Distributors
Topar Films
Turtle Releasing
Westamerica
Xerox

## Counterculture, Sexploitation, Blaxploitation and Exploitation Distributors

The Post-Code era also saw the emergence on many "fly by night" indies who catered to the youth market within the various categories of counterculture, exploitation, blaxploitation and sexploitation. Few survived for long and many distributed a handful of pictures, then folded. This was typical for porn companies. Others specialized in specific genres like Terry Levine's Aquarius, whose main product was martial arts films. Some directors attempted to market their own pictures. Tom (*Billy Jack*) Laughlin of Taylor-Laughlin Distributing was an example. He tried to entice theaters into booking his counterculture pictures by offering more generous terms than was common practice at the time. His rental policy enabled exhibitors to recoup between two to four times their up front guarantee with the remaining box-office grosses to be split on a conventional 40/60 basis with the distributor.

There were some holdovers from the Production Code era like A.I.P. which continued to make low budget exploitation but with an increased amount of sex, violence and nudity. Roger Corman's New World produced similar product which was directed by upcoming New Hollywood filmmakers. The majority of the movies these companies released were rated R or X. Since mainstream theaters were no longer required to book movies with a Seal, they often played these pictures. Prints lingered around for years at the bottom half of double-bills or as the second or third feature in drive-in fare. Grind-houses played them until the copies were too faded or worn to project.

In the counterculture genre, the distributors included Abel-Child Productions, Cinema V, Grove Press, Fanfare, Leacock-Pennebaker, Maron Films, Sigma II, and Regional Films. Among their releases were *Putney Swope*, *More* and *WR-Mysteries of the Organism* from Cinema V. Fanfare distributed *The Gay Deceivers* and *Wild Wheels*. Leacock-Pennebaker had *Monterey Pop* and *Don't Look Back*. Sigma II titles included De Palma's *Greetings* and *Hi Mom!* as well as sexploitation movies like *The Love Doctors*. Regional Films handled *Can Heironymus Merkin Ever Forget Mercy Humppe and Find True Happiness?* and *The Activist*. Sherpix marketed Warhol's *Lonesome Cowboys*, Paul Morrissey's *Trash* and Condon's *The Stewardesses* in 3-D. They also released one of the first hard-core features, *Mona* in 1970.

In the exploitation and horror field were Aquarius, Bryanston, Crown International, Excelsior, Hallmark, Jack H. Harris Enterprises and Lopert. Crown International released *Blood of Dracula's Castle* and *Nightmare in Wax*. Hallmark Releasing had *Mark of the Devil* and *Last House on the Left*. Cinemation booked *I Drink Your Blood*, which was among the early splatter films. Jack H. Harris low budget titles included *Hungry Wives* and *Schlock*.

Sexploitation distributors included Audubon, Boxoffice International, Joseph Brenner Associates, Cambist, Cannon, Chancellor Films, Cinemation Industries, Constellation Films, Distinction Films, Distribpix, Inc., Entertainment Ventures, Inc., Eve Productions, Group 1 Films, Grove Press, Haven International, Sherpix and Trans-World Attractions. Titles included Audubon's *Camille 2000* and *The Libertine*. Boxoffice International had *The Secret Sex Lives of Romeo and Juliet* and *Weekend Lovers*. Lee Hessel's Cambist titles were *The Female* and *The Minx*. Cannon had *Incest* and *Guess What We Learned in School Today*. *Submission* and *Potpourri* were marketed by Chancellor Films, Inc. Jerry Gross's Cinemation had *Fanny Hill*, *Female Animal*, *Grimm's Fairy Tales for Adults* and the blaxploitation movie, *Sweet Sweetback's Baadasssss Song*. Distinction Films released *Eugenie ... The Story of Her Journey into Perversion* and *Nana*. Distribpix had *Kiss Me Mate*, *Three Sexeteers* and *Four on the Floor*. Entertainment Ventures, Inc., pictures were *The Ribald Tales of Robin Hood*, *Thar She Blows* and *Trader Hornee*. Eve Productions marketed Russ Meyer's

*Harry, Raquel and Cherry* and *The Vixen*. Group 1 Films had *House of 1000 Pleasures* and *Diary of a Rape*. Grove Press distributed the "art house sexploitation" films like *I Am Curious, Yellow* and *I Am Curious, Blue*. J.E.R. Pictures had movies with titles like *Depraved, The Degenerates* and *The Flesh Game*. Troma, Inc. distributed *Sweet and Sour* and *Hot Nasties*.

Most of these indies booked titles in multiple genres. Grove Press also handled counterculture films and Cannon released sexploitation. A few mainstreamed their operations. Cannon's hit film, *Joe* (1970), inspired the company to move out of the exploitation field. They became a mini-major under the management of Golan-Globus in the eighties before folding. New World and New Line eventually mainstreamed their operations too. Most of the movies released by these companies during this era were bottom of the barrel product, but there were occasional quality pictures. Cinemation distributed Ralph Bakshi's *Fritz the Cat* in 1972 which grossed $4,000,000. They also reissued Elia Kazan's *Baby Doll* (1956) in 1969. Bryanston had Morrissey's *Flesh for Frankenstein* and *Blood for Dracula*. Sherpix reissued the fifties 3-D classic *House of Wax*.

With the advent of home video in the eighties, most indies folded or switched to that venue. There were fewer of these companies in subsequent decades engaged in theatrical exhibition. Since the corporations that marketed these pictures and most of the labs they were processed in are long gone, many of these features are probably lost outside of private film collections. These small time indies came and went but made an impact on exhibition when they flooded the market with second-rate R and X product for a decade.

Detailed below is a list of indie distributors who catered to the youth demographic from 1968 to 1979. Several merged over the years including Four Star and Excelsior, Gemini and Maron and National General and Cinema Center Films. Commonwealth United distributed their product through A.I.P. in 1971. Troma, Inc., moved from hard-core porn into R rated sex comedies like *The First Turn On* (1982) and campy horror films such as *The Toxic Avenger* (1985), both of which I edited when I was their post-production supervisor in the eighties. They are one of the few remaining exploitation distributors engaged in theatrical exhibition.

| | |
|---|---|
| A. Sterling Gold Ltd. | ACF |
| Abbey Theatrical Films | Adair Films |
| ABC Interstate | Adelphia Pictures Corporation |
| Abel-Child Productions | Adpix, Inc. |
| Abkco Films | Adventure Productions |
| Able Films | AEA |
| Ace Booking | AFC Distributing |

*(Indie distributors, continued)*
A.I.P.
Ajay Films
Alcyone
Allen, Jason
Alexander International
All-Film Enterprises
Allstar Producers
All State
All-Scope
Altura Films International, Inc.
Amalgamated Gigantic
American Cinema
American Continental Films
American National Enterprises
Ane
Andy Warhol Films
Angelika Films
Angels
Anonymous Triumvirate
Anthenaeum Film
Apollo Productions
Apple
Aquarius Releasing, Inc.
Aquila
Argos Films
Arthur Productions
Ariane Films
Artimis
Art in Motion Productions
Artisan Releasing Corporation
Artists International
ASF
Asom
Associated Artists
Astro Releasing
Asthena Films
Atlantic Releasing
Atlas Films
ATV-ITC
Audio Brandon
Audubon Films, Inc.
August Films
Aurora City Group Inc.
Bardene International
Barely Proper Distribution
Barrister Productions
B.M.P. Producing
BCP

Beacon Releasing
Beattie Releasing, Inc.
Belford
B.E. Productions
Betram W. Lee
Bil-Ko
Blazers Co.
Blueberry Hill Films
B.M.P. Producing
Bona-Fide Productions
Borden Releasing
Boxoffice International Film Distrib.
Brandon
Joseph Brenner Associates, Inc.
Brian Distributing
Brain Distribution Corporation
Brode
Brode, Seymore
Bruck, Jerry
Bryanston Distributors
Buckley Brothers
Buffalo Films
Burbank International
Burt Martin Films
B&W Distributors
Cal-Tex
Cal-Vista International
Camscope
Camelot Entertainment
Campbell Devon Productions
Cambist Films
Cannon Releasing Corporation (Cannon-Happy)
Caribou Films
Casino
C-B Productions
Centaur Releasing
Centro Distributing
Centronics
Centrum International Film Group
C.G. Productions
Chancellor Films, Inc.
Charles Films, Inc.
Cheerleaders Company
Cherokee
Chevron Pictures
Christiana Productions
Chris Releasing
Chuck Vincent Productions

Ciem, Inc.
Cinamerica Releases, Inc.
Cinar Productions
Cine Artists International
Cinecom
Cine Globe, Inc.
Cinema Center Films
Cinema Financial Corp.
Cinema V
Cinemagic Pictures
Cinema Horizons
Cinema International
Cinema National Corp.
Cinema Shares International
Cinema 10
Cinematix
Cinemation Industries, Inc.
Cinema-Vu
Cinemax
Cinemedia International
Cinepix-USA, Inc.
Cineprobe-Variety Films (merger)
Cinetex
Cinevision Films, Ltd.
Cineworld Corporation
Citel-USA
Citrus Productions, Inc.
Clamil Productions
Claridge
Clark Film
Clover Films (Clover/Liberty)
C.M.B. Films
CMPC
Coast Industries
Cock-Rock Releasing
Colby
Coliseum Films, Ltd.
Colmar, Ltd.
Command Cinema
Commonwealth United
Conner Distribution
Constellation Films
Contemporary Films
Conqueror Promotion
Coralta
Corwin-Mahler
Countrywide Distribution
Coralta
J. Cornelius Crean Films Inc.

CPA Investors IV
Craddock Films
Creative Coalition
Crismar Associates
Cristiana Productions
Crown International Pictures, Inc.
Crystal Pictures
CUC
Sean S. Cunningham Films
Cupid
Cyanide
Dal-Art
Dalia Productions
Dana Don
Dandilion
Dandrea Releasing-Marvin Films
  (merger)
Daniel Bourla Film Enterprises
Dauntless Productions
Desert Productions
Directors Enterprises
Donald A. Davis Productions, Inc.
DHS Films
Dick Ross and Associates
Dimension Pictures
Dingletone-Dabema
Diplomat Pictures
Directors Enterprises
Distinction Films
Distripix, Inc.
Distributed thru Lesure Media
Dominant
Don Henderson Film
Dorad
D/R Films
Duffy, Kevin
Dundee Productions, Inc.
Eagle International
Eden
E.C.U. Inc.
808 Pictures
Eisenlohr, David C.
E.K. Corporation
Elevated Entertainments
Ellman Film Entertainment
El Sol/Craig
Emco Films, Inc.
Emerson Film Entertainments
Enchanted Filmarts

*(Indie distributors, continued)*
Entertainment Pyramid
Entertainment Systems
Entertainment Ventures, Inc.
Entertainment World
E.O. Productions
Epoc
Equal Opportunities Company
Eroica Entertainments, Ltd.
Espana Films
Essex Distributing, Inc.
EUC
Europix International Ltd.
Evart Releasing
Eve Productions
EYR Films
Excelsior
Exquisite
Faces International
F.A.I.
Fairbanks, Jerry
Falcon Productions
Fanfare Corporation
Far West Films
Fanzia Records Releasing
FDC
Feazell Ltd.
FGM Export
Field Films
Filmaco Inc.
Film Enterprises, Inc.
Film Gems
Film Group
The Film League, Inc.
Film-Makers Internat'l Releasing Co.
Film Productions, Inc.
Film Ventures International
Filmways
Finest Films, Inc.
Fipco
First Artists Company
First Asian Films of California
First Musical Company
1st Southern Cinema
James Flocker Productions
Format Films
Four Star-Excelsior (merger)
Four Star International
Frank-Russell

Frederick
Freena
Freeway Films Corporation
Futurama
G.A. Film
Gail Film Company
Gamalex Associates
Gamma III
Gateway Films
Gemini Film Distribution, Inc.
Gemini/Maron (merger)
Gendon Films
Geneni
George Gund Release
General film Corporation
Gerard Damiano Productions
Geunette
Giant 4
Gibson, Stephen
Gillman
Glenn, Dan
Globe Pictures, Inc.
Gold Key Entertainment
Golden Circle
Golden Eagle Films, Inc.
Goldstone Film Enterprises, Inc.
G.P. Management
Grads
Graffiti Productions
Grand Corporation
Grand National
Grand Range, Ltd.
Green, Joseph
Greydon Clark
Group 1 Films
Group 3
Grove Press
GSF Productions, Inc.
Hallmark Releasing
Hampton International Pictures
Harold Robbins International
Harnell Independent Productions
Haven International Pictures
Hawthorne Films
H.B. Halicki
Headliner
Hemisphere Pictures, Inc.
Herman Cohen Productions
Hershman

Hexter
H.G. Entertainment
HIFCA
Hitite Films
HK Film Corporation
HMS Film Corporation
Hollywood Cinema Associates
Hollywood Cinemart
Hollywood International Film Corporation of America
Hollywood Star
The Honey Company
Horizon Films
HSP
Hudson Valley Corporation
Hye Arts International
Idalene
I.A.E.
Imago Films
Independent International Pictures Corporation
Independently Released
Independent Producers
Indepix Releasing
In-Frame Films
Instant Distributors
Institute for Adult Education
Intercontinental Releasing
International Amusement Corporation
International Cinema Corporation
International Cinefilm
International Co-Productions, Inc. (Pisces Group)
International Producers Corporation
International Talent
Interwest
IPC
I.R.M.I. Films
Irwin Yablans Company
ITC
Jack H. Harris Enterprises, Inc.
Jacobs, Edward
Jama Productions
Jaquar
Jaylo International
J.C. Crean Films
J.E.R. Pictures, Inc.
Jerand Films Inc.

Julio Tanjeloff Productions
Inish Kae, Ltd.
Jordan, Kelly
Kemal Enterprises, Inc.
Kaleidoscope
Kathleen Productions
K.B. Productions
Kelly-Jordan
Kenmore
Key Films (Key International)
Killing Her Now Company
Kirt Films
Knuts Productions
Kroger Babb
Kung Fu Films
Kybo Productions
L.A.N.A. Films
Lang
LBJ Film Distributors, Inc.
L.C.S. Distribution
Leacock-Pennebaker
Leabell-Brunswick
Leisure Media
Leisure Time Booking
Lemming Productions
Lendor
Leon Film Enterprises
Levitt-Pickman Film Corporation
Lewis Motion Picture Enterprises
L. Five Films
Libra Films
Lima Productions
Lodie Distributing
Lopert
Lovina
L-P Corporation
L-T Films
Lustig Productions
MacRoden Films
Magellan Ltd.
Magna Pictures Corporation
Mago
The Magus Film Group
Malibu Productions
Howard Mahler Films
Maltese
Mammoth Films
Manson Distributing
Maron Films Limited

*(Indie distributors, continued)*
Mars
Marshall
Marvin Films, Inc.
Matterhorn Films
Mature Pictures Corporation
Mayfair Film Group
MB Productions
McLead Films
Medallion
Medford Film Corporation
Media Cinema
Meridan Films Ltd.
Merrick International Films
Merritt-White Ltd.
Metromedia Productions
MFD Corporation
Mid-Broadway
Midwest Film Productions
Minotaur Films
Minsky
Mirage Film, Inc.
Mitam Productions
Mitchell Brothers Film Group
M.J.L. Productions
Modern
Monarch Releasing Corporation
Montgomery Productions
Moonstone
Motion Picture Marketing, Inc.
The Movie Company
MPO Vid
MSW Presentations
MTPS
Mushroom
Mutual Film Service, Inc.
Mutual General Film Company
National Entertainment Corporation
National Entertainment of Detroit
National General-Cinema Center
   (merger)
National Leisure Corporation
National Productions
National Showmanship
New American
New Day Pictures
New Line Cinema
Newport
New World Pictures

New Yorker Films
NMD Films
NMO Film Distributing
No Moss Productions
Northwest
Nova Productions
Nu-South Films
Oakshire
Omni Pictures Corporation
Orrin Pictures
Ourada
Oxford Films
Pace
Pacific Coast Films
Pacific Grove
Palomar
P & L Management
Pantages
Paragon Pictures
P & C Inc.
Paul Mart Productions, Inc.
Peacock
Peeble Productions, Inc.
Penelope Productions
Penthouse Productions
Peppercorn-Wormser
PG Films
Phantasy Films
Pharoah
Phase One Films, Inc.
Phoenix International Films
Photographer Productions
Pic American Corporation
Pierce, Chas.
Pine-Thomas
Pinelope Productions
Pinnacle Productions
Pioneer Productions
Plaintain Films
Plateau Productions
Platter Productions
Playboy Productions
Plaza Pictures
Plitt
P&L Management
Plura Distribution
Plymouth Distributors
P.M. Films
PMK Production

Poinciana Productions
Poolemar Productions
Pop films
Porta
Portrait Releasing
Power & Communications
PPP Releasing
Preacherman
Preemore, Inc.
Premier Productions
Prestige
Prentoulis
PR Film Service
Producers Commercial
Producers Distribution Corporation
Productions Unlimited
Pyramid Pictures
Quality Film
Max L. Raab
Radim Films
R.A. Enterprises
R.A.F. Industries
Rainbow Distributors, Inc.
Regent
Regional Films
Re-mart International
Renn Productions
Renzy, Alex De
Republic Arts
Return to Campus Productions
Richard A. Enterprises
Richmark
Rising Sun Enterprises
Rittmuller, Meisel
Rogers
Romatt Releasing Company
Ronin Films
Rook, Albert E.
Rosebud
Ross, Kelly
Ted Roter/Film and Stage Productions
Royal Films International
R & S Film Enterprises
Russ Meyer Films International
Sabastian
Saeta
Sagittarius Productions
Sal/wa-Stagestruck

Salt Water
S.A.M. Distribution
Sam Lake Enterprises, Inc.
Sands Distributing Company
Saturn Pictures
Saxton Films
SCA Distributors
Schnell
Schoenfeld Film Distributing
Schooner
Scope III Inc.
Scotia International Films, Inc. (Scotia American)
Screencom International Corporation
Screening Room Productions
Seaberg Film Distributing, Inc.
Sequoia
S.J. International
Silver Screen
Specialty Films
Seventh Seal
Shaw
Shermart Distributing Company
Sherpix Inc.
Sigma II
Silver Screen Productions
S.J. International
Skinner, Peter
Sorrogate Releasing
Southern Star Productions
Specialty Film
Spencer Productions
Sperling
Sprague, Peter J.
SRC Films, Inc.
Standard Films
Starline
Steinman-Baxter
Stellar Film IV Corporation
Starmaker Inc.
Starmaster, Inc.
Stratford
Steko Motion Pictures, Inc.
Stu Seagall & Associates
Stuart Ducan Productions
Sullivan, M.D.
Sunset International
Sunshine Unlimited
Superior Films

*(Indie distributors, continued)*
Supreme Mix
Surety Releasing Corporation
Taft
Target International Films
Taurus Film Company
Taylor-Laughlin Distributing
TBS Film Distributors
TEA
Ted Mann Productions
Telefilm Company
Theatre Exchange Activities, Inc.
Thomas Enterprises
Three-D Vision
III LQJ Corporation
Times Film Corporation
Tinc Productions
To Be Productions
Tomorrow Enterprises
Topar Films
Topaz Films Corporation
Tower Film Corporation
Traom, Inc.
Transamerican
Trans-International Pictures
Trans-Lux Distribution Corporation
Trans-National
Transvue Pictures Corporation
Trans World Attractions
Tricontinental Film Center
Troka, Inc.
Troma, Inc.
Trio Releasing
Turner, Mary E.
Turtle Releasing
21st Century
Tynman Films
U-M Distributors
Unisphere Releasing Corporation
United Film Distribution
United International Pictures
United Marketing

United Productions
United Theaters United World
Universal Film Exchange
Unusual
UPRO
U.S. International
Vagar Films
Valiant International Pictures
Van Guard Releasing
Variety Films
Vaudio Inc.
Venture Distribution
Victoria Capital
Virgo International
Viola Films
VIP Distributors
Voyage Productions
Vortex, Inc.
Walnut International Productions
Wargay Corporation
Washita Films
Wayne, Hagen
Weiner
Weis
Westamerica Film Distributors, Inc.
Westbury
Western International
Westland
William Mishkin, Motion Pictures,
    Inc.
William Thompson Pictures Corp.
Winter Film
Wolf Lore Cinema
World Amusement
World Northal
World-Wide Films
WSF
Xanadu Productions
Xeromega
Zenith
Ziv/Tel

# Post-Code Auteurs

Thus far I've discussed filmmakers who took advantage of screen freedom. There were a number of directors who used it artistically and produced some of the finest films of the era. Most could be considered auteurs and had a great deal of creative freedom compared to those who worked within the boundaries of the Production Code. Martin Scorsese was one of the critically acclaimed directors who made controversial pictures about violent and disturbed protagonists. *Mean Streets* (1973) dealt with small time hoods and *Taxi Driver* (1976) chronicled the mental breakdown of a Vietnam veteran. Both had riveting performances by Robert De Niro. Sidney Lumet's *Serpico* (1973) dealt with the drug trade and police corruption. Francis Ford Coppola's *The Godfather* (1972) and *The Godfather Part II* (1974) were excellent dramas that examined the family structure of organized crime.

What's interesting from a historical perspective is what these top quality R rated films had in common. All contained explicit sex, violence and strong language which would not have been permitted under the 1966 modified Code. They were also extremely grim and made from a liberal perspective. The screenwriters suggested that the pathology of the characters was a result of society and the "system" rather than personal character flaws. None of these movies had the vibrant color cinematography of "Old Hollywood" product although the dark and gloomy imagery worked within the context of the themes. Advocates of New Hollywood would cite these examples as the justification for the abandonment of industry self-regulation. Other quality R and X rated films that expanded the limits of screen freedom included Ken Russell's *The Devils* (1971), William Friedkin's *The French Connection* (1971), Sam Peckinpah's *Straw Dogs* (1971) and Mel Brooks' *Blazing Saddles* (1974).

## Backlash

> In the aftermath of the appalling real-life violence that has infected our culture, several critics have seconded Pauline Kael's feeling that "at the movies, we are gradually being conditioned to accept violence…. Surely, when night after night atrocities are served up to us as entertainment, it's worth some anxiety.[18]

> Alarmed moralist saw the fall of the Roman Empire all over again…. There was the argument that pornopix promoted sexual imagination; against that argument that community culture was being polluted.[19]

> Valenti makes the point that there is "no mass audience anymore" and filmmakers are in a state of uncertainty.[20]

The change in motion picture content in the Post-Code era had a backlash. On the Left, feminists continued to campaign against pornography which they believed degraded women. On the Right, conservatives claimed movies had become gory and decadent. Even centrists wondered whether there was a connection between violent behavior, sexually transmitted diseases, substance abuse and motion picture content.

There was little evidence that an individual movie could make a viewer change his behavior except in extreme or unusual circumstances.[21] Whether the enormous volume of agit-prop, pornographic and violent films de-sensitized audiences in the long run is a topic that continues to be debated. Some states fought what they considered the corrupting influence of modern cinema. Billy Jenkins, an Albany, Georgia, theater manager was convicted of obscenity for exhibiting *Carnal Knowledge* (1971). The case was brought to the Supreme Court which later overturned the State of Georgia ruling.

To a large extent it was a numbers game. No one could deny the brilliance of Coppola's *The Godfather* (1972) which contained more graphic violence than previous gangster films. *Carnal Knowledge* was a thought-provoking look at sexual attitudes that never would've received a Seal. *Lenny* (1974) had strong language and sexually explicit sequences for adult audiences. However, for each quality R or X rated film there were hundreds that exploited screen freedom and drove away potential moviegoers. Many of them were released by indie companies. Mainstream cinemas played product that had been relegated to grind-houses and burlesque theaters in the past. I don't want to suggest that counterculture, splatter and sexploitation distributors were intentionally undermining exhibition. Most were hustlers trying to get a piece of the action. They existed prior to 1968 but the Production Code gave them parameters to operate in. When the Seal was abandoned, the industry no longer had a self-regulating entity to prevent excesses that harmed the business in its relationship with the public and critics.

There was no coordination between distributors and exhibitors regarding the type of pictures available for bookings, which made it difficult to maintain a stable audience demographic. In one month, the majority of titles would be G or M but the next month R and X would dominate. Instead of families attending movies consistently, they went occasionally. Valenti did not mediate the various factions as his predecessors did. He remained a staunch advocate of the ratings system regardless of the consequences.

One of the major objections to the Code was that it tended to keep content restrained for middle-class sensibilities. Valenti argued that the political and cultural turmoil of the era should not be restricted from screenplays. As of 1968, there were few films that used Vietnam, black militancy and campus radicalism as subject matters. The question remained, what was the purpose of cinema? Did audiences attend theatres to escape reality or to be bombarded with the uglier side of current events? Compared to previous decades when message films were only a small percentage of the yearly product, the industry was unable to find an appropriate balance in the late sixties and early seventies. From an exhibitor's perspective, PG rated films without a political ax to grind like *Diamonds Are Forever* (1971), *The Poseidon Adventure* (1972), *The Sting* (1973), *Murder on the Orient Express* (1974) and *The Towering Inferno* (1974) tended to outgross most agit-prop or exploitation features although there were notable exceptions.

## Product Shift

Following is a chart[22] of Post-Code releases. The yearly ratings indicate which "targeted audience" was being catered to by major, mini-major and independent distributors. In the X category, I've only listed non-pornographic titles (e.g. *The Devils, The Damned*). I also included reissues of pre–1968 pictures that were subsequently classified and films that were released under different ratings (e.g. *MASH*). Some of the NC-17 films were originally X rated studio releases that were reclassified (e.g. *Last Tango in Paris*).

**1968/1969**
G rated films: 187
M rated films: 192
R rated films: 124
X rated films: 19

**1970**
G rated films: 91
GP rated films: 139
R rated films: 160
X rated films: 16

**1971**
G rated films:107
GP rated films: 201
R rated films: 183
X rated films: 5

**1972**
G rated films: 90
GP/PG rated films: 218
R rated films: 200
X rated films: 8

**1973**
G rated films: 89
PG rated films: 194
R rated films: 270
X rated films: 7

**1974**
G rated films: 76
PG rated films: 186
R rated films: 230

**1975**
G rated films: 57
PG rated films: 160
R rated films: 205
X rated films: 3

**1976**
G rated films: 61
PG rated films: 155
R rated films: 210
X rated films: 2

### 1977
G rated films: 47
PG rated films: 147
R rated films: 157
X rated films: 2

### 1978
G rated films: 39
PG rated films: 147
R rated films: 121

### 1979
G rated films: 22
PG rated films: 146
R rated films: 165

### 1980
G rated films: 14
PG rated films: 127
R rated films: 157

### 1981
G rated films: 7
PG rated films: 103
R rated films: 193

### 1982
G rated films: 11
PG rated films: 126
R rated films: 187

### 1983
G rated films: 11
PG rated films: 124
R rated films: 196

### 1984
G rated films: 7
PG rated films: 107
PG-13 rated films: 25
R rated films: 191

### 1985
G rated films: 15
PG rated films: 75
PG-13 rated films: 66
R rated films: 196

### 1986
G rated films: 9
PG rated films: 83
PG-13 rated films: 70
R rated films: 223

### 1987
G rated films: 11
PG rated films: 101
PG-13 rated films: 70
R rated films: 301

### 1988
G rated films: 10
PG rated films: 108
PG-13 rated films: 85
R rated films: 339

### 1989
G rated films: 7
PG rated films: 87
PG-13 rated films: 86
R rated films: 362

### 1990
G rated films: 7
PG rated films: 74
PG-13 rated films: 91
R rated films: 366
NC-17 rated films: 17

### 1991
G rated films: 12
PG rated films: 88
PG-13 rated films: 108
R rated films: 339
NC-17 rated films: 10

### 1992
G rated films: 10
PG rated films: 90
PG-13 rated films: 87
R rated films: 399
NC-17 rated films: 6

### 1993
G rated films: 16
PG rated films: 98
PG-13 rated films: 96
R rated films: 362
NC-17 rated films: 2

### 1994
G rated films: 11
PG rated films: 112
PG-13 rated films: 92
R rated films: 379
NC-17 rated films: 1

**1995**
G rated films: 16
PG rated films: 97
PG-13 rated films: 99
R rated films: 437
NC-17 rated films: 4

**1996**
G rated films: 12
PG rated films: 97
PG-13 rated films: 86
R rated films: 402
NC-17 rated films: 2

**1997**
G rated films: 14
PG rated films: 90
PG-13 rated films: 102
R rated films: 354
NC-17 rated films: 2

**1998**
G rated films: 21
PG rated films: 66
PG-13 rated films: 100
R rated films: 436
NC-17 rated films: 2

**1999**
G rated films: 23
PG rated films: 59
PG-13 rated films: 102
R rated films: 473
NC-17 rated films: 1

**2000**
G rated films: 21
PG rated films: 51
PG-13 rated films: 125
R rated films: 530

**2001**
G rated films: 15
PG rated films: 44
PG-13 rated films: 33
R rated films: 493
NC-17 rated films: 1

An analysis of the chart indicates that the G rated film was incrementally abandoned by the industry with the exception of Disney pictures and other children's product. The G rating became so associated with juvenile films that many distributors preferred the PG rating even if there was no justification for it (e.g. *Star Wars*, *Close Encounters*, *Superman*). While many movies were in the PG or PG-13 category, the amount of restricted films increased each year. Distributors seemed to ignore the problems exhibitors faced. Cinema owners that initially supported the ratings system discovered audiences were being split into categories which affected overall attendance. Eugene Picker, the President of the National Association of Theatre Owners (NATO) noted in 1971, "Has the nature of many of our recent films, especially those displaying the so-called permissiveness, served to alienate vast numbers of people who previously favored us with their patronage?"[23] The box-office take of R rated films like *Easy Rider* was substantial but if you catered to the youth audience, you might lose the remaining family trade. That's how individual film grosses could be up but attendance down. By 1971, it was approximately 25 million a week which was paltry compared to the early sixties. Picker continued, "Have we placed too heavy an emphasis on appealing to the younger sector of the population only to find that we are the victims of their fickleness of taste and this after we have virtually disregarded the over 30's who constitute the major consumer segment in the American market?"[24]

As previously mentioned, attendance had been in decline since the advent of television. It was reduced from approximately 90 million a week in 1948 to 45.9 million a week by 1952.[25] It increased to 49 million in 1954 after the introduction of new technology like Cinerama, 3-D, CinemaScope and VistaVision. It leveled off to 45–46 million for the next few years then began to drop again. By the mid-sixties attendance was around 41 million per week. Most of the above processes were phased out with the exception of the anamorphic and 70mm formats.

Whether retaining the Production Code Seal combined with a classification system to encourage general attendance would've prevented the drop to 25 million by the early seventies is unknown. Screen freedom and its excesses did not reverse the decline although it did increase box-office revenue for targeted viewers. Valenti admitted, "This backbone following is found in the 12–29 age group, which, although representing only 40 percent of the 12-and-under population, accounts for 73 percent of total theatre admissions."[26] This demographic shift was caused in part by his policies. Weekly attendance continued to drop and was approximately 22 million out of a population of 200 million by 1979.

Other factors contributed to distributor's attitudes at the time. By the mid-fifties, the studios had stopped competing with television and began to merge the two mediums. In 1955, they started selling their libraries of "A" pictures for broadcast. This became a key ancillary market for films. By 1958, over 3,500 old feature films had been sold or leased for television broadcast. In 1966, the ABC airing of *The Bridge on the River Kwai* garnered high Nielson ratings with 60 million viewers. The network had paid Columbia $2,000,000 for two showings. After this breakthrough, the studios sold their prestigious titles as television events. Fox sold *Cleopatra* to ABC for $5,000,000 for two broadcasts which finally put the picture in the black. Network showings of *Ben-Hur, My Fair Lady* and *Gone with the Wind* were also very profitable for the distributors. ABC's theatrical division produced the movies *Too Late the Hero, They Shoot Horses, Don't They?* and *The Last Valley* for cinema release.

The majors formed subsidiaries to produce television shows and "Movie of the Week" specials. Hollywood became a "TV town" and theatrical exhibition was no longer their sole means of income. In some cases, television rights were pre-sold to recoup part of the budget. For instance, NBC paid Avco-Embassy two million dollars for the right to show *Day of the Dolphin* (1973) after its theatrical release. Cinema owners didn't profit from these deals and were in a constant battle to retain customers with

# John Travolta   Olivia Newton-John

 **is the word**

PARAMOUNT PICTURES PRESENTS
A ROBERT STIGWOOD/ALLAN CARR PRODUCTION
JOHN TRAVOLTA   OLIVIA NEWTON-JOHN in "GREASE"
and STOCKARD CHANNING as Rizzo   with special guest appearances by EVE ARDEN, FRANKIE AVALON
JOAN BLONDELL, EDD BYRNES, SID CAESAR, ALICE GHOSTLEY, DODY GOODMAN, SHA-NA-NA
Screenplay by BRONTE WOODARD   Adaptation by ALLAN CARR   Based on the original musical by JIM JACOBS and WARREN CASEY
Produced on the Broadway Stage by KENNETH WAISSMAN and MAXINE FOX in association with ANTHONY D'AMATO   Choreography by PATRICIA BIRCH
Produced by ROBERT STIGWOOD and ALLAN CARR   Directed by RANDAL KLEISER   DOLBY SYSTEM®   PANAVISION®   A PARAMOUNT PICTURE
[PG] PARENTAL GUIDANCE SUGGESTED   Soundtrack Album available on RSO Records & Tapes   Read the paperback from Pocket Books   © 1978 PARAMOUNT PICTURES CORPORATION
SOME MATERIAL MAY NOT BE SUITABLE FOR CHILDREN

Pressbook ad slick for *Grease* (1978).

the competition from other forms of entertainment in the subsequent decades.

Ironically, there was a revival of mainstream entertainment after the counterculture, exploitation, blaxploitation and sexploitation cycles had run their course. Less than a decade after they were made, films like *Greetings, I Drink Your Blood, Putney Swope* and *Deep Throat* seemed dated and amateurish. The industry drifted away from activism and politics in the late seventies. There was a resurgence of epic adventures featuring spectacular special effects and technology. Movies like *Star Wars* (1977), *Close Encounters of the Third Kind* (1977), *Superman* (1978) and *Grease* (1978) were PG rated films that became some of the top grossing pictures of all time which indicated there was still a general audience to cater to. Attendance increased and admissions were up by 6.5 percent in 1978 although ticket price inflation was a factor in box-office grosses. Prices had doubled since 1968 and it cost $2.50 per adult to see a movie. As A. Alan Friedberg, the subsequent President of the NATO, noted in 1979, "More movies were made to quench the entertainment thirst of the moviegoer and fewer were made a) for the purpose of transmitting messages or b) for the purpose of accommodating the artistic ego of some producer, director or star."[27] It would appear that general audiences did not abandon cinema so much as New Hollywood directors and exploitation distributors abandoned the general audience. Despite the fact that the industry was ending on an upbeat note at the close of the seventies, the increase in attendance was irregular since PG rated films were only part of the release schedule. Exhibitors were nervous about the future and had already implemented changes in reaction to the earlier product and demographic shift. They would have long term effects on cinema and the moviegoing experience.

# 3. Multiplexes and Twinning

In the first fourteen months of the post–Code era (November 1968–December 1969), there were 103 G rated films, 154 M rated films, 87 R rated films and 32 X rated films (studio and indie) available for booking. This posed a problem for movie palaces, big screen houses and drive-ins whose primary income was derived from pictures that admitted all ages. R and X rated films like *Easy Rider* and *I Am Curious, Yellow* could fill a large theater in some instances but many were only modest successes. Restricting children and disenfranchising older viewers meant empty seats and a loss of revenue. This is not to suggest that there weren't profitable general audience pictures being made but the number of adult movies continued to increase and Jack Valenti gave speeches indicating this was the trend. Since Hollywood was no longer making a uniform product, it made the survival of single screen houses uncertain. If the future of exhibition was going to be targeted and specialized viewers, theatre owners had to make changes to stay in business. The end result was multiplexes and twinning.

## Jerry Lewis Cinemas

As an industry, the motion picture producers are cutting their own throats. Kids have to get into the habit of going to the movies, so when they grow up, they will consider moviegoing a standard part of their lives— Jerry Lewis[1]

The concept of the multiple theatre complex originated with James Edwards of Edwards Cinemas who opened the first twin theatre in the late thirties. It made no impact at the time. Thirty years later, Stanley Durwood's American Multi-Cinema (AMC) opened the Parkway Theatres in

# Only 54 areas left in the entire United States. After these are awarded, there will be no other areas available

# Join Jerry Lewis

## in the most profitable segment of the entertainment industry.

There were 158 areas, at first. Now, more than 100 have been sold. And, in less than a two-year period.

But, we expected it. Because there's big money to be made with Jerry Lewis Cinemas. And, now we're asking you to join us before all the areas are sold out.

What are Jerry Lewis Cinemas? They are fully automated mini-theatres. With seating capacities from 200 to 350. They're luxurious, plush and easily accessible. And, can be completely operated by only two people. Profitably.

Now, take a look at their track record. It's almost unmatched.

Since the Jerry Lewis Cinema program was launched in 1969, it has become one of the fastest growing theatre chains in the world.

Currently, mini-cinemas are operating or under construction in every part of the country. And, Jerry Lewis Cinemas have already been introduced in England, France, Italy and West Germany.

Because of their size, these theatres can be installed almost anywhere. In office buildings, shopping centers and stores. And, they can be constructed on new sites as well. Fast.

Now, we're giving you the opportunity to become an Area Director for Jerry Lewis Cinemas. You'll be given exclusive territory to open and operate from 10 to 20 mini-cinemas. You can manage them yourself, joint-venture or license them to individual owner-operators. The choice is up to you.

And, we'll do everything we can to insure your success from the start.

We'll train you in all aspects of theatre operation. From advertising to accounting. From theatre procedure to promotions.

We'll even book your films, supervise in lease negotiations and help secure a prime site for your cinema.

Sound good? It is good.

Look into this unusual opportunity. But, do it now. Time is important. Although only 54 areas are left, one might be near your own home town.

## INVESTMENT INFORMATION

The minimum cash investment for an AREA DIRECTOR is $50,000. This includes the cash we require for your own Jerry Lewis Cinema, which will be used as a showcase and in addition, can return substantial profits to you. A portion of this investment will be refunded upon performance.

There are also opportunities available for Individual Exhibitors to open one or more mini-cinemas. Cash investment for each is $10,000 to $15,000 depending on the theatre's seating capacity. Additional working capital needed. Balance may be financed.

For Complete information
CALL COLLECT.

# (212)-752-6622

or Mail coupon

V1–72

NETWORK CINEMA CORPORATION
505 Park Avenue, New York, New York 10022

Please contact me for an immediate appointment.

MY PHONE NUMBER IS . . . . . . . . . . . . . . . . .

I am interested in: (please check one)

. . . . . Area Director . . . . . . . . . One Cinema

Name . . . . . . . . . . . . . . . . . . . . . . . . .

Address . . . . . . . . . . . . . . City . . . . . . . . . .

State . . . . . . . . . . . . . . . . . Zip . . . . . . .

## Be Our Guest at Caesars Palace, Las Vegas - Jan. 12-16

Jerry Lewis Cinemas are having their Annual National Convention for 350 Area Directors and Exhibitors at that time. We invite you to experience first hand the acceptance of our nation-wide Mini-Cinema program. Speak with our people. Listen to their success stories.

If you sign up and qualify for our Mini-Cinema Program * we will reimburse all your

expenses for travel, room and meals for the entire weekend for two people, PLUS you will be our guest for the Dinner Show Opening Night, January 13, starring Jerry Lewis. Meet Jerry Lewis in person as he celebrates his 40th Anniversary in Show Business, during this fabulous four week engagement. For complete details and reservations, Call Mr. Noel, COLLECT (212) 752-6622.

* For a Twin Cinema, Joint Venture or Area Director.

Network Cinema Corp. — National Headquarters—505 Park Avenue, New York, 10022 / (212) 752-6622 • West Coast Sales Office—1900 Avenue of the Stars, L.A., Calif. 90067 / (213) 277-2605

*Variety* ad for Jerry Lewis Cinemas.

Kansas City's Ward Parkway Shopping Center on July 12, 1963. It was a twin cinema with a single box-office. Durwood's idea was to build 300 and 400 seat cinemas near suburban outlets. The postwar trend began in the fifties as more and more middle-class families moved away from the large cities and settled in comfortable and safe suburban communities like the one where I grew up. Durwood's theatres contained average sized screens but limited seating. He opened the first four-theater complex in 1966 and six-plex in 1969. The screen sizes in these multi-cinema buildings tended to be the same as in smaller single houses, approximately 30–35 ft. wide.

At the time the multi-cinema was considered a novelty rather than a permanent fixture for exhibitors. It took comedian Jerry Lewis to create the first franchise. In 1969, Lewis was concerned that theaters were no longer catering to family viewers and children. The amount of R and X rated product meant that families who did attend were bombarded with posters and trailers for films that weren't suitable for children. There were two types of coming attractions sent to the managers on cores with colored cardboard bands; Green Band and Red Band. Green Band trailers were suitable for all viewers. Red Band were intended for adults only. Sometimes the projectionist would mix them up after the bands were removed. I recall seeing a Red Band trailer for the X rated film, *The Killing of Sister George* prior to the feature *Stop the World, I Want to Get Off* in 1968 at age 11. The trailer displayed Susannah York's naked breasts getting fondled. I thought it was amusing but my parents and other adults complained to the manager. Even the Green Band trailers for films like *The Wild Bunch* were graphic as were the one sheet posters for exploitation and sexploitation product. Complaints about explicit trailers forced CARA to classify them like the features.

Lewis formed a partnership with the Network Cinema Corporation in 1969 to build mini-cinemas for the family trade. They were called "Jerry Lewis Cinemas" and had a seating capacity of 100–350 per house. They differed from later multiplexes in that they were advertised as "intimate" and "luxurious," similar to Art houses. Like the Edwards Cinemas, they had average sized screens with curtains. A low end estimate was around 28 ft. wide. While these were not movie palaces, they did offer the "movie-going experience" on a limited basis. The architecture made good use of the available space and resembled miniature large screen cinemas rather than the shoe box units of later years. I recall seeing some films in these theaters in the early seventies and the presentation was acceptable, at least compared to later multiplex operations. Lewis's concept was that these could be "mom and pop" operations with a staff of two. Everything was automated including the projection system (covered in Chapter 4). When the operator turned on the projector, the house lights would dim and the curtains open simultaneously. There was a filmed logo indicating it was Jerry Lewis cinema.

The first 350 seat theater was built in Old Bridge, New Jersey, and by 1973 there were 190 theaters. The minimum cash investment for a participant was $50,000 although the company would accept a $10,000 down payment with the rest financed. Other locations included Greenville, South Carolina; Peabody, Massachusetts, and Mount Airy, North Carolina.

However, in October of 1980, Jerry Lewis Cinema Corporation filed for bankruptcy. While the concept of mini-cinemas was the wave of the future, Lewis made a series of errors. His company did not offer enough technical support to members, which made it difficult for small time exhibitors to compete with the majors. Concerns like dealing with distributors, booking terms and operating concessions were left to the managers to sort out in many cases. Another problem was the stipulation that owners only book general audience pictures. While 103 were released in 1969, there were fewer made each year. By 1980 only 14 G rated films were available and the quality of the product was often poor. Titles like *Song of Norway* (1970) and *Daisy Miller* (1974) were critically panned box-office flops. Buena Vista's movies had declined in the seventies too although it would improve in the eighties and nineties under new management. There were some Lewis cinemas that expanded their bookings to M (GP or PG) films but it was too late to save the franchise. After 1980, some theaters continued to operate under new ownership but most became run-down. As a final irony, a few Jerry Lewis cinemas became grind-houses that played exploitation.

## Twinning

A cheaper option for many houses was "twinning." Compared to the "luxurious" Jerry Lewis mini-cinemas, many twinned theaters were horrible. Those that went this route were in trouble financially and often modified them economically. The common pattern was to construct a wall down the center of the auditorium. The large screens were removed and replaced by two smaller ones, often no wider than 20 ft. Each half resembled a "shoe box" and seating was uncomfortable. When the Beach Cinemas I attended as a youth were twinned, the aisle seats became the center row and faced the wall rather than the screen.

The projection booth remained in place except that the machines were at an extreme angle to the screen resulting in "keystone" distortion.

Either the right or left side of the image was soft in anamorphic presentations. The curtains, an integral part of the moviegoing experience, were removed from most cinemas. Acoustics was another problem. Audiences could hear the sound from the adjacent theater. This corner cutting method didn't help many twinned theaters which folded anyway. All but one of the single screen cinemas I used to attend were gone by the late eighties.

## Multiplexes

A number of companies began building mini-cinemas in the seventies and eighties following Durwood's concept. One could not expect a small theater complex to have the ornate atmosphere of a Thomas Lamp or C.W. Rapp picture palace of the twenties with its old world aristocracy. However, the architectural design of many multiplexes resembled the "shoe box" twinned theaters rather than "luxurious" Jerry Lewis venues. Most made poor use of the limited space. Any competent interior decorator could've generated better results. It would seem that the design emphasis was on the lobby and concession areas whereas the actual theater was merely functional. Rather than having a wall to wall screen, many units had a tiny one centered at the end of the aisle. Few, if any, had curtains. The screens were usually masked off for 1.85. A black drape would be lowered to crop the top of the screen for the 2.35 anamorphic ratio which defeated the whole purpose of Panavision. Technical specs were often well below average. Many screens fell short of even the minimum 400:1 screen contrast ratio as specified by SMPE Standard 196M. The design was so bad that stray light from the exit sign and other unwanted reflections (lens flare, dirty port glass) made the screen image murky. Kodak implemented a Screencheck system to try and resolve these problems, but it was not always employed since many managers didn't care. It was used on an individual film by film basis by production companies like Dreamworks. Lucas's THX corporation also had a theater check system although they concentrated on sound and speaker quality.

One of the major chains that built these cinemas throughout the U.S. was Cineplex Odeon. It started as Canada's Cineplex theater circuit which had opened the first 18-plex in Toronto. In 1984 it opened the Beverly Center Cineplex in a Los Angeles shopping mall with 14 screens. In 1985, the company bought out the Plitt circuit and Cineplex Odeon became one of the major theater chains. Cineplex houses had small screens with limited seating. As the numbers of cinemas increased, the size of the screens decreased. Other multiplex chains included AMC, General Cinema Corporation, Hoyts, Carmike, Landmark Theatres, United Artists Theatre circuit, Chakeres Theaters, Marcus Theatres and Kerasotes Theatres.

Any screen smaller than 30 foot wide undermined the impact of the projected motion picture, especially for big budget spectaculars like *Superman*. Anamorphic widescreen films suffered the worst and the illusion of peripheral vision and viewer participation was completely absent. No one complained about the lack of quality and comfort in these complexes. Those that did stopped attending. The targeted youth audience didn't seem to mind. For adults, attending a multiplex screening was often a frustrating experience when teenagers talked throughout the presentation as if they were in their living room. In the nineties, some people made cell phone calls during the presentation. It's hard to blame them since many of the small auditoriums resembled screening rooms rather than theaters. There were no ushers to quiet them.

The ballyhoo that used to be part of the moviegoing experience disappeared in most complexes. While pressbooks were still sent to theaters, they stopped suggesting newspaper contests and other gimmicks utilized in the past. Local businesses that catered to the family trade did not want to be associated with graphic R rated product. Program books, souvenirs, window cards, banners and other items used to decorate the lobby were rarely used or phased out entirely. Even the one sheet poster was reduced in size and the artwork lackluster. The elaborate paintings of illustrators like Jack Davis (*It's a Mad, Mad, Mad, Mad World*) were replaced with simpler concepts. In the nineties, computer generated imagery was used in the key artwork. Few pictures were promoted as events. There was little opportunity for display items given the available space. There was barely enough room for the posters of the multiple films that were playing which made it difficult to promote any one title.

There were some multiplex owners who cared about presentation and showmanship although they were often local independents. Nelson Page's Galaxy Theatre Corporation was founded in the late eighties with the premise that where you saw a movie was as important as what movie you saw. Starting with one single screen house, the company expanded to 8 locations with 21 screens in the New Jersey area. The largest one was in the Guttenberg location which had a 42 foot wide silver screen. It was installed to premiere my feature, *Run for Cover* in 3-D in 1996. Organ music was played on the Mighty Wurlitzer on weekends prior to the show. Even in the smallest unit which was 12 foot wide, curtains were retained along with art deco lighting which made it resemble an art house rather than the warehouse appearance of many competitors. There were other chains around the country that compromised between the single screen

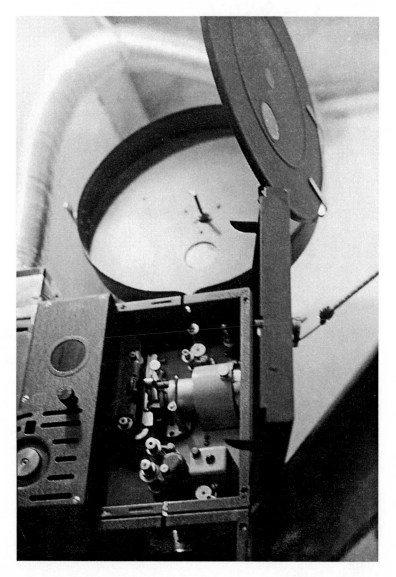

**Film was enclosed in a magazine in the reel to reel system which kept out dirt and dust.**

house and multi-cinema concept and kept at least one large theater for big budget presentations. However, these were the exceptions to the rule and the national chains continued to build generic structures with inferior presentation and architecture. At their worst, these type of multiplexes were the cinematic equivalent of fast food restaurants in suburban malls.

# 4. Projection

The proper presentation of a motion picture involves more than technical competence ... the projectionist is, in effect, presenting an illusion created by artists, actors, writers, etc.[1]

## *Reel to Reel Projection*

Through 1970, the majority of theaters in the U.S. utilized reel to reel projection. This format offered the best quality for motion picture exhibition. There were many reasons for its superiority compared to contemporary systems. First and foremost, was the requirement of a qualified union operator to run the machines. Most projectionists were skilled technicians who had to know about screen luminance, film formats and machine maintenance. They had to know how to utilize carbon-arc lamphouses, maintain even screen light, change formats from 35mm to 70mm and accurately crop and focus the image depending on distributor specifications.

Release prints were shipped to the theater on 2,000 ft. reels. Most contained less footage than that so they wouldn't unravel. Magnetic stereo prints were often no longer than 1,500 ft. to compensate for the extra thickness. There were numerous types of projectors available through 1970 from different companies. Simplex and Century were the most common ones. Others included Motiograph, Brenkert, Ballantyne, Cinemeccanica and Kenoton. The Norelco company offered a dual system unit that had larger outer sprockets for 70mm and smaller inner sprockets for standard 35mm presentations. Incorporated into the machine were head clusters for 70mm six track magnetic and 35mm four track magnetic stereo. It used a curved gate to improve focus on large screens. Some industry personnel consider it the finest reel to reel projector ever built. Cinemeccanica and Century also offered 35/70 units.

Projectionists threaded the film into the gate and enclosed the reels in upper and bottom magazines. This prevented dust and other airborne pollutants from accumulating on the reels. The only part of the machine that physically touched the film was the optical sound drum. As long as it was kept clean and the gate maintained, there was little that could scratch a print. 35mm magnetic four track stereo prints continued to be manufactured for big budget films through 1983. To project them, a "Penthouse" attachment was installed on the top of the projector between the upper sprocket and reel arm. These had an additional drum roller to stabilize the magnetic heads which played back the four discrete channels of stereophonic sound. The rear channel contained a 12K tone and audio switcher which would turn off the track when it was wasn't being used so track hiss would not come out of the speakers. Ideally, magnetic heads should be cleaned and de-gaused to prevent track damage. Penthouses were also used in the later digital formats. While not every theater was meticulous, most could project a print over a hundred times without displaying too much wear. Many theaters returned the prints to the exchange in near mint condition as evidenced by the number that have survived in private film collections.

Reel to reel projection required a "changeover." At the end of each reel were a series of cue marks in the upper right hand portion of the frame. They were usually circles although Technicolor dye transfer prints contained a star pattern. They were spaced out 12 ft. and 1 ft. from the last frame of picture. When the projectionist saw the first set of cues on screen, he would turn on the second projector which was threaded on the number 8 in the academy leader. After seeing the second set of cues, he would change over to the second projector. The light and sound would turn off on the first unit. This required some skill which was part of the projectionist's training. In most theaters it was rare to see countdown leader or other visual distractions during the changeover process.

## Automation

There was always a drive towards automation by theater managers. In the fifties, the reel capacity had to be increased to a full hour to show interlocked dual projector 3-D. Some theaters retained the large reels and assembled a six reel, two hour feature onto two large reels. To make an automatic changeover, they used cue tape. It was a short strip of metal tape fastened onto the edge of the film at a specific location. At the reel change mark (usually the end of the third assembled reel), the film passed two electrical contacts and the cue tape completed a circuit between the contacts. In essence it acted as a switch which turned off the first projector, lamphouse and sound and turned on the second unit . No operator was required once the first unit was turned on. The reels were usually enclosed in oversized magazines which kept the prints clean. Cue tape could also be used to dim house lights and open the curtains. As previously mentioned, Jerry Lewis cinemas used automated projection with cue tape functions.

The automation movement began in 1967 during a conference of NATO in Florida. President Sherril C. Corwin announced that various manufacturers were developing methods to eliminate the "human error" in motion picture presentation. I found no evidence that this was a problem at the time and it appears the real agenda was to save money in exhibition. Initially, the International Alliance of Theatrical Stagehands and Motion Picture Machine Operators of the United States and Canada (IATSE) trade union supported the technology. At the time, it appeared that their job would be simplified without a loss of salary or benefits. In twin theaters, *Film Daily's* Merlin Lewis stated, "One projectionist can handle two sets of projectors without any worries, once he has automated changeovers.... This is an efficient use of manpower, it is good economics for the theatre owners, and it is a substantial raise in pay for the projectionist without adding anything to his work load."[2] Had they known what was really in store for them in the eighties and nineties, projectionists would've fought automation to ensure their survival.

A number of companies offered systems in the era. *Century Projector Corporation's Automated Projector and Theatre Control System* utilized three control panels, one for each projector. When the projectionist pushed the Start Show button, the lamp lights, auditorium lights, curtains and projector motor turned on simultaneously. *National Theatre Supply's PEC 1000 Automation Equipment* had similar functions but included automatic screen masks which changed the ratio from 1.85 to anamorphic 2.35. This was useful if flat trailers or shorts were played before a Panavision feature. *Purdue Motion Picture Equipment* was custom made to adapt existing booth equipment from various manufacturers. The film was assembled onto two one hour reels. Automatic changeovers were incorporated into the system with a delayed timing device in the box controlling the projector. *Cinemeccanica's Victoria 18 Projector* assembled the entire two hour feature onto one reel in a magazine with a 13,000 ft. capacity. In each of these systems, the reels remained enclosed in oversized magazines on the top and bottom of the projectors to keep out dust and dirt. By 1968, there were approximately fifty theaters in the United States that used some form of automation. Merlin Lewis continued, "One mistake should not be made, however. Automation *per se* does not put a better picture on the screen. That depends upon getting good prints from the exchange, and equipping the theatre with the best projection and sound equipment obtainable."[3]

In the seventies the *Eprad-Sabre* unit rewound the assembled large reels at high speed through the projector as did the knock-off *Sword System*. These units fell out of favor since they often damaged the film. Another problem associated with large reel projection was accumulated dirt where the sections were spliced together. However, these early automated formats were still preferable to the Platter systems that replaced them in the eighties and nineties.

## Platters

"Platters" as developed by the Christie, Cinemecannica, Goldberg, Neumade Neuexel 2000, Strong and Speco companies were not designed to improve presentation. They were a labor saving device. Their origins date back to a non-rewind cake-stand system invented by Willie Burth, a German projectionist. It was offered by Philips Cinema (later Kinoton) in the sixties. This was followed by the Potts and Christie units. Platters worked as follows: The release print was assembled on a make up table ("MUT") which utilized a guillotine tape splicer. The head and tail academy leaders were removed from the print and the reels spliced together. The sprocket holes were manually punched into the tape with the guillotine. Many splicers did not create an overlap in the splice which meant that the sound would make an audio pop at each section unless blooping ink was used.

After the feature was assembled onto a large horizontal plate known as "the brain," it was threaded through a series of rollers into a top roller that twisted the film into the upper sprocket which lead to the film gate. It was important to leave enough space between the top roller and upper sprocket since the twist could cause stress on the film. There was an 8 to 10 foot span between rollers and platter system. If everything was set up correctly, the brain fed the film on the rollers to the projector. The take-up was another horizontal plate. In the case of digital stereo prints, the top roller lead to the Penthouse decoder before the upper sprocket. Rewinding was unnecessary since after the film was taken up on one plate, the operator only had to switch platters before the next show.

**Static electricity caused dirt to accumulate on the film in the platter system.**

There were inherent problems with platters. First was the length of the space the film had to travel in the open air. Keeping the reel enclosed in a magazine was far preferable in the reel to reel method. Film was also subject to a static charge from the rollers and plates which was especially troublesome in post–1993 estar base film. The static caused dirt and airborne particles to attach themselves to the print. Dust settled on the print when not in use. Older tri-acetate film tended to become brittle and warped as it aged. Film was designed for vertical, not horizontal projection. The Turner company was reluctant to book their classics, restorations and archival copies in theaters that utilized platters.

Platters increased the potential of scratches. Prints could get lines during the make-up assembly or due to improperly positioned guide rollers. A vertical scratch throughout the entire feature could result from a misthread. Sometimes the film would get tangled up in a "brain wrap" which was caused by static build up and film jams as it came out of the center-feed pay-out mechanism. Estar film could ruin the projector or rollers since it had greater tensile strength and didn't break easily.

Other difficulties originated at the MUT. Residue tape was left in the punched holes and the sticky glue attracted dirt. Some operators removed fade ins and fade outs if they occurred at the head or tail of the reel rather than finding the frameline in the black image. Assembling and disassembling prints from theater to theater also increased wear. Frames were removed from the heads and tails of the reels or the wrong leaders were reattached after the booking. Prints were often sent to sub-run houses in filthy, scratched condition. Some multiplexes even used the same print on two screens with an automation system which synchronized the projectors so they started and ran at the same speed. The film was pulled across the room on rollers from the first projector to the second. In other setups, the platter plates were in adjacent rooms or on another level. The film traveled on rollers from room to room or through a hole in the floor. Obviously, these increased wear and accumulated dirt and dust.

I encountered a very strange booth when I booked my feature *Space Avenger* in Washington, DC. The room had a series of platter projectors inside but no porthole windows for the screens. The light was reflected with a periscope to the theaters below. Unfortunately, the mirrors were so dirty that it darkened the image. My release copies were made at the Beijing Film Lab in the dye transfer process, and had rich colors and contrast but were barely visible. One critic complained about the poor quality of the print in his review, unaware the fault was with the lens system. One of the platters was set up improperly and cracked the sprockets of my first reel.

The main problem with platters was they didn't require a qualified operator. This devastated the projectionist's union which was the first craft in the business to join the American Federation of Labor in 1906. By 1978, they had lost a great deal of clout and control over performance. Since changeovers and rewinding were unnecessary, theaters began to use untrained staff to run the machines. In some cases the managers turned them on and returned to the floor. While these individuals knew how to thread up the unit, few had any additional skills. To insure a good performance, projectionists had to know how to change Xenon bulbs and align them so there were no hot spots. For stereo films, they needed to run Dolby tones and set levels. There were 35mm image test films for cropping, jitter/weave, uniformity of screen focus and ghosting. Managers and staff did not know how to adjust the equipment. Film damage could occur from rubbing on the platter surface during make-up, excess tension on an undercut roller or the wrong loop size. A misaligned roller or gate could also cause print shedding when emulsion debris skived off the film. General maintenance like oiling the gears, cleaning the sound drum and projection gate was ignored. The projector port hole window became dirty and lenses were not cleaned. Since I have my own home screening room with reel to reel projection, I can verify that proper exhibition is a lot more complicated than simply turning on a switch.

I've had bad experiences with inept operators during the exhibition of my features. When I booked *Space Avenger* for a midnight run at the

Bleecker Street Cinema in 1991, I visited the booth and heard a loud chattering sound coming from the projector. I asked the manager/operator when the unit had been oiled last. He looked at me bewildered and said, "oiled?" I brought some Simplex oil and lubricated the gears while the projector was running which splattered on me but made the machine run smoothly.

Another problem was "Green" prints sent to the theater directly from the lab. New prints tended to buckle a bit and require focus adjustments until the booth temperature stabilized the emulsion. This was especially true of pre–1993 tri-acetate stock. The film drifted in and out of focus but no one was in the booth to make the adjustments. This was very distracting for audiences. Recently, Kodak has addressed these concerns by introducing improved Vision estar base stocks 2383 and 2393. Incorporated into the film was an anti-static layer to reduce dirt attraction and a scratch-resistant backing.

Even chains that used professionals stretched their abilities to the limit. One projectionist would be responsible for five to ten theaters and no one was monitoring the performance of any individual screen. Sloppy projection and bad presentation became common. Horizontal emulsion scratches that looked like a cat clawed the print ("platter scratches") were typical in poorly maintained and understaffed theaters. 70mm magnetic stereo prints were susceptible to "oxide flaking." When I saw *Die Hard* in New York City, the marquee advertised it as being in 70mm. A 35mm Dolby stereo print was shown instead. I visited the projection booth where the operator showed me the 70mm print which had shredding tracks from an improperly set up platter. The expensive print was barely a week old and already ruined. In 2001, a new $27,000 70mm print of *2001: A Space Odyssey* was damaged at New York's Loews Astor Plaza by a manager/operator who didn't know how to run the large format copy.

There were remedies. The platter and roller surfaces could be treated with Staticguard. In the eighties, coating the print with Scotchguard or Imageguard gave it protection against scratches, although archivists worried it might accelerate deterioration by locking in residue developing chemicals and not letting the emulsion "breathe." Film Guard was a lacquer that not only kept the print clean but obscured scratches on the film. It was applied with media rollers attached to the projector. None of these were done universally. A manager could not expect a person working for the minimum wage to have any projection skills nor motivate them to learn about proper film handling. Professional projectionists were not treated with respect by many chains nor their craft given the importance it warranted as part of the moviegoing experience.

I'm not suggesting that all multiplexes had bad projection and platters couldn't be operated efficiently in short runs. Most managers preferred the system since it saved them money. In practice, they were not
the ideal method for quality exhibition for the reasons stated above.

## Carbon-Arc Lamphouse

For most of cinema history, the standard source of projector illumination was the carbon-arc lamphouse. It generated the required 16 foot-
lamberts as specified by the SMPTE. The way the system works was as
follows: Carbon rods were positioned inside the lamphouse. The arc was
struck by bringing the carbons together and the burning gas ball that
resulted was the illumination. A technical explanation is that expendable
carbon electrodes were gripped and fed together maintaining an arc supplied electrically from a power supply with a drooping voltage character-
istic. The positive electrodes were either copper-coated or bare depending
on where the current is lead into the electrode. The burning rate varied
from 6 in to 60 in/h. The negative electrodes were generally copper-coded
with a slower burning rate between 2½ to 4 in/h.

A cylinder mirror reflector in the back of the lamphouse was used to
focus the light and maintain even screen brightness. The burning gas ball
had to be at a constant location in relation to the reflector. It was also
important that the arc lamp was aligned with the projector optical system.
The carbon-arc crater had to be centered with the reflector, the film aperture and projection lens in the horizontal and vertical plane. Alignment
kits were available and the operator needed to know how to use them,
especially in machines that used both 35mm and 70mm formats. A heat
shield in front of the opening prevented film damage. Carbons were available uncoated in 9, 10, 11, and 13.6mm sizes. The length was 20 inches
although 18 inchers were used for specific lamphouses. Union Carbide was
among the companies that manufactured them. They no longer make them
but carbons are still available from National Specialty Products and the
Marbel Company in Nashville, Tennessee.

Carbon Arcs generated a light that was very close to the color temperature and wavelengths produced by the sun and produced a continuous spectrum. It was appropriate for the Technicolor films and other
processes utilized in the fifties and sixties. Many older projectionists still
swear by them as the best light source. The carbon rods were inexpensive
to purchase but a qualified operator was required which was an asset of
the reel to reel system. Someone was always present in the booth monitoring

# YOUR NATIONAL CARBON ENGINEER...

*Sells you the best <u>product</u>—gives you the best <u>service</u>!*

The illustration shows a NATIONAL CARBON Sales Engineer using the Motion Picture Research Council's Projector alignment tool to position the mirror on the optical axis of the projection lens.

These Sales Engineers—equipped with complete service kits containing the most modern test equipment—are trained to solve screen lighting problems and help the industry achieve the ultimate in picture quality. This is an important part of NATIONAL CARBON's continuing program of service to the industry.

For best projection results, use "National" projector carbons—for dependable, free technical service, call on NATIONAL CARBON. For details, ask your NATIONAL CARBON supply dealer or write: National Carbon Company, Division of Union Carbide Corporation, 270 Park Avenue, New York 17, N. Y. *In Canada:* Union Carbide Canada Limited, Toronto.

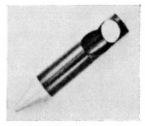

With the Motion Picture Research Council's projector alignment tool it is possible to determine within a few minutes—while the show is on — if the optical train is in alignment, or what adjustments need be made.

"National" and "Union Carbide" are registered trade-marks for products of

## NATIONAL CARBON COMPANY

Magazine ad for National Carbon Company.

the performance. Maintenance was required and the interior of the lamphouse, reflector and stack had to be cleaned daily to remove residue carbon dust since the arc flame gave off smoke, soot and intense heat. Silver polishing the carbon jaws and scraping the melted copper away were other standard operating procedures.

There were a number of lamphouses available depending on the size of the screen and distance from the projection booth. The Single-Feed Coaxial Trim Carbon-Arc was used for smaller screens in the thirties and forties. The amperage range was generally from 40 to 46 A. This was not bright enough for 3-D projection or the wide screen films of the fifties and the unit was discontinued. The Split Feed Ball and Cylinder Clutch Coaxial Trim Arc Lamp replaced it for small and medium sized theaters and was appropriate for 3-D, CinemaScope and 1.85 cropped presentations. The amperage range varied from 45 to 85 A direct current.

The Rotating Positive Carbon-Arc Lamphouse was used in medium to large indoor theaters and most drive-ins in the fifties and sixties. The amperage range varied from 75 to 160 A with 100–110 A the best for most houses. The Blown Arc was a special type of unit used in movie palaces or large screen theaters where the greatest amount of illumination was required. The amperage range varied from 140 to 160 A.

There were some potential problems with these units. An improperly focused reflector or damaged heat shield could cause carbon burns on the release print. The dark areas of the frame would be speckled with white dots. While this was uncommon, when it happened it usually occurred at drive-ins which utilized the Rotating Positive Carbon Arcs. In general, carbon-arc lamphouses offered excellent quality through its fifty year history. I don't recall any large screen cinema in the sixties having a poor illumination or a dark screen image. Unfortunately, carbon-arc lamphouses were inappropriate for the automated projection systems of the seventies, eighties and nineties. The carbon rods within the unit had a limited lifespan and could not be used for extended running times. This was not a problem in reel to reel projection but not an option for automated platter systems since the carbons could not be changed while the film was being projected.

## Xenon Lamphouse

The Xenon lamphouse that replaced it was developed by the Zeiss-Icon Company in Germany in 1954. It was used extensively in that country but was not incorporated into US theaters until the seventies. It worked as follows: When gas vapors were used as a conductor in an electric arc, radiation was emitted. Xenon gas was utilized because it formed a continuum covering all visible colors in its line spectrum. To the naked eye it looked like a bulb inside the lamphouse. It was powered by a rectifier and generated a colder light than the carbon arc. It tended to be "bluer" than the "whiter" carbon arc illumination, especially as the bulb aged. It was acceptable for the "colder" color design of the Eastmancolor films in the seventies which lacked the warm, saturated hues of Technicolor movies. The dye transfer process was abandoned in 1975 and the style of cinematography changed which will be covered in the next chapter.

Xenon lamphouses did not require a qualified projectionist to operate them. Once they were turned on, no further monitoring was required. This was a liability since its always preferable to have the operator in the booth during the performance. To replace them did require some competence and protective face gear was necessarily in case the bulb exploded. When a new bulb was put into the lamphouse, a counter would indicate how many hours of operation were left after each screening. Depending on the bulb, they were good for a substantial amount of time, 2,000 to 6,000 hours. There were different models available including 1,600 watts, 3,000 watts and 5,000 watts according to screen size and distance. The Xenon Vertical Arc utilized a silver surfaced reflector for the lower powered bulbs. The Xenon Horizontal Arc was used for larger screens and had a 5,000 watt capacity. The Strong Electric Company designed a 6,000 watt Xenon for drive-in use. To reduce the heat transmitted to the film, a front or rear surfaced "dichroic" reflector was used in the higher power lamps. This reflected the infared heat portion of the spectrum out through the back of the mirror and was exhausted by the ventilation system.

In theory, Xenon lamphouses were an acceptable source of illumination, especially for the small screen multiplexes and twinned theaters of the seventies and eighties. In practice, problems arose when multiplex managers cut corners. Minimum maintenance like cleaning the reflectors to remove dust was ignored. If the lamphouse was not perfectly aligned with the projector or was set to the wrong distance from the film, the light would enter the lens at an angle. Mis-directed light bounced around the lens, reducing contrast on screen. Unqualified operators were unable to realign them or set them up properly to begin with.

Some theaters installed rectifier power supplies that were inadequate to support a Xenon bright enough to properly light the screen image. Others used 1,600 watt lamps when the cinema needed a 3,000 watt source of illumination. Compared to the cheap carbon rods, replacement bulbs were very expensive depending on the watts which is why they used the least expensive ones. As the Xenon bulb aged, it darkened. Some cinemas used them beyond their capacity. The end result was a dark projected image well below the required 16 foot lamberts of screen brightness. Combined with inept platter projection, improperly set up Xenon lamphouses were responsible for the overall decline in presentation in the last three decades.

# 5. Cinematography

In 2000, Ridley Scott's *Gladiator* was released in U.S. theaters. It was photographed in the Super 35mm format by John Mathieson. This retrograde process was a variation of Howard Hughes' SuperScope method of the fifties. The entire Academy 1.33 silent aperture frame was exposed during principal photography. After the negative was conformed, the film was optically enlarged to the anamorphic 2.35 format by cropping the top and bottom of the frame and blowing up the image. The end result was a grainy release print. Mathieson's photography was typical of many post–1968 features. Scott was fond of de-saturated, muted colors. Flesh-tones were often orange or bluish tinted. Since the Super 35 system was designed to have multiple aspect ratios derived from it, the widescreen compositions lacked the dramatic use of width and space common in the best Panavision or 70mm films. The release copies were three generations removed from the negative and had weak contrast. These factors caused the viewer to watch the film objectively with little emotional impact.

Nine years earlier, Robert A. Harris' restoration of *Spartacus* was given a theatrical release in 70mm. The film was shot in the large format Technirama process in 1959 by the brilliant cinematographer Russell Metty. The camera utilized a horizontal negative exposing a wide eight sprocket image (similar to a still camera) with a 25 percent anamorphic compression. From this element, optically derived first generation 70mm prints were manufactured along with 35mm anamorphic dye transfer reduction copies in 1960. In both cases, the resolution and sharpness was improved due to the large format pre-print. Harris' version was reissued in 70mm and the quality was spectacular and far superior to the release copies of *Gladiator*. Flesh-tones were vibrant as were the skies and dramatic high key lighting. The rich colors and contrast increased apparent sharpness. Viewers watched the film subjectively as if they were visiting ancient Rome. The moviegoing experience of these two pictures was quite different and it was obvious that the standards of color cinematography and release print methods had changed over the decades.

## *The Classic Studio Style*

Since the majority of contemporary features are in color, I'll focus on this format instead of black and white. From 1934 to 1968, Technicolor set the standard for quality color motion pictures.[1] Many historians depict the process as a method of principal photography via the three strip camera. Others associate it with the vibrant colors of particular films shot with that unit like *Singin' in the Rain* (1953). Technicolor was actually a release print method that enhanced specific kinds of photography. Different types of negatives were used over the years to achieve various looks.

Some of the early Technicolor movies downplayed the use of primary colors . It was thought that the vibrant dyes might cause eyestrain. *Sweethearts* (1938) and *A Star Is Born* (1937) adopted a subdued color scheme. However, these films featured saturated flesh-tones like the majority of subsequent Technicolor films through the late sixties.

Sol Polito and Tony Gaudio's cinematography of *The Adventures of Robin Hood* (1938) had a saturated color design that emphasized bright primary colors as did Harold Hal Rosen's camerawork on *The Wizard of Oz* (1939). These pictures set the standard for one type of Technicolor look that was adopted by MGM, Fox, Columbia and other studios in the forties and early fifties. Features like *Anchors Aweigh* (1945), *Cover Girl* (1944) and *The Gang's All Here* (1943) had intense colors that were visually stunning. Natalie Kalmus, Henri Jaffa and others were the color consultants on these pictures and assisted the cinematographers and art departments in generating the "Glorious Technicolor" look. This is what many people associate with the process today.

It was not the only look available. Some cinematographers opted for a more realistic color design. Ray Rennahan's camerawork on *For Whom the Bell Tolls* (1943) and Victor Milner and William V. Skall's photography on *Reap the Wild Wind* (1942) avoided garish primaries but retained the saturation and rich contrast.

The problem with Technicolor films in the three strip era was the camera itself. The extensive lighting required to expose the multiple B&W negatives limited depth of field and made low key lighting effects difficult. The switch to color negative in 1952–1953 was a major improvement. Kodak and Anscocolor introduced dye coupler negative and print stock

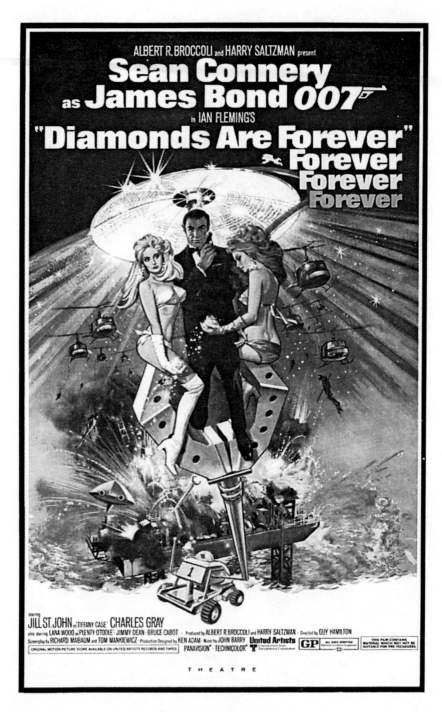

The classic studio style continued to be used on some films like Ted Moore's slick cinematography on *Diamonds Are Forever* (1971).

in 1951. The early Super Cinecolor features used the former but made the prints in their proprietary three strip method via B&W separations derived from the color negative and dyed onto duplitized double emulsion stock. *This Is Cinerama* (1952) was one of the first features to be shot with the Kodak color negative. Since there was no interpositive or internegative stock, the fades were made in the printer while the positive was exposed. By 1953, the only method available for optical effects was to make black and white separations of each color then reprint them with the effects onto color negative. The quality was very grainy and contrasty. As a result, fades and dissolves were only used for the few frames that were necessary then cut back to the camera negative within the same shot. This resulted in an visual "pop" on screen which was apparent in Fox CinemaScope films.

Technicolor adapted their matrix printers so that they could be made from Kodak or Ansco color negatives and A&B rolled the originals so that first generation fades and dissolves could be incorporated into the dye transfer release prints. In the sixties, they developed an auto-select single strand printer for the same purpose.

After the introduction of Cinerama, VistaVision, Technirama and Todd-AO large format negatives, the quality of both Eastmancolor positives and dye transfer reduction release prints were upgraded. The TV competition was the inspiration. Depth of field (foreground to background sharpness), resolution and color rendition were all improved. Kodak continued to develop their color negative stock throughout the era. The speed of the emulsion doubled from 25 to 50 which allowed wider exposure indexes and subtle lighting effects.

Fifties color photography emphasized wide screen composition and improved sharpness. While high key studio lighting was still common, many productions were shot on location. Lionel Lindon's superb Todd-AO photography in *Around the World in 80 Days* (1956) was a good example. The exposure range of color negative allowed flexible lighting design and enabled directors like John Ford to advance the art of cinematography. Winston Hoch's lyrical VistaVision camerawork on *The Searchers* (1956) had a three-dimensional quality that enabled audiences to experience the film as if they were on location. Its haunting imagery remained with the viewer after leaving the theater. Robert Surtees was another color stylist who utilized 65mm negatives effectively. His Todd-AO camerawork on *Oklahoma!* (1955) along with the anamorphic 65mm formats on *Ben-Hur* (1959) and *Mutiny on the Bounty* (1962) enhanced their appeal. Charles Lang photographed some of the best westerns of the fifties and sixties including *Gunfight at the O.K. Corral* (1957) and *One Eyed Jacks* (1961), both in VistaVision. He also shot some of *How the West Was Won* (1962) which was filmed in three panel Cinerama with an infinite depth of field and illusion of peripheral vision. Lang was equally adept at thrillers as illustrated with his atmospheric Technicolor photography in *Charade* (1963) and *Wait Until Dark* (1967).

Other notable cinematographers that utilized the classic studio look included Russell Harlan (*Rio Bravo*, 1959, *The Great Race*, 1965), Harry Stratling (*My Fair Lady*, 1964), Daniel Fapp (*West Side Story*, 1961) and William H. Clothier (*The Alamo*, 1960, *Cheyenne Autumn*, 1964). All of these cameramen created breathtaking visual beauty that was aesthetically pleasing and artistically integrated into the narrative. An example of creative color design was the dance sequence in *West Side Story*. As Maria swung her arms around, the hues separated into superimposed colors that strobed. The image then turned hot red as the scene switched to the high school gymnasium where the teenage gangs competed for dominance on the dance floor. As Tony walked in, the red was dissolved out and the colors returned to normal. Director Robert Wise and Daniel Fapp's use of primaries added to the intensity of the drama.

In the sixties, most of the large format processes were phased out with the exception of 70mm. Simultaneously, improvements in Panavision anamorphic lenses enabled both Eastmancolor positives and dye transfer prints to simulate the fine grain imagery of the 35mm print downs. Ted Moore's slick Panavision photography on *Thunderball* (1965) looked superior to any CinemaScope production. While flesh-tones were toned down a bit, the overall sharpness and color remained vibrant for most of the decade. Freddie Young's camerawork on David Lean's *Lawrence of Arabia* (1962) was an example of the spectacular quality that was typical for the era. Films printed in Eastmancolor also simulated the Technicolor look. Joseph F. Biroc's photography in *The Russians Are Coming, the Russians Are Coming* (1966) which was printed at De Luxe also had saturated colors. A list of major cinematographers who utilized the "classic studio look" and their films is contained in Chapter 10.

## The Contemporary Style

Cinematography went through major changes in the late sixties and early seventies. Improved high speed stock enabled cameramen to shoot with less light. Kodak's 5251 was an EI 50 tungsten balanced film which was twice as sensitive as previous stocks. In 1968, the stock was further modified with 5254 which was tungsten-balanced with an E 100 rating which allowed cameramen to underexpose the negative to a greater degree

# THE ACCLAIM IS GREATER THAN EVER!

LAWRENCE OF ARABIA IS

"A REALLY EPIC SPECTACULAR! IF YOU'VE NEVER SEEN IT, *WHAT ARE YOU WAITING FOR? IF YOU HAVE SEEN IT, YOU'LL ENJOY IT EVEN MORE THIS TIME AROUND!* One of David Lean's most fascinating works. Forceful and dynamic, with sweep, majesty and splendor!" —BOB SALMAGGI, Group W Network

COLUMBIA PICTURES Presents The SAM SPIEGEL-DAVID LEAN Production of LAWRENCE OF ARABIA starring ALEC GUINNESS · ANTHONY QUINN · JACK HAWKINS · JOSE FERRER · ANTHONY QUAYLE CLAUDE RAINS · ARTHUR KENNEDY with OMAR SHARIF as 'ALI' and introducing PETER O'TOOLE as 'LAWRENCE' SCREENPLAY BY ROBERT BOLT · PRODUCED BY SAM SPIEGEL · DIRECTED BY DAVID LEAN · Photographed in SUPER PANAVISION 70® · A Horizon Picture in TECHNICOLOR®

WINNER OF 7 ACADEMY AWARDS INCLUDING BEST PICTURE!

Freddie Young's breathtaking cinematography on *Lawrence of Arabia* (1962) represented the "classic studio style" at its best.

than in the past. Directors of photography took advantage of these developments and created a different type of lighting design. This "contemporary style" coincided with New Hollywood. Many of the old standards were rejected or phased out. The next breed of cinematographers were not advocates of traditional camerawork.

Among the innovators was Conrad Hall, who began shooting pictures in the late fifties and early sixties. He was among the first cameramen to break the rules. In *Cool Hand Luke* (1967), he allowed the sun to create flares in the camera lens which no studio cinematographer would permit. In an interview on American Movie Classics, Hall remarked that he wanted to change the look of Westerns in *Butch Cassidy and the Sundance Kid* (1969). Rather than using polarization filters to generate vivid blue skies and saturated colors typical in John Ford films (i.e. *Cheyenne Autumn*), he wanted to "pale it out" which indeed he did by overexposing the negative with back light. The film had de-saturated colors and a rustic look. He won an Oscar for his efforts.

William A. Fraker was a relative newcomer to the field. He utilized diffusion in *Paint Your Wagon!* (1969) which inspired a trend of similar camerawork, most notably by Vilmos Zsigmond whose background was exploitation films (*The Sadist*, 1963). In 1971 Zsigmond photographed *McCabe and Mrs. Miller* with extreme de-saturation and diffusion. The film was notable for its absence of primary colors. *Deliverance* (1972) featured a similar look. While both were printed in the dye transfer method, the release copies were very different from what was typically associated with that process. Although Douglas Trumbull's special effects were impressive in *Close Encounters of the Third Kind* (1979), the main body of the film had Zsigmond's de-saturated flesh-tones and dark interiors. Fellow cinematographers awarded him the Oscar for another picture that was quite different from the "Glorious Technicolor" look of earlier winners like *A Man for All Seasons* (1966). Perhaps the most notorious example of the new style was Zsigmond's photography in *Heaven's Gate* (1980). As critic Roger Ebert noted, "It is so smoky, so dusty, so foggy, so unfocused and so brownish yellow that you want to try Windex on the screen. A director is in deep trouble when we do not even enjoy the primary act of looking at his picture."[2] The movie's one sheet tag line was "What one loves in life are the things that fade." Ebert's description fit many movies from that era.

Another newcomer was Gordon Willis. He was called the "Prince of Darkness" by film crews. He used very little light on set and portions of his compositions were often in total darkness. The *Godfather* films of 1972 and 1974 were examples of his work along with *The Parallax View* in 1974.

The story of a gambling man and a hustling lady and the empire they fashioned from the wilderness.

WARREN BEATTY & JULIE CHRISTIE

McCABE & MRS. MILLER

WARREN BEATTY · JULIE CHRISTIE in The Robert Altman-David Foster Production of "McCABE & MRS. MILLER"
Also Starring RENE AUBERJONOIS · Screenplay by Robert Altman and Brian McKay · Produced by David Foster
and Mitchell Brower · Based on the novel "McCabe" by Edmund Naughton · Directed by Robert Altman
PANAVISION® TECHNICOLOR® From Warner Bros. A Kinney Services Company

**Vilmos Zsigmond's cinematography on *McCabe and Mrs. Miller* (1971) was an example of the "contemporary style."**

All three were printed in the dye transfer process which helped to reduce apparent grain in the underexposed negatives. In the case of the *Godfather* pictures, this style enhanced the subject matter, which dealt with the sinister underworld.

Others included John A. Alonzo, who was originally a television cameraman. He shot Polanski's *Chinatown* (1974) with diffusion and soft focus. Michael Chapman's grainy photography on *Taxi Driver* (1976) and Victor J. Kemper's work in *Dog Day Afternoon* (1975) were examples of gritty realism that worked within the context of the films. Both began their careers in the seventies. Bruce Surtees, the son of Robert Surtees, also contributed to the new style with his dark, low key photography on *Joe Kidd* (1972) and *The Outlaw Josey Wales* (1976). The imagery of these films was the opposite of the look his father gave *The Graduate* (1967) and *Sweet Charity* (1969).

A number of experienced cinematographers also experimented with new types of photography. Freddie Young developed a process of pre-exposing color negative film (pre-fogging) to mute the colors in *The Deadly Affair* in 1967 as an experiment. Charles Lang adopted a diffused style of photography for *Summer and Smoke* in 1961 which Geoffrey Unsworth adapted for *Cabaret* (1972) and *Superman* (1978). The former won the Oscar but the latter was blown up to 70mm and grainy. Both pictures were different from the high key lighting and razor sharp imagery Unsworth utilized in *2001: A Space Odyssey* (1968) which was shot in 65mm. Arthur Ornitz was another veteran who created the illusion of source lighting in pictures like *Serpico* (1973) and *Death Wish* (1974). The overall murky quality of these projected images distanced viewers from the story compared to earlier Technicolor movies which absorbed audiences into the dramas and used color dramatically. When excessive grain and poor contrast were noticeable on screen it called attention to itself and made it difficult to suspend your disbelief. Classic cinematographers like Lionel Lindon and Robert Surtees changed their style and adapted to the new look although later features were lackluster compared to their earlier work.

In the Post-Code era, other trends developed in the aforementioned categories. Many counterculture pictures not only rejected traditional narrative structure but standards of photography. Films like *The Activist* (1969) were shot "cinema-verite" as was *Woodstock* (1970) with five cameramen including director, Wadleigh. De Palma's *Hi Mom* (1970) was filmed with minimal light and contained a hand held black and white sequence photographed by Robert Elfstrom which spoofed hippie guerrilla theater.

Sexploitation and exploitation pictures also had an impact. A number were shot in 16mm and optically enlarged to 35mm. *The Texas Chainsaw*

*Massacre* (1974) was among the 16mm blow-ups and was quite grainy. Some used TVC's Chem-tone process that pushed the latitude of under-exposed negatives in processing. These techniques lowered the bar as to what was acceptable for exhibition.[3] Those who advocated the contemporary style took a relativist attitude regarding quality. In reality, they merely replaced one set of standards with another. When I was young, I used to sit a few rows from the screen which enhanced the illusion of peripheral vision and gave the projected image greater impact. I had to move to the back rows while watching many seventies movies since the prints were so de-saturated and murky you could see obvious grain on screen.

The fact that the contemporary style had become standardized was not immediately apparent to audiences. Throughout the late sixties and early seventies, many classic features were reissued to theaters prior to television broadcast. Among them were the James Bond thrillers, Disney animated classics and epics like *Around the World in 80 Days, My Fair Lady, The Ten Commandments* and *Lawrence of Arabia*. The vibrant color of these pictures gave the impression that both types of cinematography would co-exist.

By the early eighties the competing cable and home video formats phased out theatrical revivals with the exception of some high profile restorations and occasional "special editions." After a film was available on cassette for rental, it was difficult to book them in cinemas. Even the Disney company released their animated classics on tape and ended the cyclic reissues. The absence of classics with studio lighting and vibrant color in first run theaters made it obvious that movies had changed. While the seventies still offered pictures with traditional cinematography (e.g. *Blazing Saddles, The Towering Inferno*), the eighties institutionalized the styles introduced in the earlier part of the decade. In general, the majority of films had de-saturated flesh-tones and color with a shallow depth of field. The grainy release copies of *Cocoon* (1984) was a typical example. The expanded exposure latitude gave some cameramen an excuse to use as little light as possible. The trouble was, the art of cinematography was dependent on the art of lighting.

Andrzej Bartkowiak's camerawork on *Prince of the City* (1981) and *The Verdict* (1982) was so dark I could barely see the expressions on the actors' faces. Large format negatives, 35mm print downs, increased depth of field and other advancements from the fifties were lost over the succeeding decades. In the nineties, Technicolor developed a proprietary bleach-bypass process that left some imaging silver in the film. This gave deeper blacks but further de-saturated the color. *Seven* (2001) was among the titles that utilized this look. Personally, I found it aesthetically ugly.

There were some exceptions and pictures like *Grease* (1978), *My Favorite Year* (1982) and *Dances with Wolves* (1990) simulated the look of pre-seventies features but they were period films. The location work of many contemporary stories did not lend itself to the elaborate lighting design of studio sets. The use of color was rarely dramatic as it was in films like *Vertigo* (1958) where Robert Burk's imagery was integral to the theme. Advocates of the new look claimed that post-sixties camerawork was more "realistic." This argument didn't hold up to scrutiny since movies by their very nature were not photographed realism. Film emulsion did not replicate what the human eye saw. The choice of stock, lenses, filters and lighting design all altered the location of the shoot.

In my opinion, the color of most post-seventies features tended to be functional instead of artistic. The movies of Alfred Hitchcock, Walt Disney, Michael Powell, David Lean and John Ford all had unique imagery. Post-code movies in the same genres had less distinct cinematography. An overall blandness was apparent in most releases. Some were unpleasant to watch with excessive grain and poor contrast. The changing styles of motion picture visuals did not affect box-office revenue. Audiences became accustomed to it and in the case of the targeted youth audience had no frame of reference to what films used to look like. A list of notable cinematographers and their features that utilized the contemporary style is contained in Chapter 10.

## Color Cinematography Oscars

The Academy of Motion Pictures Arts and Sciences also contributed to the success of modern photography. As the new breed of cameramen gained influence, they voted for others who followed their trend. Detailed below are the Academy Award winners for color cinematography. Prior to the mid-sixties, there were categories for B&W and color but they dropped the former in 1967. I've indicated whether the feature was photographed in the classic or contemporary style. I omitted the years prior to 1939 along with 1993 since the Oscars went to black and white films which is not the subject of this analysis.

1939  Ernest Haller, Ray Ranahan *Gone with the Wind* (classic style)
1940  Georges Perinal *The Thief of Baghdad* (classic style)
1941  Ernest Palmer, Ray Rennahan *Blood and Sand* (classic style)
1942  Leon Shamroy *The Black Swan* (classic style)
1943  Hal Mohr, W. Howard Greene *Phantom of the Opera* (classic style)
1944  Leon Shamroy *Wilson* (classic style)

**1945** Leon Shamroy *Leave Her to Heaven* (classic style)
**1946** Charles Rosher, Leonard Smith, Arthur Arling *The Yearling* (classic style)
**1947** Jack Cardiff *Black Narcissus* (classic style)
**1948** Joseph Valentine, William V. Skall, Winton Hoch *Joan of Arc* (classic style)
**1949** Winton Hoch *She Wore a Yellow Ribbon* (classic style)
**1950** Robert Surtees *King Solomon's Mines* (classic style)
**1951** Alfred Gilks, John Alton *An American in Paris* (classic style)
**1952** Winton C. Hoch, Archie Stout *The Quiet Man* (classic style)
**1953** Loyal Griggs *Shane* (classic style)
**1954** Milton Krasner *Three Coins in the Fountain* (classic style)
**1955** Robert Burks *To Catch a Thief* (classic style)
**1956** Lionel Lindon *Around the World in 80 Days* (classic style)
**1957** Jack Hildyard *The Bridge on the River Kwai* (classic style)
**1958** Joseph Ruttenberg *Gigi* (classic style)
**1959** Robert Surtees *Ben Hur* (classic style)
**1960** Russell Metty *Spartacus* (classic style)
**1961** Daniel L. Fapp *West Side Story* (classic style)
**1962** Freddie Young *Lawrence of Arabia* (classic style)
**1963** Leon Shamroy *Cleopatra* (classic style)
**1964** Harry Stradling *My Fair Lady* (classic style)
**1965** Freddie Young *Doctor Zhivago* (classic style)
**1966** Ted Moore *A Man for All Seasons* (classic style)
**1967** Burnett Guffey *Bonnie and Clyde* (classic style)
**1968** Pasqualino De Santis *Romeo and Juliet* (contemporary style)
**1969** Conrad Hall *Butch Cassidy and the Sundance Kid* (contemporary style)
**1970** Freddie Young *Ryan's Daughter* (classic style)
**1971** Oswald Morris *Fiddler on the Roof* (contemporary style)
**1972** Geoffrey Unsworth *Cabaret* (contemporary style)
**1973** Sven Nykvist *Cries and Whispers* (contemporary style)
**1974** Fred Koenekamp, Joseph Biroc *The Towering Inferno* (classic style)
**1975** John Alcott *Barry Lyndon* (contemporary style)
**1976** Haskell Wexler *Bound for Glory* (contemporary style)
**1977** Vilmos Zsigmond *Close Encounters of the Third Kind* (contemporary style)
**1978** Nester Almendros *Days of Heaven* (contemporary style)
**1979** Vittorio Storaro *Apocalypse Now* (contemporary style)
**1980** Geoffrey Unsworth, Chislain Cloquet *Tess* (contemporary style)
**1981** Vittorio Storaro *Reds* (contemporary style)
**1982** Billy Williams, Ronnie Taylor *Ghandi* (contemporary style)
**1983** Sven Nykvist *Fanny & Alexander* (contemporary style)
**1984** Chris Menges *The Killing Fields* (contemporary style)
**1985** David Watkin *Out of Africa* (contemporary style)
**1986** Chris Menges *The Mission* (contemporary style)
**1987** Vittorio Storaro *The Last Emperor* (classic style)
**1988** Peter Biziou *Mississippi Burning* (contemporary style)
**1989** Freddie Francis *Glory* (contemporary style)
**1990** Dean Semler *Dances with Wolves* (classic style)
**1991** Robert Richardson *JFK* (contemporary style)

1992  Phillippe Rousselot *A River Runs Through It* (contemporary style)
1994  John Toll *Legends of the Fall* (contemporary style)
1995  John Toll *Braveheart* (contemporary style)
1996  John Seale *The English Patient* (contemporary style)
1997  Russell Carpenter *Titanic* (contemporary style)
1998  Janusz Kaminski *Saving Private Ryan* (contemporary style)
1999  Conrad Hall *American Beauty* (contemporary style)
2000  Peter Pau *Crouching Tiger, Hidden Dragon* (contemporary and classic styles)
2001  Andrew Lesnie *The Lord of the Rings: The Fellowship of the Ring* (contemporary style)

After 1968, only four motion pictures won awards for films that utilized variations of the classic look. Recently, Peter Pau's *Crouching Tiger, Hidden Dragon* (2000) combined the two styles for the martial arts fantasy and Donald McAlpine's colorful lighting design in *Moulin Rouge* (2001) were among the few features that had vivid colors but they remained the exception to the rule.

## Release Print Technology

While the style of lighting and cinematography was an aesthetic choice, the changes in release print technology had an impact on its use. Prior to 1968, copies were either made in the dye transfer process at Technicolor or via the contact positive method at the competing labs like Metrocolor and De Luxe. Many positive release prints were struck directly off the camera negative in both 35mm and 70mm at a slow printing speed. Dye transfer matrices were also derived from the master element resulting in first generation sharpness in both processes.

There was a quality difference between Eastmancolor and Technicolor. While the former was technically sharper than the latter, the color was more vibrant and the contrast superior in the dye transfer prints which generated excellent "apparent sharpness." There was a serious problem in the contact printing method. Striking hundreds of copies off the original wore it out quickly. Release prints made in the dye transfer process did less damage since the negative was only used to make matrices.

In 1968, Kodak introduced Color Reversal Intermediate 7/5249 (CRI). This new type of internegative was derived from the camera negative. Second generation release prints were made from them. While acceptable, they lacked the contrast and resolution of first generation copies. Labs found it difficult to process and some referred to it as "CRY." 20th Century–

Fox and their subsidiary De Luxe was the first facility to use them for general release prints. Eventually other labs followed.

While camera negative wear was reduced, CRIs were not appropriate for the underexposed negatives of the seventies and eighties. For example, Gordon Willis' *The Godfather* (1972) looked quite nice in the original run of dye transfer prints. A second run of release copies were made from a CRI at Movielab. These prints were grainy and murky compared to the Technicolor copies.

Technicolor shut down its dye transfer line in 1975 and developed the continuous high speed printer in 1976 for which they received an Academy Award. This machine was able to crank out Eastmancolor release prints from CRIs at the rate of 2,000 feet per minute. The speed was increased in later years. To properly expose a positive required contrast adjustments. For example, night scenes required a darker exposure to generate rich blacks. CRIs incorporated the color timing derived from the answer print but copies were exposed at a "one lite" setting. The contrast was inferior to camera negative prints where each shot had a separate exposure. The high speed also affected image steadiness on screen. As print orders increased, labs coordinated their efforts to handle the overload. It was not uncommon for reels of the same feature to be made at different facilities with inconsistent color and contrast. The days of "Glorious Technicolor" were over with the exception of 70mm blow ups. One of the advantages of that format was the printers did not operate at high speeds and timing adjustments could be made.

In the post–Technicolor era, many labs cut corners in processing. Few did archival washes which affected image stability. Sloppy handling resulted in off-color reels. Because of the poor quality of general release copies, studios made a few camera negative prints for press screenings. Referred to as "EK (Eastman Kodak) Showprints," the critics reviewed copies that the general public rarely saw. When the Paramount Center of the Arts played *Dances with Wolves* (1990), program director Robert Frischmuth announced he had secured a "Showprint" for the screening. The quality was excellent except for one reel which was from a general release copy. It was off-color and grainy compared to the rest of the film.

A contributing factor in lab sloppiness was the reduced number of facilities. In the eighties and nineties many folded including Movielab, Guffanti, Precision, Studio Film Lab, TVC and others. Video editing was introduced in the eighties. Rather than making a "work print" of the 35mm or 16mm dailies, producers transferred them to tape with a time code. They assembled the final version by video "insert editing" and the cutter conformed the negative via the matchback system using the timecode to splice each shot rather than edge numbers on the side of the film. Later, the AVID system was adopted for computer editing and a similar match-back of the negative rolls. Television commercials started using videotape instead of 16mm prints for broadcast. Many facilities lost their customer base with these changes. The lack of competition among the surviving labs increased costs and the overload of work made them cut corners.

In the eighties, Kodak replaced the round shaped grain in film stock with tubular shaped grain ("T-Grain"). The smaller grains meant an increase in sharpness. 5245/7245 was the first stock to use this in all of its layers in 1989. Simultaneously, intermediate stock improved. The camera negative was copied onto the new interpositive stock which incorporated the color corrections in the timing ribbons. From the interpositive, an internegative was manufactured. Release copies were struck from them on high speed printers and the final product was three generations removed from the camera negative. CRIs were phased out. Print orders continued to increase and some labs coated the internegative with chemical solutions to prevent scratching which also affected contrast.

Although Agfa and other companies offered estar base stock prior to 1993, Kodak switched to it that year with *The Fugitive*. The estar stock was advertised as being more durable for platter use. Manufacturers claimed it was archival and not subject to hydrolysis (aka "vinegar syndrome") as was tri-acetate or decomposition like nitrate in bad storage. However, it scratched easier and was more subject to static charges, especially on platters which could result in a "brain wrap." In large runs, the static caused dust particles to get printed into the release copy. Both *Titanic* and *Grease* had dirt contained on their emulsion which was noticeable in scenes when the sky was light. In the nineties, Kodak introduced two new print stocks, Vision (2383) and Premiere (2393), which featured an increase in contrast and color saturation. While current high speed release copies are better than ones in the past, they are still inferior to first generation prints of the fifties and sixties or dye transfer copies from any era.

## Back to the Future

The June 15, 1997, issue of *The Hollywood Reporter* contained an article by Scott Hettrick entitled, "Technicolor says it may go back to the future." The lab had revived the famous dye transfer process ("DT") which generated the "Glorious Technicolor" prints of features like *The Wizard of Oz* (1939) and *Goldfinger* (1964). It took a few more years before the machines were available for industry use. In the June 20, 1997 issue, they announced that Warner Bros. was making new dye transfer prints of *Batman and Robin*. One print played the Astor Plaza theater in New York City and other venues. The color quality was quite good although the use of the process was not extensively promoted.

Over the next five years, a handful of new features and classics had limited print runs in the new dye transfer system. Among them were *Godzilla, Bulworth, The Wizard of Oz, Gone with the Wind, The 13th Warrior, Toy Story II, Pearl Harbor* and *Funny Girl*. Robert A. Harris' restoration of *Rear Window* and reedited version of Coppola's *Apocalypse Now* were reissued in DT prints too.

Significant changes had been made. The pinbelt which transferred the dyes from the matrix to the blank receiver stock had been shortened to a loop of about twenty one feet. The machines ran at the rate of 800 feet per minute. The top speed they operated at in 1974 was 330 feet. The negative was submerged in the liquid gate chemical which eliminated base scratches. While wet gate matrix printers had been used in the past, they had problems with "shorelining" which caused defects on the surface of the liquid. The new matrix stock, printers and processing yielded sharper images and better tone scale latitude including shadow detail delineation.[1]

According to the Technicolor patent of December 14, 1999 (US6002470), the new equipment contained a plurality of large diameter rollers with an elevator mechanism for adjustment and a rectilinear film path for the film sandwich which transferred the dyes from the matrix to the blank stock which allowed for high speeds compared to the pre–1975 line. One of the inventors was Richard J. Goldberg, who was also the Special Assistant to the president of Technicolor and a major source of information in my previous book on the process.

The Fuji Photo Film Company also contributed to the system with a stain preventing device. The apparatus had a rotatable plate cylinder on which the matrix was mounted on a squeeze roller to remove washing liquid which contained dye from the surface of the receiving material. It uniformly applied the dye solution to the matrix.

The cost of utilizing the dye transfer process was expensive compared to the high speed method. A set of matrices cost over $3 per foot compared to the $2 per foot average to make an interpositive/internegative for contact printing. The release prints were cheaper at .15 per foot. Eastmancolor positives averaged .20 per foot. Matrices had a limited life. A high end estimate was approximately 400 copies before they wore out which meant that multiple sets would have to be made for large print runs of 2,000 which was common.

The advantages of the dye transfer process were the same as in previous eras. The contrast, color saturation and apparent sharpness were superior to contact positive prints made on the high speed printer and they didn't fade. The revival of Technicolor's famous system seemed to be the solution to decades of sub-standard general release prints. Why didn't it make the impact anticipated?

Part of the problem was poor advertising. Other than the *Rear Window, Gone with the Wind* and *Apocalypse Now* reissues, the use of the process wasn't promoted by the lab or distributors. Few people were aware that they were seeing dye transfer copies of *Pearl Harbor* which looked quite good because the cinematography featured saturated flesh-tones and color. It was almost as if the use of DT was an industry secret. Quality control was another issue. *Gone with the Wind* was not derived from the nitrate three strip camera negative which still existed in 1997. A strange format was created for this release. The 1.33 image was centered within black borders in an anamorphic 2.35 x 1 ratio. This color internegative was three generations removed from the camera negative and the matrices derived from it were contrasty. The dye transfer prints were rushed through the lab to meet a release date and had inconsistent color from reel to reel. Frameline artifacts were noticeable in the window-boxed image that would've been cropped by the projector if the image was exhibited full frame with a 1.33 ratio.

The reissue of *The Wizard of Oz* was more successful since the matrices were derived from the original nitrate three strip negative. Only 50 prints were made in the DT process. The rest of the run were Eastmancolor prints derived from a color internegative with the 1.33 image centered in a 1.85 x 1 frame with black borders. Theaters didn't advertise which copies they were showing.

*Rear Window* was the most successful use of the process for a classic revival. Matrices were derived from a restored internegative and supervised by archivist Robert A. Harris. The quality was excellent and the dye transfer prints were actually sharper than the originals from 1962 and 1970. Harris allowed me to inspect dye transfer prints from these years to delineate the quality difference. It was clear that to use dye transfer effectively, there needed to be qualified personnel supervising the release and enough lead time to make it worthwhile.

The main problem was that the aesthetics of modern cinematography was not appropriate for the process. The quality difference between a dye transfer print of *Godzilla* and a conventional high speed general release print was not distinct enough to warrant the expense. The Technicolor corporation also had a conflict of interest since they continued to offer their inexpensive high speed printing method and were involved with Digital

***Rear Window*** reissue glossy photo ad.

Cinema which would eliminate release prints entirely. In 2001, Coppola's revised version of *Apocalypse Now* was reissued in the process to critical acclaim. However, unless other major directors get behind it and cinematographers shoot with the process in mind, dye transfer may be phased out again in the near future.

# 6. The Home Entertainment Revolution

> Show business may never be the same. The distribution revolution continued throughout 1981, and the new technologies associated with cable television and homevideo came ever closer to providing showman with the so called millennium of a boxoffice in the living room.[1]

Although exhibitors survived the post–Code changes in content and demographics by twinning and multiplexing their theaters, they were less prepared for the video revolution. In the late seventies and early eighties, cinema owners were confronted with new competition from home entertainment venues.

## CATV

The first to make an impact was cable television. "Pay TV" dated back to the beginnings of the television medium. In 1948, Robert Tralton built the first cable system to receive widespread publicity which charged a monthly fee for service. The same year, the FCC put a four year ban on licensing new broadcast stations which gave the opportunity to cable TV systems (CATV) to expand. There were 14,000 subscriber homes by 1952.

Exhibitors fought back with a campaign to "Stop Pay TV" and "Save Free TV." Some theaters even put it on their marquee. The studios were reluctant to sell their newer product to the few cable systems in operation lest they incur the wrath of theater owners. The cable industry continued to grow at a slow pace throughout the sixties and early seventies. In 1963 there were 1,200 cable systems, which served 1 million homes. By 1969 there were 2,260, which served 3.6 million homes. However, it wasn't until advanced satellite technology was developed that the medium gained widespread popularity. In 1975, HBO was established and in1976, Ted Turner launched the first satellite-delivered broadcast system. In 1978 additional programming expanded channel capacity which included Showtime, USA Network, MTV and others.

Cable gained in popularity and by 1979, Showtime had tripled its size into a national pay television network of 525 cable systems with nearly one million subscribers. They also began producing their own programs which cut into network fare. HBO increased from a few hundred subscribers to six million by 1980. The number of systems grew along with the households. In 1975 there were 3,506 systems which nearly doubled by 1984 with 6,200 systems and in 1999 the number totaled 10,700. The U.S. households with cable in 1977 was 12,168,450 or 16.6 percent. In 1984 there were 37,290,870 or 43 percent and in 1999 67,592,000 households or 68 percent.

HBO and others made deals with the distributors to broadcast recent films. For example, in 1976 Columbia licensed its first five films to HBO which included *Shampoo, Breakout, Aloha, Bobby and Rose, The Fortune* and *Lies My Father Told Me.* This became such a profitable ancillary market that the studios shortened the window from multiplex bookings to cable showings which affected sub-run theaters and drive-ins. Studios also made pre-release commitments to cable stations which enabled them to utilize the publicity generated by the theatrical release. It was in their interest to get their movies on HBO or Showtime as quickly as possible which eventually ended double-bills and reissues which had a been a staple of theatrical distribution for decades.

Cable also affected free television and the three networks lost their dominance over the broadcast medium. As Paul Klein of *Variety* noted in 1982, "To the outside world it looked as if CBS aided by 18 hours (20 percent of their schedule) of high-cost features, won the November sweep with an 18.9 rating. But to the inside world, the news was that all three networks were seriously off in circulation from last year and, in an almost unbroken trend, were down over seven ratings points from 1976. The network pie is shrinking and it can never grow again."[2] The uncut movies presented on cable made the high priced purchases of new films by networks less desirable for the future. Many films had already saturated the market on pay TV before being aired on CBS or ABC, which caused a ratings drop. The "event" presentations of the sixties were gone by the late eighties.

Throughout the eighties, cable showings of recent films cut into exhibition. HBO and Showtime made feature films with major stars which also had an impact. Unlike network broadcasts, CATV airings were uncut. It wasn't critical for viewers to see the film in a multiplex when it was first released. If they missed it on the small screen at the mall, they could see it on their small screen at home shortly afterwards. History repeated itself with a twist. In the fifties, the TV medium cut theatrical attendance in half. To compete, distributors and exhibitors offered spectacular new technology to improve the moviegoing experience including Cinerama, 3-D, CinemaScope, VistaVision, Todd-AO and Technirama. Other than 70mm blow ups supplied by the studios, most exhibitors cut corners rather than improve presentations in the seventies, eighties and nineties.

While creating a new venue of watching uncut movies at home in the seventies and eighties, some disturbing trends were introduced in the nineties. Many cable stations started incorporating their logo on the side of the screen which was very distracting. American Movie Classics included commercials in the middle of their broadcasts which interrupted the story.

## Pay-Per-View

Another venue that cut into theatrical exhibition was Pay-Per-View. Like cable, its origins were in the early fifties. It was known as "Subscription Television" or "Pay-As-You-Go TV." The first to try it was Zenith Radio Corporation in 1949. The FCC granted permission for a test of "Phonevision" in 300 Chicago households which aired a scrambled signal. The telephone lines were used for ordering the desired program which was then de-scrambled to the customer for viewing. The next two companies to try it in 1953 were Skiatron Electronics & Television Corp. and International Telemeter of which Paramount was a fifty percent owner. Skiatron was demonstrated at the Belmont Plaza Hotel and had an arrangement with Western Union to function as the billing agent. An IBM punch card was used for billing and de-scrambling on New York's WOR-TV during off hours. International Telemeter was tested at Palm Springs, California, in 1954. A box was installed in each house at a cost of $21.75. To watch a scheduled movie on TV, $1.35 in coins had to be dropped into the box. The first feature offered simultaneously in theaters and at home in this system was Paramount's *Forever Female*. It cost less to see it in the Plaza Theater at $1.15 which was the house selected for this test.

As with cable, exhibitors knew a threat when they saw it and banded together into a "Joint Committee on Toll TV" with Trueman T. Rembusch and Alfred Starr as co-chairmen to petition politicians and the FCC to try and kill off this emerging competition. The Telemeter system tests were canceled when the company announced there was a lack of product.

Paramount had withdrawn its features. The company struggled along through 1955 when it folded. The same year, RKO sold its backlog of classics to C & C Television Corp. which was operated by Matty Fox. The studio made $15,200,000 on the deal with included 740 features. They were the first to offer "A" features for broadcast on free TV. The others had held back their top titles in the early days of the medium and most distributors only offered "B" Westerns and other low end product which gave pay-per-view a temporary lead of "A" pictures for broadcast in their system.

The impact of Fox's deal was noted by Donald La Badie. "More than a few observers felt that the chances of the coin-box medium had been hurt by the increase in quality entertainment on free television and the first sale of a major studio library, promising an imminent availability of fresh feature material."[3] Columbia followed and released their features and shorts through their subsidiary, Screen Gems. UM & M acquired 1,600 Paramount shorts. MCA purchased 123 Gene Autry and Roy Rogers films from Republic, David Selznick offered 12 titles to NTA and 139 J. Arthur Rank product went to ABC. The following year the two holdouts unloaded their libraries. Paramount sold its backlog of pre–1948 titles to MCA for $35,000,000 with a provision for an additional $15,000,000 later. Universal also unlocked its vaults and sold 600 films to Columbia for Screen Gems broadcast for a minimum guarantee of $200,000,000.

In 1957 there was another attempt with the "Telemovies" system in Oklahoma. New features and reruns were broadcast but they charged a flat monthly fee of $9.50 which made them closer to a cable station than a subscription TV format. It ended one year later. In 1958, two closed circuit toll TV systems were proposed but neither became operational. Photographic Analysis, Inc. claimed to offer a format that eliminated special wiring under the name Selectavision, Inc. (no relation to the videodisc format). An injunction against them due to stock fraud charges shut them down. The second system was offered by Video Independent Theaters in Oklahoma but it was not successful either. Exhibitor pressure on the FCC gave them a short-term victory the same year when the House Interstate and Foreign Commerce Committee adopted a resolution that asked them to withhold action on experimental licenses until Congress legislated on the legal and public issues involved.

This didn't affect our neighbors up north and General Precision Equipment was used for a "Pay-As-You-Go" home television test in Toronto, Canada in March 1960. Under sponsorship by Famous Players Canadian Corp., consumers participating in the system were required to insert the equivalent of one dollar in coins. Feature films along with sports events and other subjects were broadcast. Approximately 3,000 subscribers signed on for the initial cable installation. By 1961, there were 5,800 units in oper-ation and according to industry reports, it had no effect on neighborhood theatres.

Stateside, exhibitors continued to pressure the government and FCC into preventing its reintroduction. They also started negotiations with dis-tributors to reissue post–1948 features to theaters in an attempt to keep them off the networks. They proposed a national advertising campaign to promote these revivals. Theater owners suffered the first of many setbacks in February of 1961. The Federal Communications Commission autho-rized the nation's first full scale tryout of pay television. Hartford Phonevi-sion in a joint venture with RKO utilized Zenith's decoding system for the experiment. The UHF rather than VHF bandwidth was used. First-run fea-tures, educational and sports programs were aired with a cost range of 25 cents through $3.50 with the majority running between 75 cents to $1.50. The charge for installation was under $10. The system operated at a loss through 1969.

Another brief entry was Subscription Television Inc. in 1964 which did not survive the year. It offered sports and theatrical performances as well as movies. As always, product was difficult to come by as theater own-ers continued to combat them behind the scenes. The FCC remained cau-tious in granting permission to new broadcast systems due to the continued failure of these early ones. From a consumer's perspective, the quality of these broadcasts was not worth the installation costs or fee. Most people had B&W sets and they could see the same movie on a big screen in color at their local cinema at less expense.

Networks also competed with pay television and theaters by pur-chasing large blocks of recent films for broadcast. In 1964, Seven Arts acquired TV distribution rights to 215 Universal post–1948 features. NBC signed with Fox and MGM for 60 theatrical pictures. The programs *Sat-urday Night at the Movies* and *Monday Night at the Movies* became popu-lar shows in this era along with the *Late Show* and other venues. Like many adolescents, I was glued to tube watching as many films as I could around the clock. Theater owners organized again into a "Crusade for Free TV" committee headed by Roy Cooper. Their lobbying did not prevent another setback in December of 1968. The FCC granted permission for pay sys-tems to operate on a far greater scale than in the past. A few companies came and went including Wometco Home Theater in New York and National Subscription Television in Los Angeles in the late seventies and early eighties.

Pay-per-view as we know it today started with Showtime in 1973 which charged subscribers a flat monthly fee of $1.50 plus an extra $3 per film. The biggest difference was that more people had color sets and saw the broadcasts in color rather than B&W. Other companies like Viewer's Choice, HBO, Time/Warner, Blockbuster Ticket, and Starz! offered pay-per-view services over the years. By 1988, 10 million homes subscribed to one of the services although much of its popularity was with sporting events like the World Wrestling Federation's Wrestlemania and boxing matches. Pay-per-view was also utilized in hotels and motels throughout the country. Current features along with softcore X product were popular in these venues. Prices were comparable to videocassette rentals in most cases. For example, Blockbuster Ticket charged $3.99 per film.

Another development was "Video on Demand" which differed in that customers could access a movie anytime they wanted rather than at a scheduled hour. Another company, Pay Per View.com, offered a similar service to moviegoers connected to the internet by higher bandwidth means such as ADSL and DSL technologies. The price was only $1 per film. Miramax was the first company to release one of their titles by conventional broadband. *Guinevere* was offered online for people to legally download through its distribution partner, SightSound Technologies. Payment was by credit card. Two plug-ins were needed and the file size was only one-tenth the file size of the DVD. The quality of the picture was much lower as a result. There were also websites like AtomFilms and iFilm that offered independent product.

Cable industry insiders anticipate a future "Magic Box" that companies will install in living rooms. Inside the box will be a computer that enables customers to download any show on its hard drive and play it back at their leisure. Since the signal is digital, the quality will be identical to the original broadcast. In 1999, startup companies TiVo and ReplayTV introduced the first prototypes. They were so sophisticated that viewers could freeze frame a video picture which simultaneously copied the rest of the show for future screening. These early boxes cost between $400 to $700 along with a monthly subscription fee of $10–$20. In 2000, ReplayTV stopped making the boxes but TiVo continues to promote the system. Microsoft, Motorola, Open TV and Liberate Technologies are developing similar products which will drive down prices.

## Home Video

Along with cable and pay-per-view, new home entertainment formats changed the movie going experience in the living room. Consumer videocassette recorders were introduced in the mid-seventies but were expensive. It wasn't until affordable systems were developed at the end of the decade that they became popular. Competing videodisc systems were offered simultaneously which redefined the concept of television.

## Videotapes

In the early days of TV, shows were either done live or aired on film. The only method to save a live broadcast was to make a kinescope of it in 35mm or 16mm. A motion picture camera was adapted to the video scanning rate and filmed off a studio monitor. The contrast was poor and image subject to video distortion of the time. *The Honeymooners* "lost episodes" shown in syndication was an example of this technology and while the quality was poor, it was still a record of the show that would not otherwise exist.

In 1956, the Ampex Quadraplex video recorder was introduced which was the first commercially successful unit. It utilized two inch tape with 4 rotating recording heads for B&W monochrome video picture and mono audio signal. The broadcast bandwidth was 525 lines of resolution. The system had many problems. To assemble footage on video, editors used diagonal razor cuts and spliced the tape which meant the number of times it could be played was limited. The tape had no long term archival stability but was viable for short term use. Ampex model UR-1000 cost stations $50,000. The first videotape broadcast was the CBS airing of *Douglas Edward and the News* on November 30, 1956 in New York. It was shipped to the West Coast and CBS Television City in Hollywood which rebroadcast it three hours later. The following year, color videotape was developed. Videotape continued to be used on a limited basis in the fifties due to the cost of the equipment. It was cheaper to broadcast 16mm prints on a film chain.

Ampex used its patents to monopolize the business until the sixties when they got some competition from Sony which invented the Helical scan which laid down the video signal diagonal on the tape. Video insert editing was developed so the footage could be assembled by recording segments from one tape to another rather than physically splicing it. Sony also came out with one inch videotape in 1964 which reduced costs. Simultaneously, transistors replaced tubes in studio equipment Ampex developed their one inch videotape machines and other companies offered their brands but none were compatible. They also had to contend with color which was standardized in the mid-sixties. NBC began broadcasting in color on a limited basis in 1955 under the guiding force of David Sarnoff,

Chairman of the Board of RCA. Milton Berle's variety show was among the programs that aired to the few people who owned color sets which was less than 50,000 at the time. CBS also did limited color broadcasts in an alternate incompatible system while ABC remained in B&W. Over the next decade, color TV gained momentum and by 1966, the three major networks had converted and the syndication stations were also in the process of switching formats. Color videotape was utilized by NBC, CBS and ABC along with many local stations within the next few years.

Consumer color sets took a while longer to establish itself since the early ones were expensive. 1970–1977 was considered the replacement period when the older sets were discarded and new ones purchased. The number of sets doubled from the previous 5 million per year rate. In 1972 there were 8,845,000 color TVs sold vs. 8,239,000 B&W units. In 1973, color set sales outpaced B&W by 2,774,000. Households with color monitors increased proportionately. Only 7 percent had them in 1965 which was increased to 41 percent in 1970. By 1985 91 percent of households owned at least one color TV. Broadcasts of recent features had more appeal to viewers when they were shown in their original format rather than in B&W. Theaters lost their semi-exclusivity of showing color entertainment.

The next development was a portable video recorder/player for both studio and home use. Original Ampex machines were the size of a refrigerator and expensive to maintain and operate. In 1971, the Sony U-matic Video Cassette Recorder (VCR) was introduced which used ¾" rather than one inch tape. The bandwidth was a reduced 340 lines of resolution but acceptable for broadcast. An innovation was putting the tape in large 9 inch by 5½ inch cassettes rather than the reel to reel format of earlier systems. The machines were much larger than current home units and expensive. I have one in my home and it measures approximately 2 ft. by 1½ ft. wide by 8 inches deep and weighs 60 lb. They were durable since this one still operates. Tapes were limited to one hour recording time. They were used in libraries and schools but few private homes since they were not consumer friendly. Many TV stations used them for news broadcasts and they replaced 16mm filmed records of current events.

In 1975, the first practical consumer videocassette player/recorder was introduced which started the home video revolution. Early home entertainment formats should've advertised with a "buyer beware" warning. There were many competing systems and only one survived into the nineties. Sony's Betamax utilized ½" videotape and 240 lines of resolution which was inferior to both one inch and ¾" but acceptable for amateur use. Within a year, the company had sold 30,000 units. However, in 1976, JVC introduced a competing ½" video format known as Video Home

System or VHS which also had 240 lines of resolution. The first machine offered to the public was the JVC HR-3300 in the fall of 1977. Both systems had separate video and audio portions of the tape contained in magnetic flux variations based on azimuth helical scan technology but were incompatible. There were notable differences. At the SP speed, Betamax had a one hour recording limit whereas VHS was two hours. Beta's larger head drum resulted in better fidelity recording. Only video heads inside the head drum rotated in Betamax. On VHS the whole drum spun which increased friction on the tape. Beta also had larger chroma bandwidth and better color. In 1977, four Japanese electronic companies began to build VHS machines including Matsushita. Next, RCA joined the format and slower recording speeds were implemented with LP running time of four hours and EP with six hours. RCA also reduced the price of their VHS machines, forcing Sony to do the same.

The formats were sub-licensed and sold under other manufacturers. Beta was sold under the brand names of Sony, Zenith, Sanyo, Sears and Toshiba. VHS used the trade names of RCA, General Electric, JVC, Hitachi, Curtis Mathes, Magnavox, Panasonic, Quasar and Sylvania. After a slow start, the numbers of households who owned VCRs jumped dramatically from 14 percent in 1985 to 66 percent by 1990. In 2000, 85 percent of U.S. households had machines.

Home video was almost stopped in its tracks in 1976 when Universal and Disney sued Sony. They claimed that home videotaping of their movies and programs off the air was a copyright infringement. Ironically, the suit only involved Betamax, not later VHS manufacturers. Their attitude about home entertainment was also hypocritical since both companies offered Super 8 and 16mm prints of their films for sale to film collectors. The court battle dragged on for years. In 1979, the U.S. District Court for the Central District Court of California determined that home taping was legal but the Ninth Circuit U.S. Court of Appeals reversed that decision in 1981. The case went to the U.S. Supreme Court in 1984 which ruled that it was not copyright infringement although the market had been established by then and they had little choice. In 1980 it was estimated that 1,500,000 homes had some kind of VCR. Too many consumers owned the machines to outlaw it. If they had succeeded in attaching a surcharge to each player or tape, it would've damaged the emerging industry.

The decision stated that the protection given to copyrights was wholly statutory and individuals could reproduce a copyrighted work for a "fair use," namely, private and non-profit. They also determined that companies that sold VCRs were not liable for any use of the machines that might be construed as illegal by third parties. It was a victory for consumers, movie buffs and film collectors. Disney and Universal ended up selling their libraries in the various video systems and profiting from them.

While Sony handled their legal problems, they continued to upgrade the system with Beta Hi-Fi but Panasonic and JVC quickly offered VHS Hi-Fi formats. In 1981, the camcorder was offered by a number of manufacturers including Canon, Nikon, JVC and Panasonic. These cameras eventually replaced Super 8mm home movie units although few people knew that the Kodachrome film it used lasted much longer than the videocassettes which deteriorated over the years. Betamax sales were only a quarter of the market in the eighties even though Sony's machines were less expensive and videophiles preferred them. In 1988 Sony threw in the towel and began manufacturing VHS player/recorders and videotapes. The Betamax format was phased out over the next few years costing those that invested in it a great deal of money.

The popularity of home entertainment increased when some studios offered pre-recorded cassettes of feature films and programs for sale in both VHS and Beta. 20th Century–Fox was one of the first to offer their library through their subsidiary, Magnetic Video. *Fantastic Voyage* (1965) and other classics could be purchased. Other studios released titles through this company. In 1978, Allied Artists made 500 films available in videocassette in the price range of $49–$79. Avco-Embassy also signed a five year contract with Magnetic Home Video which gave them access to their library. In 1980, they licensed 250 titles from UA and made a deal with the British producer, Sir Lew Grade for his features. The same year CBS Enterprises entered the field and sold videocassettes of MGM and Lorimar movies. Warner Bros. and Paramount formed their own home video divisions. VHS and Beta versions were available for most films. Although they were expensive and the quality was poor, film buffs liked the idea of owning tapes of classics for home viewing. 16mm and 8mm sound formats were the only methods of collecting licensed movies prior to videocassettes. 8mm was phased out although 16mm remained a popular format for purists. The home video business grew in leaps and bounds and grossed 10 billion at the retail level by the late eighties.

During the same era, the Fotomat chain of retail photography stores tried renting Disney titles to consumers. Magnetic Video, Paramount and Warner Home Video companies also adopted rental policies. This was a cheaper option for most people who didn't want to own the movie. At first, patrons had to join a video club but this was later abandoned and anyone could rent a video with prices that ranged from $1 to $2 per day. By the mid-eighties, cassette rentals were a highly profitable business. It was cheaper to rent new films than see them in theaters and the returns from this ancillary market often exceeded box-office revenue. The VHS system was upgraded with stereo sound and Dolby noise reduction which eventually surpassed the quality of the abandoned Betamax system. All videocassettes had a limited life and rental tapes deteriorated rapidly from overuse. Degraded cassettes clogged the heads of VCRs with shedding oxide.

Cassette companies complained about the pay-per-view competition in the eighties. The simultaneous release of popular titles on cassette and subscription TV cut into the retail market. Video distributors had little choice but to live with it as did exhibitors. Some industry insiders believed the extensive advertising cross promoted both venues.

## Laserdiscs and DVD

Two videodisc systems were introduced around the same time. In 1978, Philips introduced the laserdisc format. The 30 cm optical analog dual sided aluminum disc was the size of a phonograph record and contained micropits of peaks and valleys which carried the video and audio information. The aluminum was encased in plastic and read by a laser which decoded the information in the player's signal processing circuitry. This technology lead to compact discs and DVDs years later. Laserdiscs contained 425 lines of resolution and had superior video and audio quality to both VHS and Betamax in the analog format.

MCA and its partner, Philips, released laserdiscs through their company, DiscoVision. Initially, the discs were only available in the CAV format which offered still frame and slow motion capabilities. The playing time was limited to a half hour per side. The first machines were made by Magnavox which was Philips line of consumer products and released in Atlanta, Georgia, in 1978. The players were expensive at $750. Titles from Universal's library were offered including *Airport, The Sting* and *High Plains Drifter*. While the quality was better than videocassette, the transfers were the same as the ones used for that format. *Airport* was pan/scanned and *High Plains Drifter* was the edited television version. The defect rate was very high for both players and discs. In 1980 Pioneer began producing laserdisc machines.

The actual discs were cheaper than VHS or Beta videocassettes of the same feature. The CAV release of *Jaws* had a $15.95 retail price in 1978 and was spread onto five sides and three discs. Abbott and Costello's *Buck Privates* was sold for $9.95 on four sides and two discs. Stereo analogue sound was incorporated onto the tracks which had much better audio than either

Laserdiscs were a high end home entertainment format until they were replaced by DVD in 1995.

tape format. *Sgt. Pepper's Lonely Hearts Club Band* was one of the early stereo titles in CAV on five sides, three discs and the same $15.95 as mono features. The movie was terrible but the sound quite good when played through a home stereo receiver. Paramount and Warner Bros. also licensed some titles on the DiscoVision label including *Bonnie and Clyde, Dirty Harry* and *Saturday Night Fever*. While Disney litigated against Sony's videocassette recorders, they simultaneously released films on laserdisc for home use including *Adventures with Chip and Dale* and *On Vacation with Mickey Mouse and Friends* both at $9.95. The average VHS pre-recorded cassette cost upwards of $60 in comparison. In 1980, the prices increased on the discs with movies like *The Jerk* priced at $24.95 in CAV on four sides and two discs. Laserdisc collectors discovered that there was information contained on the "dead side" of the disc that wasn't part of the feature film. Manufacturers needed a video signal on both sides of each disc for the machine to operate so they incorporated random material rather than blank footage. The coating could be removed with a solvent and the "dead side data" uncovered which was often a part of another movie.

CLV was developed in 1981 to expand the running time to one hour per side but did not offer still frame and other special effects functions of

CAV. The extended play versions of *Smokey and the Bandit* on two sides and one disc and *Jaws* on three sides and two discs ran $29.99. Unfortunately, DiscoVision discs were subject to "laserot." Over time, dust and dirt became trapped between the recorded surface and reflective layer as it oxidized. This caused speckling of the image. Early players heated up the discs which might have been a contributing factor. Drop outs and laser lock were other problems caused by minor scratches or manufacturing flaws. Most DiscoVision titles are no longer playable and the company stopped manufacturing them in 1982. MCA sold them as a durable format and I recall how upsetting it was to discover my copies of *Jaws* and *Psycho* completely deteriorated a couple of years after purchasing them.

Pioneer took over the format and kept it alive for another fifteen years. They lowered the price of the players to below $300 and tried to reestablish a market niche for laserdiscs. They succeeded up to a point although they never approached the popularity of VHS. The problem of laserot was addressed with superior manufacturing standards although it was never completely resolved and some discs continued to deteriorate. At least there was a chance that many post–DiscoVision laserdiscs would last for a while. From a collector's point of view, they were less stable than 16mm B&W or Technicolor prints of the same title.

Criterion was an innovative corporation that improved the quality and added features. They released special editions of movies which included second channel audio narration by the directors, actors and other participants. Screenplays, stills, deleted footage and other extras were contained on the discs. It was a clever marketing plan to sell them as a high-end videophile system to film buffs and collectors. The quality of Criterion discs was great but so was the price. They resurrected the CAV format for some releases but priced them higher than some videocassette releases. Other companies followed their lead. Rather than mastering the films from sub-standard, third generation release copies exhibited in theaters, laserdiscs were derived from first generation color interpositives, black and white fine grain masters or other pre-print. Criterion also mastered films in their original aspect ratio. For widescreen films, black bands were contained on the top and bottom of the picture area which was referred to as "letterboxing." *Manhattan* was the first feature released on laserdisc in this format in 1984. Letterboxed discs offered the correct composition but also limited the resolution since much of the available video signal did not contain picture information. It was better than panning and scanning but no substitute for real anamorphic imagery projected in theaters. On the other hand, there was more effort and showmanship put into Criterion's laserdisc releases than there was in general release copies shown in multiplexes.

In 1980 the Philips and Sony corporations agreed on a compact disc standard for digital audio with 16 bit/44.1kH2 sampling. They offered 70 minutes of audio recording time. CDs were launched in 1982–1983 and eventually replaced vinyl records. The laserdisc format incorporated this technology and added digital sound but retained the analog picture. In 1995, Dolby digital (AC-3) was implemented in the format. Later players incorporated CD and laserdisc formats in one unit. CDs also had deterioration potential. Radio stations that played compact discs discovered that with extended use, some developed pinholes which made them useless. I wish I was aware of this when I sold all of my vinyl soundtrack albums and rock records and replaced them with CDs. I would advise collectors to save their original records as back ups to the CDs. In some cases the analogue vinyls have a smoother sound than digital recordings. I find the soundtrack record of *From Russia with Love* more appealing than the compact disc version although this is purely subjective.

The laserdisc format was rendered obsolete in 1995 when Digital Video Discs (DVD) were introduced. DVDs contained 500 lines of resolution and a digital video signal. They were the size of a compact disc. They had a capacity of 133 minutes (4.7 million bytes) on a single layer disc and over four hours on dual layer discs. Some of the early titles were subject to digital artifacts due to compression. This problem seems to have been addressed and DVDs are gaining in popularity. The archival stability of this format is unknown. As with the Beta, people who purchased laserdisc machines and titles got burned. I was one of the consumers that had invested heavily in the format with a large library of discs, many of which deteriorated.

DVD appears to be the first system aside from VHS that has established itself in the marketplace. DVD movie sales went from $416 million in 1998 to approximately $3.1 billion in 2001. Players are under $200 which is cheaper than either videodisc format ever was and consumers like the fact that its the same size as a CD rather than the obsolete vinyl record width. Many video stores are renting them and some libraries stock them for residents to take out for free. A compromise was incorporated into many releases which offered both letterboxed and pan/scan version on the same disc.

DVD was the subject of a heated debate between consumers, computer hackers and copyright owners. Discs contained an algorithm which scrambled the signal so it could not be played back on systems it wasn't licensed to. However, it wasn't long before people unscrambled it which was technically a violation of the 1998 Digital Millennium Copyright Act. With the advent of digital videotape and recordable DVDs in the near

future, it will be easy for anyone to make an unlimited number of dupli-
cates of a copyrighted digital program with no loss of quality. History
repeated itself as the same issues relating to the Universal vs. Sony Betamax case resurfaced. As Simon Garfinkel noted in Technology Review
magazine, "Things have gotten nasty as this new crime gets its tryout in
the legal system. Last year, eight major film studios, all members of the
Motion Picture Association of America, sued the magazine 2600 for post-
ing on its Web site a program that unscrambles DVDs."[4] They won the
case but it's currently on appeal and the earlier Supreme Court decision
which legalized home videotaping will undoubtedly be cited. Technological advancements continue to outpace distribution and copyright practices.

## Selectavision

The other disc system of the eighties was RCA's Capacitance Electronic Disc (CED) which was introduced in March of 1981 as Selectavi-
sion. Laserdisc fans labeled it "needle vision," which was accurate. A vinyl
record contained the microscopic peaks and valleys in grooves. A diamond
stylus with titanium electrodes read the information which was decoded
by the player's signal processing circuitry. The disc was in a protective
plastic sleeve and inserted into the player. It offered between 240–270 lines
of horizontal resolution and an analog picture and audio which was slightly
better than videocassettes but inferior to laserdiscs' 425 lines. The first
players cost $499.95 but subsequent models ran $399.95 in 1982 and finally
$299.95. This made them cheaper than laserdisc players at the beginning
but compatible by the early eighties. Other companies produced players
including Hitachi and Toshiba.

Many consumers, myself included, purchased the CED system initially because more movies were available than on laserdisc. Approximately
1,700 titles were in the catalogue in its five year history. The average retail
price was $19.98 for single disc titles and $34.98 for double discs which
was cheaper than videocassettes and laserdiscs. RCA hired Gene Kelly to
promote the format. Kelly was a better spokesman than Ray Charles, who
pitched the sound quality of laserdiscs in television commercials. The format offered decent analogue stereo sound with a CX noise reduction but
never had digital capability like laserdiscs. Of the discs I purchased, I recall
the pan/scanned copies of *Cleopatra* and *Ben-Hur* looking and sounding
good for their time.

CED introduced a significant innovation in January of 1984 when they released *Amarcord* in the "letterboxed" format. Film collectors liked it but some consumers found the tiny image distracting. As previously mentioned, a letterboxed version of *Manhattan* followed on laserdisc which was inaccurately promoted as the first title to be mastered by this method. Other CED letterbox releases were *The Long Goodbye*, *Monty Python and the Holy Grail* and *The King of Hearts*. In the nineties, some VHS titles were available in the format including the *Lawrence of Arabia* restoration and an expanded version of *It's a Mad, Mad, Mad, Mad World*.

Like laserdiscs, CED discs also had deterioration problems. The diamond stylus cartridge was allegedly good for 1,000 hours but the discs had a limited life. RCA claimed they were good for 500 plays but that was not my experience. CEDs were subject to "video virus." Tiny dust particles became glued to the surface of the disc which was caused by a combination of high temperature and humidity. This made the stylus skip which resulted in jump cuts. Summer weather played havoc with the discs. RCA sold 500,000 players before canceling the format in June of 1986. Once again, video customers lost their investment in a defunct format. Most of the CED discs I owned developed problems. Rental copies were even worse. I ended up selling my entire collection for a dollar a disc in the late eighties along with most of my laserdiscs.

## *The Moviegoing Experience at Home*

As the quality of home video formats improved, TV sets were upgraded. They became so sophisticated that they were renamed "television monitors." Tube sizes increased from a 25" diagonal maximum to 27" and 35" units. Sleek new designs with multiple video/audio inputs improved signal quality. Manufacturers included Sony, Sanyo, Sharp, RCA, Zenith, Mitsubishi and many others. Some companies offered gimmicks to try and simulate the big screen experience at home. One of the stranger ones was sold in the mid-eighties. A series of large plastic magnifying lenses were available to place in front of a standard 20 or 25 inch screen that would enlarge it to 35 inches or more. The image was distorted and viewers had to sit directly in front of the screen. Don Adams, of *Get Smart* fame, was the spokesman and standees containing his image could be seen in many electronic stores. I purchased one for the fun of it in 1986. A variation was a lens placed in front of a smaller 12 inch television that projected it onto the wall. The resulting image was very dark.

The next step in home cinema was the development of front and rear screen projection sets. Sharp developed an LCD video projector that contained a zoom lens which displayed the image on a reflective screen or the wall at various sizes. Others projected the image via mirrors onto a concave silver screen. The most popular of these formats was a unit that reflected the three color lenses into a superimposed image on a rear projected screen. The quality of these systems was quite poor since the NTSC bandwidth was never designed to withstand that level of magnification. Depending on the source of the signal (cable, videotape or disc), watching a large screen video presentation could be an eyestrain.

In the late nineties, digital technology was adapted into home receivers. Referred to as DTV (digital television) there were a number of systems available. The low end formats were 480I (interlaced) with 236,000 displayable pixels-per-frame and the 480P (progressive scan) with 304,000 displayable pixels-per frame. There was also a 720P (progressive scan) which provided 829,000 displayable pixels per frame. They offered better resolution than standard NTSC analogue but were not high definition. 1080I & P was the digital high definition format standardized by the International Telecommunications Union (ITU) for international high definition production and program exchange. It offered 1.421,000 displayable pixels per frame and transmitted in the interlace mode for electronically generated programs and in the progressive mode for film programs. Unfortunately, HDTV software (movies, programs) on videotape or DVD have not yet been produced. In terms of broadcast, CBS, NBC, HBO, MSG, Warner Bros., PBS, DirectTV and the Discovery Channel will use 1080I. ABC plans to use the 720P and Fox the 480P formats. The 1080I & P sets are the most expensive and are in the range of $10,000. The other formats are less expensive in the $3,000 range but are not HD.

The difference between HDTV and NTSC can be summarized as follows: Television pixels (picture element) are composed of three color dots of color: red, green and blue. Combined together on the phosphor screen the three separate colors appear to blend into a single color. HDTV pixels are square rather than the rectangular shape utilized in NTSC analogue. There are 4½ square HD pixels for the same area of each rectangular analogue pixel which accounts for the superior sharpness. It also has 5.1 channels of digital sound (left, center, right, left rear, right rear) compared to NTSC's MTS analogue dual channel stereo sound. The aspect ratio is 16:9 which is similar but not identical to 35mm 1.85 cropped widescreen but wider than conventional TV's 4:3 image. Flat and anamorphic feature films will have to be adapted to the new size with some letterboxing necessary for the anamorphic 2.35 format. In 1999, the first HD compatible digital VCR was released in the U.S. market by Panasonic, model PV HD-1000.

In the future, digital recordings might render current VCRs obsolete but will improve the quality of feature films on tape.

At some future point, HDTV will be a major force in the marketplace. It will change the movie going experience at home and affect exhibition. Cinematographers may start to compose their frames for the 16:9 ratio and fewer anamorphic movies will probably be made. As with all electronic products sold after 1975, I urge caution before investing in a system that might not survive.

# 7. Distribution Changes in the Seventies, Eighties and Nineties

Distribution practices changed in the post–Code era. In the mid-seventies, a different type of booking system was implemented which gradually replaced regional exhibition. Rather than making a limited run of 400 copies, distributors began striking upwards of 900 prints and released them simultaneously in major markets. While saturation bookings had been tried in the past, it was a high risk proposition since the cost of prints and advertising could not be amortized. It was hit or miss in the first few weeks and if the film failed to perform it was pulled. In regional bookings the movie might play better in some areas than others resulting in extended runs. The distribution expenses could be controlled to a greater degree. Pictures like *Jaws* (1975) and *Superman* (1978) were distributed via saturation although they were pre-sold titles based on a best selling novel and comic book.

Despite the risk, saturation releases began to dominate exhibition throughout the eighties and nineties. From a distributor's perspective, it helped advertise the ancillary markets which were more profitable and less expensive than theatrical bookings. Roadshow presentations with reserved seat tickets were phased out although 70mm blow ups remained a popular format through the early nineties. There was no "window" between first run 70mm showings of pictures like *The Empire Strikes Back* (1980) and 35mm general release copies. Both types of prints played simultaneously. The surviving big screen theaters had to compete with multiplexes playing the same product which contributed to their demise.

In general, booking terms were an advance or guarantee that the exhibitor made to the distributor for the right to play the picture and a 60/40 split of the proceeds. Advertising was either paid for by the distributor or a co-op deal was arranged and the percentage pro-rated accordingly. In big budget pictures, the advances and guarantees could be very high and distributors demanded a greater percentage of the first two weeks. In some cases the split was 90 percent to the distributor and 10 percent to the cinema owner. Throughout the decades, exhibitors petitioned Washington to assist them in their grievances against the distributors with little success. As NATO president Ted Solomon noted in 1976, "the consent decrees have worked 95 percent in favor of the distributor," essentially as a direct result of "that big stock — the bid — which most of them use to their great advantage in extracting unreasonable, unbearable and vicious terms."[1]

Among the controversial practices Solomon was referring to was blind bidding, a problem that pre-dated the seventies. Studios forced theater owners to make bids on blockbuster films prior to the trade screening. In many cases, the final product was poor and theaters got stuck playing extended runs of bad films after paying the distributor a non-refundable down payment. Distributor and exhibitor relations were strained. Theater owners petitioned their local representatives and in 1979, 16 states passed legislation against it. By 1982, 24 states had banned blind bidding.

Another trend was runaway production costs following the decline of the low budget counterculture and blaxploitation cycles. In the late seventies, movies like *Close Encounters* ($21,000,000), *Superman* ($35,000,000), *Sorcerer* ($22,000,000), *A Bridge Too Far* ($24,000,000), *The Wiz* ($24,000,000) and *1941* ($27,000,000) pushed financing beyond the limits of most big budget films of the sixties. The studios forgot that Fox almost went bankrupt over *Cleopatra* in 1963 and it took them years to recover. The studio looked like a ghost town with all production on hold during this debacle. At least it was an entertaining picture with spectacle and good performances. The above films would have to become the top grossing pictures of their era to be profitable when the expenses of prints and advertising were added to the negative cost. *Close Encounters* ($82,700,000 initial US gross) and *Superman* ($82,500,000 gross) justified their costs but the others all failed to recoup their production budgets in their theatrical runs. *The Wiz* and *Sorcerer* lost a great deal of money for their studios. The eighties also had a series of expensive duds like *When Time Ran Out* (1980), *Raise the Titanic* (1980) and *Legend of the Lone Ranger* (1981). Hollywood continued its high stakes gambling and boom or bust trend into the nineties with a significant difference.

In the fifties, sixties and seventies, the budgets of films like *The Ten*

*Commandments, Ben-Hur, Cleopatra, Close Encounters* and *Superman* were displayed on screen with spectacular sets, costumes and special effects. However, in the eighties and nineties, above the line fees encompassed much of the negative cost with outrageous salaries for the stars. The rest was squandered by undisciplined directors and producers. When they failed to perform, like UA's *Heaven's Gate* (1980), the producing companies folded. Andrew Sarris's *auteur theory* was somewhat discredited by this disaster. According to Steven Bach's 1985 book, *Final Cut: Dreams and Disasters in the Making of Heaven's Gate,* the cost overruns were caused primarily by the director's artistic indulgence. Perhaps a catastrophe of this sort was inevitable in the long run following the demise of the studio system in 1948. By the late fifties, few stars or directors were under contract to the major studios. Many features were made by independent production companies who had more autonomy than in the past when Thalberg, Zanuck, Warner and others controlled every aspect of production. John Wayne's Batjac and Kirk Douglas's Bryna corporations were among those that produced their pictures in this manner. UA was also known for the amount of creative freedom it gave its producers and directors. Unfortunately, no matter how talented some filmmakers were, they needed someone to keep them in line. On the strength of Cimino's Oscar winning *Deer Hunter,* he was given a free reign and went way over budget. The final cost was estimated at $44 million with a US theatrical gross of $1.5 million. This scenario would be repeated many times throughout the eighties and nineties. Perhaps cinematic artistry was dependent on a set of standards and practices from which filmmakers could either expand upon or deviate from. The financial and artistic "free for all" in the post–Code era did not always generate the anticipated results.

It was difficult to determine where the one hundred million dollars went on titles like *Waterworld* (1995) since it didn't translate into production value. Kevin Costner was one of the expensive stars that made films like this one and *The Postman* (1995) which were too expensive and did poorly at the box-office. What's curious from a corporate perspective is how some actors and directors continued to command huge fees and get substantial backing after making so many bombs in a row. This was not necessarily a reflection on their talent but on the business acumen of industry leaders. Directors who were fiscally irresponsible seemed immune from pressure to stay within budgets or make pictures where the cash outlay translated into production value, spectacle and lush photography.

In 1997, James Cameron's *Titanic* broke the two hundred million dollar mark. The budget had doubled since the commencement of principal photography and it took two studios to finance it, Paramount and Fox.

Fortunately, the movie was a smash hit and became the top grossing pictures as of that date. It was also one of the best films of the nineties which was not a great decade for the art form. Many subsequent big budget features didn't pay off. *Thirteen Days* (2000) was not popular despite its attempt to mimic the style of *JFK* (1991) with the same star (Costner). Recent pictures like *Lord of the Rings* have surpassed the budget of *Titanic*.

All of this had an impact on exhibition. Distributors imposed onerous terms on exhibitors to try and recoup as much as they could up front. They varied depending on the location and number of seats. In major markets, huge guarantees were demanded regardless of how the film performed. While none of this was new, the stakes were higher. Even in smaller markets, the deals were tough. At multiplexes, Fox made them pay 90 percent for the first four weeks of *Star Wars: The Phantom Menace* with a guaranteed twelve week run. Although the theater's percentage was pro-rated upwards in subsequent weeks, the film had to continue to perform for them to make money. Attendance usually dropped off during extended runs. The distributors had the ancillary markets and foreign sales to recoup their expenses whereas the multiplex chains went into the red. The only option for theater managers was to raise ticket and concession prices and cut corners in performance. Staff was reduced to a minimum which meant that projection suffered, the machines weren't maintained and the theaters were dirty. Over-priced junk food was the difference between profit and loss in some locations. Erratic profit prevented many chains from upgrading their equipment with state of the art digital sound and other improvements.

Print quality continued to decline as the numbers increased. There was no way of making thousands of top quality materials at high speeds within the deadlines the studios imposed on the labs. Distributors didn't seem to care since they considered theatrical exhibition as paid advertising for the ancillary markets. The notion of giving audiences a "show" was obsolete in many cinema-plexes around the country.

## *Demise of the Large Screen Cinemas and Movie Palaces*

Most of the large screen cinemas folded in the late seventies and eighties due to the lack of mainstream product along with the multiplex and home entertainment competition. In my area, New York City lost its grand Roadshow houses. My favorite was the Rivoli, a Dimension 150 theater with an enormous 74 × 29 ft. deeply curved screen with curtains and 1,600 seat capacity. Projection was reel to reel with carbon arc illumination. It was located at 49th Street and Broadway. It had an Egyptian facade which was built for the premiere of *Cleopatra* in 1963. Previously, it had premiered *Oklahoma!* (1955) and *Around the World in 80 Days* (1956) both in Todd-AO. The booth was redesigned so its axis was center to the screen rather than at an angle. The horizons were straight rather than curved upwards as they were in most large screen houses. I saw *2001: A Space Odyssey* in 70mm there in a 1977 reissue. The impact was awesome, a truly spectacular experience. The acoustics were as impressive as its imagery. Since the theater was wide rather than long, audiences could hear the rear channel tracks at an appropriate sound level, rather than blasting from the back of the auditorium.

In the eighties, the theater was twinned and curved screen removed. The balcony was redesigned as the second theater but the main seating arrangement remained the same although the wide screen was flat. The projectors were automated and the carbon arc lamphouses replaced with Xenon illumination. The presentations were still impressive. I saw *The Thing* in 70mm in 1982 which featured sharp imagery and excellent stereophonic sound. One of the last films to play there before it folded was my own low budget exploitation film, *The Class of Nuke 'Em High* in 1986. Allegedly, UA Communications, Inc. altered the Egyptian facade so it wouldn't be declared a landmark. It was demolished in 1987 and another piece of cinema history was gone.

Also on Broadway were the Warner Cinerama I and II on 46th Street. Cinerama I had a huge curved screen with curtains whereas Cinerama II had a large flat silver screen with stadium seating and played 3-D titles like *House of Wax* in 70mm in 1981 and *Andy Warhol's Frankenstein*. Both were torn down around the same time. Down the street was *The National* which exhibited *Alien* (1977) in 70mm and *Criterion* which were also demolished. Other than the Astor Plaza and Ziegfeld, New York City's large screen cinemas and movie palaces are gone and it's no longer the showplace of the nation.

Radio City Music Hall stopped showing films on a regular basis in 1979. The lack of quality general audience pictures and declining attendance made it impossible to fill the 5,900 seats. Their last first run release was *Crossed Swords* in 1978 which I attended. It's a shame they couldn't have found a better feature for their swan song as an exhibitor. They were a latecomer to the 70mm format. Most Roadshow releases were very long and they avoided booking them since the Hall's presentations always included a stage show which expanded the total running time. Ross Hunter insisted *Airport* play in 70mm so the management installed the projectors in 1970 to play on their 69 ft. × 31 ft. screen. In 1975, the theater screened revivals of *Gone with the Wind*, *2001: A Space Odyssey*, *Doctor Zhivago* and *The Sound of Music* in the large format. The theater continues to operate as a performing arts center for live shows, occasional film premieres and event presentations. I saw *Napoleon* there in 1981 and the restoration of *A Star Is Born* in 1982, both memorable events.

Throughout the country other movie palaces fell like dominoes. The Jayhawk State Theatre of Kansas closed in 1976. The Alabama Theatre in Birmingham was a 2,200 seat house that went bankrupt in 1987. Fortunately, it was renovated into a performing arts center in 1998. The 1,446 seat Atmospheric Tampa Theatre in Florida closed in 1973.

In Chicago, the Varsity Theater closed in 1988 and was gutted to become a pharmacy. It was one of the largest suburban houses ever built. It was designed as a French royal chateau of Francois I. It had Italian marble and antique tapestries. Also in Chicago was the State-Lake which was a 2,700 seat palace. After it folded in the eighties, it was gutted to become a TV studio. The Coronado Theatre in Rockford, Illinois, was an atmospheric style 2,400 seat cinema that stopped showing movies in 1984 and switched to concerts and live performances.

The Embassy Theatre in Fort Wayne, Indiana; Palace Theatre in Columbus, Ohio; 2,047 seat Fox Theatre in Stockton, California; 4,000 seat Fox Theatre in Atlanta; Landmark Theatre in Syracuse, New York; 1,200 seat Missouri Theatre in St. Joseph Missouri and Old Greenbelt Theatre in Greenbelt, Maryland, all ended their theatrical runs in the seventies. The Liberty Theater in Columbus, Ohio, was converted into a disco and the 1,110 seat McHenry Theater in Baltimore, Maryland, became a Goodwill Thrift store in the same era.

In the eighties, the 2,053 seat atmospheric Plaza Theatre in El Paso, Texas; Crocker Theatre in Elgin, Illinois; Fox Theater in Stevens Point, Wisconsin; Major Theater in Washington, Kansas; Embassy Theatre in Lewistown, Pennsylvania; Bonn Theater in Bonnieville, Kentucky, and New Theater with Art Nouveau architecture located in Fort Smith, Arizona, were among those that folded. The 1,200 seat State Theater in Portland, Maine, became a porn house in the late sixties then closed in 1989. The Orpheum Theatre in Phoenix, Arizona, also stopped booking films in the late sixties. It had Spanish architecture and 1,400 seats.

Recently, the 2,190 seat Orpheum Theatre in Los Angeles finally closed its doors. Fortunately, a number of these palaces were declared landmarks or were purchased by non-profit organizations to restore and reopen them as performing arts centers. Since I attended some of these houses prior to their demise, I was fortunate to have experienced their grandeur.

A large percentage of movie palaces survive in the Los Angeles area including the Mann Village Theater, El Capitan Theatre and the Aero. Many are used for premieres, usually with first generation prints struck off the negative. Since Hollywood is isolated from the rest of the country culturally, many insiders may not be aware of the quality difference between the presentations they see and what the average moviegoer experiences in multiplexes. A list of surviving movie palaces and large screen single houses is contained in Chapter 10.

## Decline of 70mm

In the late seventies, there was a revival of general audiences pictures as previously mentioned. Steven Spielberg and George Lucas were among those responsible for this return of mainstream entertainment and spectacle. Lucas's *Star Wars* (1977) and other epics made the 70mm process popular again. Even though it was a blow-up of a 35mm anamorphic negative, the special effects were made in VistaVision and the image quality was good. 70mm (2.21 × 1 ratio) made the projected image sharper than the decompressed (2.35 × 1) 35mm Panavision image. The large frame spread out the energy of the lamphouse over a bigger area of the film. The technical specifications were 0.870 × 1.912 inches for a 70mm frame vs. 0.690 × 0.825 inches for an anamorphic frame. A longer focal length projection lens was used in 70mm which meant that the steadiness of the image was greater since the magnification was less. The six channel magnetic stereo sound was also an asset. I saw the film in this format at New York's enormous Loews Astor Plaza and it was a great show and memorable movie going experience. This even applied to the occasional 1.85 blow ups from spherical 35mm (non-anamorphic) negatives that were printed with black borders on the side of the 2.21 × 1 frame. 70mm copies were printed at a slow speed which allowed for contrast changes and a better exposure than the high speed 35mm prints which were standardized after 1976.

While the 70mm blowups lacked the resolution and fine grain sharpness of first generation copies struck from 65mm camera negatives, they still offered superior quality to the 35mm general release prints. The sound was universally good and the picture quality impressive depending on the style of the photography and format the film was shot in. For example, the fully exposed and extensively lit negative of John Carpenter's *The Thing* (1982) generated a fine grain blowup. An underexposed negative with defused lighting that was shot "flat" resulted in excessive grain when

*2001* 70mm flyer, ca. 1977.

optically enlarged as evidenced in *Cocoon* (1985). Other 1.85 blowups looked fine since their photography leant itself to the format. *Hair* (1979) and *The Right Stuff* (1983) were nice presentations.

Star Wars also revived interest in 35mm stereo sound. The Dolby split optical track system was used extensively after this feature and became standardized in the eighties. It offered a limited number of tracks but was still better than standard mono. The dual variable area optical stripes contained noise reduction to reduce hiss. Both left and right channels were discrete while the center and surround tracks derived via signal processing. Ultra-Stereo offered a compatible system and was used on many independent features although neither was as impressive as the six discrete tracks of 70mm. By the early eighties, 35mm four track magnetic stereo sound was phased out. The last films to use it were *Scarface, Yentl* and a reissue of *Fantasia* in 1983 and *Against All Odds* in 1984.

Additional big budget Panavision features were given 70mm presentation. Spielberg's *Close Encounters of the Third Kind* (1977) played New York's Ziegfeld and featured a "sensurround" effect when the ship landed. Other titles included *Superman* (1978), *Grease* (1978) and *Raiders of the Lost Ark* (1981). 1.85 blow ups included *The Cotton Club* and *Gremlins*, both in 1984. The opening credits of *Superman* featured the rear channel whoosh of the titles which made the audience at the Loews Astor Plaza spontaneously applaud. The monster giggling filled the auditorium in *Gremlins* and made viewers feel they were surrounded by them. Most big budget films had a limited number of 70mm blowup prints struck. The format reached its peak in 1985 with 34 titles given large format presentation. It was a marketing tool that enabled showmanship to survive the mini-theater trend. Many post–1980 multiplexes kept one large screen for these presentations. Unfortunately, even this was temporary.

In 1990, Warren Beatty's *Dick Tracy* introduced the first digital sound system, CDS. Developed by Kodak, it contained 6 digital channels on the film but no backup optical track. In 1991, the Dolby Stereo Digital SR-D system was introduced that contained the 6 channels in an encoded area between the sprockets. A backup Dolby optical track was on the print for theaters not set up for the process. Spielberg's *Jurassic Park* featured the strangest of the new systems, called DTS, in 1993. A throwback to the old Vitaphone process, a timecode was printed outside the perforated area that was synchronized to a separate CD-ROM containing the digital tracks. In the same year, Sony's Dynamic Digital Sound (SDDS) was utilized on *The Last Action Hero*. The 6 or 8 tracks were contained on two optical stripes on the edges of the film. The most practical of these processes was the Dolby system since the area between the perforations was subject to the least amount of wear during projection. All of these formats had a failsafe system that triggered the sound to standard Dolby optical if the digital tracks didn't register. This happened during a screening I attended of *Gone with the Wind* in 1997. The difference in sound quality was quite noticeable with the digital track much cleaner than the analogue.

All of these processes offered quality stereophonic sound but there was a trade-off. The discrete multiple tracks was one of the primary assets of 70mm. Since it was possible to have upwards of six tracks in 35mm, many theaters stopped showing large format prints. Although there were some 65mm productions in the nineties (*Far and Away*, 1992, *Hamlet*, 1996) and notable restorations (*Lawrence of Arabia*, 1989, *Spartacus*, 1991, *My Fair Lady*, 1996), the process was gradually phased out and equipment removed due to the lack of product. Another problem was the increased environmental restrictions on the solvents used for magnetic striping. Most of the companies that offered this service stopped after 1995 although enough remained to make new magnetic stereo copies of *2001* and reissue copies of *Lawrence of Arabia* and *Tron* in 1995. The same year, 70mm prints of *Vertigo* were made with a DTS timecode contained on the film and synchronized 6 track audio CD-Rom. There were no mag tracks on the copies.

*Titanic* was given a limited 70mm release in 1997 in the DTS format, but there have been no further presentations of new films. Two 70mm six track magnetic stereo prints were made of *2001: A Space Odyssey* in 2001, otherwise the format is obsolete. The digital stereo processes were better technically than the magnetic tracks but lost their impact in small theaters. Even in THX approved houses, it was disorienting to hear multichannel digital sound emitting from tiny projected images in suburban multiplexes. The whole concept of stereo was to give directional placement of dialogue and sound effects on large 50 ft. wide screens.

Following is a list of 70mm releases from 1968 to 2001 which illustrates the decline of the process. The numbers drop off dramatically after the introduction of digital sound with coincided with the building of megaplexes which will be covered later. I've indicated which ones were photographed with large format negatives and which ones were blow-ups from 35mm Technirama, Panavision, CinemaScope or flat negatives. All prints contained six channels of magnetic stereo sound but pre–1983 prints have faded.

### 1968

Charge of the Light Brigade (35mm Panavision)
Chitty Chitty Bang Bang (65mm)
Clint the Lonely Nevadan (35mm Technirama)
Custer of the West (35mm Technirama)
Finian's Rainbow (35mm Panavision)
Funny Girl (35mm Panavision)
Gone with the Wind (35mm 1.33 pan/scan reissue)
Hellfighters (35mm Panavision)
Ice Station Zebra (65mm)
The Jolson Story (35mm 1.33 reissue)
Julius Caesar (35mm 1.33 reissue)
Mayerling (35mm Panavision)
Oliver! (35mm Panavision)
The Shoes of the Fisherman (35mm Panavision)

Star (65mm)
Sweet Charity (35mm Panavision)
2001: A Space Odyssey (65mm)*
The Young Girls of Rochefort (35mm
    1.66)

### 1969
Alfred the Great (35mm Panavision)
The Battle of Britain (35mm Pana-
    vision)
Ben-Hur (65mm reissue)
Goodbye, Mr. Chips (35mm Pana-
    vision)
Hello, Dolly! (65mm)
The Longest Day (35mm Panavision)
Krakatoa, East of Java (65mm)
Marooned (35mm Panavision)
MacKenna's Gold (65mm)
Paint Your Wagon (35mm Pana-
    vision)
Seven Brides for Seven Brothers
    (CinemaScope reissue)
They Shoot Horses, Don't They?
    (35mm Panavision)
Those Daring Young Men in their
    Jaunty Jalopies (35mm Panavision)
Where Eagles Dare (35mm Pana-
    vision)
The Wild Bunch (35mm Panavision)
The Young Rebel (35mm Totalscope)

### 1970
The Adventurers (35mm Panavision)
Anne of the Thousand Days (35mm
    Panavision)
Airport (65mm)
Brewster McCloud (35mm Pana-
    vision)
Cromwell (35mm Panavision)
Darling Lili (35mm Panavision)
Kelly's Heroes (35mm Panavision)
Patton (65mm)
The Robe (35mm CinemaScope reis-
    sue)
Ryan's Daughter (65mm)
Scrooge (35mm Panavision)
Song of Norway (65mm)

Stewardesses (35mm side by side 3-
    D)
Too Late the Hero (35mm Pana-
    vision)
Tora, Tora, Tora (35mm Panavision)
Winning (35mm Panavision)
Woodstock (16mm Multiscreen)

### 1971
The Andromeda Strain (35mm Pana-
    vision)
Battle of Neretva (35mm Panavision)
The Boy Friend (35mm Panavision)
The Devils (35mm Panavision)
Elvis: That's the Way It Was (Pana-
    vision)
Fiddler on the Roof (35mm Pana-
    vision)*
The Horsemen (35mm Panavision)
It's a Mad, Mad, Mad, Mad, World
    (65mm)
The Last Valley (35mm Panavision)
Lawrence of Arabia (65mm)
Le Mans (35mm Panavision)
Light at the Edge of the World (Pana-
    vision)
Mary, Queen of Scotts (35mm Pana-
    vision)
The Music Lovers (35mm Pana-
    vision)
The Ten Commandments (VistaVi-
    sion reissue)
Utvandrarna (35mm 1.85)
Waterloo (35mm Panavision)
Wild Rovers (35mm Panavision)

### 1972
Antony and Cleopatra (35mm Todd-
    AO)
The Concert for Bangladesh (16mm)
The Cowboys (35mm Panavision)
Deliverance (35mm Panavision)
The Great Caruso (35mm 1.33 reis-
    sue)
The Great Waltz (65mm)
House of Wax (35mm side by side 3-
    D reissue)

*Indicates I saw the film in 70mm.

Jeremiah Johnson (35mm Pana-
vision)
Man of La Mancha (35mm 1.85)
Nybyggarna (35mm 1.85)
The Poseidon Adventure (35mm
Panavision)
The Professionals (35mm Panavision
reissue)
The Revengers (35mm Panavision)
Silent Running (35mm Panavision)
This Is Cinerama (35mm 3 panel
combo reissue)*
Young Winston (35mm Panavision)

**1973**

Bridge on the River Kwai (CinemaS-
cope reissue)
Camelot (35mm Panavision reissue)
Electra Glide in Blue (35mm Pana-
vision)
Jesus Christ Superstar (35mm Todd-
AO)
Let the Good Times Roll (35mm
1.85)
The Lion in Winter (35mm Pana-
vision reissue)
Lost Horizon (35mm Panavision)
The Neptune Factor (35mm Pana-
vision)
Oliver! (35mm Panavision reissue)
Playtime (35mm 1.66)
Taming of the Shrew (35mm Pana-
vision reissue)
Tom Sawyer (35mm Panavision)

**1974**

Arrivano Je E Margherito (35mm
Techniscope)
Earthquake (35mm Panavision/Sen-
surround)*
Gone with the Wind (35mm 1.33)
The Great Gatsby (35mm 1.85)
The Jolson Story (35mm 1.33 reissue)
One by One (35mm 1.85)
Panorama Blue (35mm Panavision)
Papillon (35mm Panavision)
That's Entertainment (35mm 1.33,
CinemaScope)
The Towering Inferno (35mm Pana-
vision)

**1975**

Funny Lady (35mm Panavision)
The Hindenburg (35mm Panavision)
Lucky Lady (35mm 1.85)
Paper Tiger (35mm Panavision)
Rollerball (35mm 1.85)
The Wind and the Lion (35mm
Panavision)

**1976**

Grizzly (35mm Todd-AO)
King Kong (35mm Panavision)
Logan's Run (35mm Todd-AO)
Return of a Man Called Horse
(35mm Panavision)
A Star Is Born (35mm 1.85)
That's Entertainment II (35mm
1.33,CinemaScope)

**1977**

Billy Jack Goes to Washington (Pana-
vision)
A Bridge Too Far (35mm Pana-
vision)*
Close Encounters (35mm Pana-
vision)*
Metamorphosis (35mm Panavision)
Mohammad, Messenger of God
(Panavision)
Ofeu Negro (35mm 1.33)
Star Wars (35mm Panavision)*
Tommy (35mm 1.85)
2001: A Space Odyssey (65mm)*

**1978**

Capricorn One (35mm Panavision)
Comes a Horseman (35mm Pana-
vision)
Coming Home (35mm 1.85)
Crossed Swords (35mm Panavision)
Days of Heaven (35mm 1.85)
The Deer Hunter (35mm Panavision)
Grease (35mm Panavision)
The Manitou (35mm Panavision)
The Punk Rock Movie (35mm Pana-
vision)
Sgt. Pepper's Lonely Hearts Club
Band (35mm Panavision)*
Superman (35mm Panavision)*
The Wiz (35mm 1.85)

*(70mm releases, continued)*

### 1979

Alien (35mm Panavision)*
Apocalypse Now (35mm Panavision)
The Black Hole (35mm Technovision)
The Black Stallion (35mm 1.85)
The Champ (35mm 1.85)
The Exorcist (35mm 1.85)*
Hair (35mm 1.85)*
Hanover Street (35mm Panavision)
Hurricane (35mm Todd-AO)
Moonracker (35mm Panavision)
The Muppet Movie (35mm 1.85)
1941 (35mm Panavision)*
The Rose (35mm Panavision)
Star Trek (35mm Panavision)
Tess (35mm Panavision)
Winds of Change (35mm Panavision)

### 1979 Broadway Comes to Broadway Festival

Camelot (35mm Panavision reissue)*
Hello, Dolly! (65mm reissue)
My Fair Lady (65mm reissue)*
Oklahoma! (65mm faded reissue)*
Paint Your Wagon (35mm Panavision reissue)*
South Pacific (65mm reissue)*

### 1980

Altered States (35mm 1.85)
The Blue Lagoon (35mm 1.85)
The Blues Brothers (35mm 1.85)
Can't Stop the Music (35mm Panavision)
Close Encounters (35mm Panavision reissue)
Divine Madness (35mm Panavision)
The Electric Horseman (35mm Panavision)
The Empire Strikes Back (35mm Panavision)*
Fame (35mm 1.85)
Flash Gordon (35mm Todd-AO)
Heaven's Gate (35mm Panavision)
The Island (35mm Panavision)
The Jazz Singer (35mm 1.85)
Raise the Titanic (35mm Technovision)
Saturn 3 (35mm 1.85)

Tess (35mm Panavision)
Twinkle, Twinkle Killer Kane (35mm Panavision)

### 1981

Chariots of Fire (35mm 1.85)
Dance Craze (Super 16)
Das Boot (35mm 1.85)
Dragonslayer (35mm Panavision)
Napoleon (35mm 1.33 & trptych)*
Outland (35mm Panavision)
Raiders of the Lost Ark (35mm Panavision)*
Sharkey's Machine (35mm 1.85)
Superman II (35mm Panavision)
Wolfen (35mm Panavision)
Zoot Suit (35mm Panavision)

### 1982

Annie (35mm Panavision)
Best Little Whorehouse in Texas (Panavision)*
Bladerunner (35mm Panavision)
The Dark Crystal (35mm Panavision)
The Entity (35mm Panavision)
E.T. (35mm 1.85)*
Firefox (35mm Panavision)
Ghandi (35mm Panavision)*
Grease 2 (35mm Panavision)
Oklahoma (65mm reissue)*
One from the Heart (35mm 1.33)*
Pink Floyd The Wall (35mm Panavision)
Poltergeist (35mm J-D-C Scope)*
Quest for Fire (35mm Panavision)
The Road Warrior (35mm Panavision)*
Rocky III (35mm 1.85)
Star Trek II (35mm Panavision)
Tempest (35mm 1.85)
The Thing (35mm Panavision)*
Tron (65mm)
Yes, Giorgio (35mm 1.85)

### 1983

Blue Thunder (35mm Panavision)*
Brainstorm (35mm 1.85 & 65mm)
The Keep (35mm Panavision)
Krull (35mm Panavision)

Let's Spend the Night Together (35mm)

Never Say Never Again (35mm Panavision)

Octopussy (35mm Panavision)

Return of the Jedi (35mm J-D-C Scope)*

The Right Stuff (35mm 1.85)*

The Star Chamber (35mm Panavision)

Staying Alive (35mm 1.85)

Superman III (35mm Panavision)

War Games (35mm 1.85)*

## 1984

Adventures of Buckaroo Banzai (35mm Panavision)

Amadeus (35mm Panavision)

The Bear (35mm 1.85)

The Bounty (35mm J-D-C Scope)

City Heat (35mm Panavision)

The Cotton Club (35mm 1.85)

Country (35mm 1.85)

Dune (35mm Todd-AO)

Ghostbusters (35mm Panavision)*

Give My Regards to Broad Street (35mm 1.85)

Gremlins (35mm 1.85)*

Greystoke (Super 35mm)

Indiana Jones and the Temple of Doom (35mm Panavision)*

The Killing Fields (35mm 1.85)

The Last Starfighter (35mm Panavision)*

Metropolis (35mm 1.33)*

The Never-ending Story (35mm Technovision)

The Razor's Edge (35mm 1.85)

Starman (35mm Panavision)

Star Trek III (35mm Panavision)

Streets of Fire (35mm 1.85)

Supergirl (35mm Panavision)

2010 (35mm Panavision)

We Will Rock You (35mm 1.85)

## 1985

Absolute Beginners (Super 35mm)

American Flyers (35mm Panavision)

Baby (Super 35mm)

Back to the Future (35mm 1.85)

The Black Caldron (35mm Technirama)

Bring on the Night (35mm 1.85)

A Chorus Line (35mm Panavision)

Cocoon (35mm 1.85)*

The Emerald Forest (35mm Panavision)

Enemy Mine (Super 35mm)

The Entity (35mm Panavision)

Explorers (35mm 1.85)

The Goonies (35mm Panavision)

King David (35mm Panavision)

Ladyhawke (35mm Technovision)

The Last Dragon (35mm 1.85)

Legend (35mm Panavision)

Lifeforce (35mm Panavision)*

Mad Max Beyond Thunderdome (35mm Panavision)

Out of Africa (35mm 1.85)

Pale Rider (35mm Panavision)

Rambo (35mm Panavision)

Ran (35mm 1.85)

Return to Oz (35mm 1.85)

Revolution (Super 35mm)

Rocky IV (35mm 1.85)

Santa Claus (35mm J-D-C Scope)

Silverado (Super 35m)

Spies Like Us (35mm 1.85)

Starchaser (35mm Stereoscope 3-D)

A View to a Kill (35mm Panavision)*

White Nights (35mm 1.85)

Year of the Dragon (35mm J-D-C Scope)

Young Sherlock Holmes (35mm 1.85)

## 1986

Aliens (35mm 1.85)*

Big Trouble in Little China (Panavision)

Clan of the Cave Bear (Technovision)

Cobra (35mm 1.85)

The Color of Money (35mm 1.85)

Down and Out in Beverly Hills (35mm 1.85)

The Fly (35mm 1.85)

Highlander (35mm 1.85)

Howard the Duck (35mm 1.85)

Iron Eagle (35mm 1.85)

Labyrinth (35mm J-D-C Scope)

*(70mm releases, continued)*
Legal Eagles (35mm Panavision)
Little Shop of Horrors (35mm 1.85)*
Manhunter (Super 35mm)
The Mission (35mm J-D-C Scope)
The Money Pit (35mm 1.85)
Nutcracker (35mm 1.85)
Pirates (35mm Panavision)
Poltergeist II (35mm Panavision)
Spacecamp (35mm 1.85)
Star Trek IV (35mm Panavision)
Top Gun (Super 35mm)
Tough Guys (35mm Panavision)

### 1987
Adventures in Babysitting (35mm 1.85)
Beverly Hills Cop II (Super 35mm)
Cry Freedom (35mm Panavision)*
Empire of the Sun (35mm 1.85)
Good Morning, Vietnam (35mm 1.85)
Innerspace (35mm 1.85)
The Last Emperor (35mm Technovision)
Lethal Weapon (35mm 1.85)
The Lost Boys (35mm Panavision)
Over the Top (35mm Panavision)
Platoon (35mm 1.85)
Predator (35mm 1.85)
Robocop (35mm 1.85)
The Running Man (35mm 1.85)
The Sicilian (35mm J-D-C Scope)
Spaceballs (35mm 1.85)
Stakeout (35mm 1.85)
Three Men and a Baby (35mm 1.85)
The Untouchables (35mm Panavision)
Who's That Girl? (35mm 1.85)
The Witches of Eastwick (35mm Panavision)

### 1988
Adventures of Baron Munchausen (35mm 1.85)
Akira (35mm 1.85)
Alien Nation (Super 35mm)
Beaches (35mm 1.85)
The Big Blue (35mm 1.85)
Cocoon: The Return (35mm 1.85)
Die Hard (35mm Panavision)*

Gorillas in the Mist (35mm 1.85)
Kansas (Super 35mm)
The Last Temptation of Christ (35mm 1.85)
Le Grand Bleu (35mm CinemaScope)
L'Ours (35mm Panavision)
Pathfinder (35mm 1.85)
The Presidio (35mm Panavision)
Shoot to Kill (Super 35mm)
Tucker (35mm Technovision)*
Who Framed Roger Rabbit (35mm 1.85)*
Willow (35mm Panavision)

### 1989
The Abyss (Super 35mm)
Always (35mm 1.85)
Back to the Future (35mm 1.85)
Batman (35mm 1.85)
The Bear (35mm 1.85)
Black Rain (Super 35mm)
Born on the Fourth of July (35mm Panavision)
Casualties of War (35mm Panavision)
Dead Poets Society (35mm 1.85)
Glory (35mm 1.85)
In Country (35mm 1.85)
Indiana Jones and the Last Crusade (35mm Panavision)
Lawrence of Arabia (65mm restoration)*
Lethal Weapon 2 (35mm Panavision)
The Little Mermaid (35mm 1.85)
Slipstream (35mm 1.85)
Star Trek V (35mm Panavision)
Tango and Cash (35mm Panavision)
Valmont (35mm Panavision)

### 1990
Air America (Super 35mm)
Arachnophobia (35mm 1.85)
Back to the Future (35mm 1.85)
Ben-Hur (65mm reissue)*
Bonfire of the Vanities (35mm 1.85)
Dances with Wolves (35mm Panavision)
Days of Thunder (35mm Panavision)
Dick Tracy (35mm 1.85)
Die Hard II (35mm Panavision)

Edward Scissorhands (35mm 1.85)
Fantasia (35mm 1.33)*
Flatliners (35mm Panavision)
The Godfather III (35mm 1.85)
Gremlins 2 (35mm 1.85)
Havana (35mm 1.85)
Hunt for Red October (35mm Panavision)
Memphis Belle (35mm 1.85)
Mountains of the Moon (35mm 1.85)
Narrow Margin (35mm Panavision)
Predator 2 (35mm 1.85)
Robocop 2 (35mm 1.85)
The Rookie (35mm Panavision)
The Sheltering Sky (35mm 1.85)
The Sound of Music (65mm reissue)*
Total Recall (35mm 1.85)
The Two Jakes (35mm 1.85)

*1991*
Backdraft (Super 35mm)
Beauty and the Beast (35mm 1.85)
The Doors (35mm Panavision)
Final Approach (35mm Panavision)
Flight of the Intruder (Super 35mm)
For the Boys (35mm 1.85)
Hook (35mm Panavision)
The Last Boy Scout (35mm Panavision)
Point Break (Super 35mm)
The Rocketeer (35mm Panavision)
Spartacus (35mm Technirama restoration)*
Star Trek VI (Super 35mm)
Terminator 2 (Super 35mm)

*1992*
Alien 3 (35mm Panavision)
Far and Away (65mm)
1492 (35mm Panavision)

Hoffa (35mm Panavision)
Howard's End (Super 35mm)
The Last of the Mohicans (35mm Panavision)
Lethal Weapon 3 (35mm Panavision)
Patriot Games (35mm Panavision)
Shining Through (35mm Panavision)

*1993*
Baraka (65mm)
Cliffhanger (35mm Panavision)
Geronimo (35mm Panavision)
Gettysburg (35mm 1.85)
In the Line of Fire (35mm Panavision)
Last Action Hero (35mm Panavision)
The Remains of the Day (Super 35mm)
Short Cuts (Super 35mm)

*1994*
The Lion King (35mm 1.85)
Little Buddha (35mm Technovision)
Miracle on 34th Street (35mm 1.85)
My Fair Lady (65mm restoration)*
True Lies (Super 35mm)

*1995*
Pocahontas (35mm 1.85)
The Wild Bunch (35mm Panavision)

*1996*
Hamlet (65mm)
Independence Day (Super 35mm)
Vertigo (35mm VistaVision restoration)

*1997*
Titanic (Super 35mm)

*2001*
2001 A Space Odyssey (65mm)

# Decline of the Drive-in

As noted in Chapter 1, drive-ins were approximately twenty-five percent of US theaters in 1968. By the nineties there were less than 600. Their loss was tragic since they offered affordable entertainment for the family in a unique setting. Baby Boomers who attended them have fond memories of watching movies under the stars complete with playgrounds and dinner. Drive-ins and the back aisle rows of large screen cinemas were part of the dating game for my generation. I saw more movies in ozoners as a child than indoor cinemas. I remember many entertaining double bills including *A Shot in the Dark* combined with *The Pink Panther* in 1964 and the first three *Planet of the Apes* features in a triple bill. I attached a small audio cassette mike to the speaker so I could listen to the sound-track afterwards. I also saw *Ben-Hur* in it's 1969 reissue. My father drove off with the speaker in the window after this screening, which shattered it.

There were many reasons for their decline. The change to daylight savings time limited operating hours. Increased property taxes on sea-sonal businesses caused many to fold. Late seventies inflation, the gas cri-sis and land values all had an impact. The demise of the Production Code was another contributing factor. The classification system only worked if children were restricted from seeing adult content. This was a problem in drive-ins since the screens could be seen in the surrounding areas. Drive-ins that played R and X rated films displayed nudity and were often in violation of community standards. The limited number of G and PG films made bookings difficult.

Ozoners always had limited access to quality product and often exhib-ited exploitation pictures in the fifties and early sixties to fill their bills. The level of sex and violence was far greater in the post–Code era which gave many venues a shady reputation and changed the atmosphere of the location. Admittedly, family attendance was down anyway but the deci-sion to play sexploitation product like *Inga* (1968) had ramifications. In the more conservative areas of the country, local ordinances forbade the exhibition of nudity where it could be seen from the highway. The U.S. Supreme Court decision that protected pornography as "free speech" over-turned most of this legislation. It was questionable victory for drive-ins since they ended up losing the remnants of the family trade that kept them in business. The days of double-bills like *The Pink Panther* and *A Shot in the Dark* were gone.

The cable and home video competition also affected ozoners. The window between theatrical exhibition and ancillary release was shortened which limited the amount of time owners could book sub-run titles. Many became flea markets during the daytime. Most drive-ins were forced to play movies first run which increased operating costs. Ticket prices went up and while cheaper than indoor theaters, they were no longer a bargain. Surviving drive-ins were often run down due to low profit margins which prevented the management from upgrading the site. A list of surviving drive-ins is contained in Chapter 10.

# The Megaplex

In 1995, Stanley Dunwood's company introduced the next type of theatrical venue which was known as the Megaplex. AMC opened The Grand 24 which featured new stadium style seating. This was considered an innovation although it raised the level of the projection booth and increased "keystone" distortion because of the extreme angle of the machine to the screen. Many of the megaplex buildings had larger wall to wall screens with some wider than 50 feet which filled the audiences field of view. While they still lacked curtains, this was better than the tiny 20 foot multiplex units of the last few decades. As always, there was a trade-off. The audience sat closer to the screen which meant the projector used very short focal length lenses with shallow depth of focus that magnified image unsteadiness and sharpness problems. The high speed prints with weak contrast exacerbated the situation.

Other chains built similar complexes throughout the country. While the years 1992 to 2000 produced new records in box-office sales, with a $7.67 billion revenue in 2000, 11 major cinema operators filed for bankruptcy including six of the ten top companies. Among them were Carmike Cinemas Inc., United Artists Theater Co., General Cinemas and Edwards Cinemas. Even Loews Cineplex Entertainment Corp. was in trouble. What accounts for the disparity between box-office and theater closings?

One of the reasons for high grosses was inflated ticket prices. As they increased, revenue went up but distributors, not exhibitors were making the lion's share of the profit due to their tough booking terms. Some people stopped attending because it was no longer affordable entertainment. In urban areas, ticket prices were often $10. Add to that the concessions costs and an evening at the movies for two was often in excess of $30. To pay this amount to watch a movie in a dirty theater with murky looking images and inept platter projection was not worth it to many viewers who could wait a few months and rent it on tape or DVD for $3 and see it in their home theater on a 35 inch monitor. Video masters were derived from first generation materials, not third, and had better sharpness and color rendition than many general release prints within the limitations of their technology.

Insurance companies told theater managers to keep the lights dimmed at 50 percent for the coming attraction trailers and end credits lest anyone trip on the way to their seats and sue. This was not a problem in the past when ushers coordinated the traffic before and after the show. There were even theaters that kept the lights slightly dimmed for the entire feature. I saw *Life Is Beautiful* in a Westchester cineplex that did this and the ambient light washed out the contrast of the projected image. To increase revenue and reduce operating costs, some theaters began to show advertising slides from local businesses prior to the film. Small companies paid a fee to have them displayed on screen. Century Media and National Cinema Network provided movie trivia slides between the ads but people weren't fooled. They were commercials, one of the things theaters used to avoid. All of these practices further degraded the movie going experience.

Content was another issue. The majority of films coming out of Hollywood were R rated. Distributors and exhibitors needed the teenage audience to stay in business. Studios catered to them in their advertising and some theater managers ignored age restrictions in admissions. The theaters used minimal staff which could not prevent kids from sneaking into different shows. Parents and watchdog groups complained that the industry circumvented the classification system. History repeated itself as politicians from both sides of the aisle made an issue out of it. In 1999, Republican John McCain and Democrat Joe Lieberman proposed a government rating system with fines unless Hollywood cleaned up its act. It didn't amount to anything and it was unlikely the bill would've passed Constitutional scrutiny. The logical solution was to persuade the industry to limit the number of restricted films and keep the bulk of the product in the PG or PG-13 category which could be done in the financing and pre-production stage. That way, controversial films could be marketed to adults and the rest to teenagers and general audiences. Despite promises made by distributors, restricted product continued to dominate the business. The MPAA began detailing the content within the classification listing.

Two other trends of the nineties should be mentioned. The first was "Political Correctness" ("PC"). Sixties counterculture ideology made a comeback in this guise. Once again, art was used a weapon. To a certain extent, the movies of each decade reflected presidential politics. The election of Ronald Reagan revived economic conservatism and fifties middle-class values. Counterculture and blaxploitation had fizzled out by the late seventies although there were still some movies made with a Leftist perspective like Warren Beatty's *Reds* (1981), Spike Lee's *She's Gotta Have It* (1986) and Oliver Stone's *Born on the Fourth of July* (1989). Splatter exploitation made a comeback along with 3-D. However, it was also a good era for PG entertainment devoid of political spin. Spielberg's Indiana Jones series, Lucas' Star Wars sequels, the Back to the Future trilogy and Bond thrillers were among the top box-office grossing pictures. Although the color photography lacked the richness of sixties productions, 70mm was popular which ensured some quality presentations.

This cycle ended with the election of Bill Clinton whom many in the industry supported with financial contributions. Incrementally, films became politicized again and it was rare when a picture did not contain some PC reference. Obvious examples included Mario van Peebles' *Panther* (1998) which glorified the radical group. The screenplay was by his father, Melvin, the blaxploitation director. Oliver Stone's *Nixon* (1995) also fell into the agit-prop category as did Warren Beatty's *Bulworth* (1998). The problem with these pictures was the same as message films in previous decades. The scripts depicted politics and history in simplified black and white terms with shallow characterization. Few stories had the complex narratives of a Robert Bolt screenplay or the wit of a Billy Wilder/I.A.L. Diamond collaboration.

The second trend was the over-reliance of digital special effects at the expense of drama. Many of the big budget science fiction and action thrillers contained extensive computer generated effects (CGE) but scant character development. Features like *Twister* (1996) and *Independence Day* (1996) spent little time creating sympathetic protagonists audiences could identify with and had cliché dialogue. It would appear that the targeted audience was less interested in these traditional narrative requirements since both films were box-office hits. It's interesting to compare these two films with previous special effects spectaculars like *Close Encounters of the Third Kind* (1977) which spent a large percentage of the running time developing the principals so viewers empathized with their fate.

Part of the mini-cinema concept was that multiple screens would increase the diversity of product. This has not happened in most cases since print runs were often in excess of 2,000 copies. Instead of a limited number of copies playing select theaters, the same picture played on multiple screens within a building and theaters ended up competing with themselves. Few independent or foreign pictures were given exposure. In addition, new megaplexes forced the closing of older multiplexes that lacked updated digital sound and stadium seating. Operators had borrowed extensively to construct these new screens which outpaced demand. As of 1999, there were 37,185 movie screens but many will fold in the near future due do slowing box-office sales, poor quality films, union strikes and other labor problems. It's unlikely anyone will lament their loss as people did when the movie palaces, large screen cinemas and drive-ins were torn down.

Despite the recent improvements in seating, sound and wall to wall large screens, megaplexes did not offer the spectacle or quality that large screen single houses had in the past. The high speed prints looked murky due to the generation loss and distance of the audience to the screen. 35mm dye transfer prints would improve the quality but are more expensive so few distributors manufactured them. 70mm would be another option but the megaplexes had not installed the equipment. When I saw the 1997 reissue of *Star Wars* in 35mm digital sound, it was vastly inferior to the experience of watching it in 70mm at the Loews Astor Plaza in 1977. The first reel looked faded with pink flesh-tones and the image lacked the sharpness of the 70mm blow-up two decades ago. Given the economic realities and type of product that Hollywood manufactures, we may never see large screen single houses and "event" presentations again.

# 8. Alternate Venues

While motion picture exhibition was experiencing its incremental decline with twinned cinemas, multiplexes and platters, there were still some venues that offered quality presentation and showmanship.

## Repertory Cinema

Theatres all over the country are more and more adapting to the trend to avoid product shortage and high terms demanded by major distributors. In fact, every major city offers at least one "specialized" cinema, and many cities, like Boston and New York, offer more.[1]

From the mid-seventies through mid-eighties, there was a forum that provided film buffs and general audiences a place to experience classic movies on large screens the way they were meant to be seen. It was known as Repertory Cinema. The genesis of this ten year phenomenon dated back to the fifties when some independent theaters began to show older features in double-bills. By the sixties, many large cities had at least one cinema that played classics although some were exhibiting them in the 16mm format.

What was a revival theater? By definition, they played films that were older than five years with many titles in the "classic" category from the twenties through the sixties. Films were usually booked as a series based on the work of a well known director or star. Some of the early houses were the Encore in Los Angeles and the Elgin in New York City.

One of the showmen who helped develop Repertory Cinema as a viable format was Tom Cooper in Los Angeles. He ran the Vagabond and Tiffany theaters. Cooper believed he could increase attendance by showing 35mm prints instead of 16mm and projecting them in the correct aspect

# GALA FILM FESTIVAL

### THE

# GOLDEN AGE OF THE CINEMA

## STARTING DECEMBER 17, 1954

# 55th STREET PLAYHOUSE
# NEAR 7th AVE. JU 6-4590

Early revival theater in the fifties.

ratio on a large screen. This would be an improvement over cropped 16mm prints or Children's Matinee screenings of *The Wizard of Oz* shown in 1.85 rather than 1.33. Cooper booked nostalgic theme festivals combined with heavy promotion to cater to older audiences abandoned by the industry along with film students and movie buffs.

In 1979, Cooper coordinated a 3-D festival in the original dual projector process. He contacted Warner Bros. and proposed reissuing Hitchcock's *Dial M for Murder*. The film was released in 1954 at the end of the 3-D cycle and most theaters played it flat. In a telephone interview, Cooper told me that the studio denied the film was in 3-D. After he provided them with documentation, they informed him that they only had one negative. Cooper persisted and he located both 35mm masters. He booked them at the Vagabond and promoted the event. Unfortunately, the Warnercolor negatives were faded and required extensive color correction so the opening had to be postponed. Eventually, an acceptable pair of color prints was made and Cooper's revival was a huge success.

*Dial M for Murder* premiered in New York City in 1981 at the 8th Street Playhouse which also booked other titles from the era including *Miss Sadie Thompson* (1953) and dual Technicolor prints of *Kiss Me Kate* (1954). I attended every show and the festival was an entertaining and memorable experience. It inspired me to make my own 3-D film in 1995, *Run for Cover*, starring Adam West and Viveca Lindfors. *Dial M for Murder* played other Repertory houses throughout the country and was converted into the StereoVision single strip format utilized for *House of Wax* reissues.

Other notable events included a silent comedy festival based on Walter Kerr's book, *The Silent Clowns*, published in 1975. The films of Charlie Chaplin, Buster Keaton, Harold Lloyd and Harry Langdon were shown. There was also a Sam Goldwyn festival with newly struck prints, a Fox CinemaScope series and Hitchcock retrospective. The Repertory forum expanded throughout the country and garnered a staple audience from the categories detailed above. A number of first run cinemas converted to the format rather than going the multiplex route including New York's Regency. Frank Rowley was the programmer for this house which became a Manhattan institution. Rowley was able to persuade the studios to strike new prints which he premiered. Among the notable programs was a Christmas festival, Humphrey Bogart and Bette Davis classics. Rep houses were popular near colleges. There were many near NYU which I attended from 1975 through 1979. Some offered student discounts and I went after classes three or four times a week.

New York City had the greatest number during this era. Among them

were the aforementioned Regency, 8th Street Playhouse and Carnegie Hall Cinema, all with large screens. My favorite was the Elgin located in Chelsea which was operated by Steve Gould and Chuck Zlatkin. It was the most eccentric revival theater which programmed everything from big budget studio classics like *It's a Mad, Mad, Mad, Mad World* (1963) to offbeat pictures like *The King of Hearts* (1966) and *Harold and Maude* (1972). Both had done poorly in first run theaters but found an audience there. They catered to a broad demographic including movie buffs, counterculture types, film students and senior citizens. There were discounts for the latter two categories. I practically lived there while I attended NYU and was sad when it folded in 1977. The success of the theater had increased the property value of the building and they were evicted.

The Elgin had an art deco design, 520 seat capacity and large 40 ft. wide by 20 ft. high curved Cinemascope screen. They couldn't afford masking so it looked like a trampoline but was appropriate for titles like *Lawrence of Arabia* (1962). They had state of the art projection and speakers too. Gould and Zlatkin programmed series like French night, Italian night and all night screenings of Marx brothers movies. They also pioneered the "Midnight

The 8th Street Playhouse *Dial M for Murder* 3-D festival ad.

## Nov. 16–Dec. 13
# THE FILMS OF
# SIR ALEXANDER KORDA

*Alexander Korda, born in Hungary in 1893, was primarily responsible for the international establishment of the British film industry with his productions beginning in 1933. For the next seven years, Korda produced and in a number of cases, directed many of the most outstanding films released in England during the decade preceding WWII. Knighted in 1942 by King George VI he continued as an active film producer both in England and America until his death in 1956.*

---

**Sun., Nov. 16–Mon., Nov. 17**

†**THE PRIVATE LIFE OF HENRY VIII** (1933)
Charles Laughton, Robert Donat, Merle Oberon, Elsa Lanchester, Binnie Barnes
The loves and intrigues of one of England's most colorful monarchs.
BEST ACTOR Academy Award to CHARLES LAUGHTON.
DIRECTED by ALEXANDER KORDA.
12:00; 3:45; 7:40

†*** KNIGHT WITHOUT ARMOUR** (1937)
Marlene Dietrich, Robert Donat, Irene Vanbrugh
A British scholar comes to the aid of a Russian countess being pursued by the Red Army during the Revolution.
Based on JAMES HILTON's novel.
DIRECTED by JACQUES FEYDER.
1:50; 5:45; 9:30

Charles Laughton in
*The Private Life Of Henry VIII* (1933).

*First performance during a Regency Theatre series.

†Distributed by *Samuel Goldwyn*, who has prepared new prints for this engagement.
THE SAMUEL GOLDWYN COMPANY

---

**Tues., Nov. 18–Wed., Nov. 19**

†**THE MAN WHO COULD WORK MIRACLES** (1936)
Roland Young, Ralph Richardson, Joan Gardner
H.G. WELLS creates a character of a mild-mannered clerk given super-human powers.
DIRECTED by LOTHAR MENDES.
12:30; 3:40; 6:50; 10:00

†**THINGS TO COME** (1936)
Raymond Massey, Ralph Richardson, Cedric Hardwicke
A futuristic look at a country torn apart by a destructive war.
Based on H.G. WELLS' novel.
Sets by VINCENT KORDA.
DIRECTED by WILLIAM CAMERON MENZIES.
2:00; 5:10; 8:20

■ ■ ■

**Thurs., Nov. 20–Sat., Nov. 22**

†**THE THIEF OF BAGDAD** (1940)
Conrad Veidt, Sabu, John Justin, June Duprez, Rex Ingram
An Arabian Nights fantasy in which a native boy and his genie outdo an evil sorcerer.
DIRECTED by LUDWIG BERGER, TIM WHALEN and MICHAEL POWELL.
In Color.
12:00; 4:00; 8:00

†**THE FOUR FEATHERS** (1939)
Ralph Richardson, John Clements, June Duprez
A nobleman must prove he's not a coward.
DIRECTED by ZOLTAN KORDA. In Color.
1:55; 5:55; 9:55

■ ■ ■

**Sun., Nov. 23–Mon., Nov. 24**

†**TWENTY-ONE DAYS** (1937)
Vivien Leigh, Laurence Olivier, Leslie Banks, Francis L. Sullivan
The "black sheep" of a prominent family murders his lover's husband.
DIRECTED by BASIL DEAN.
1:00; 4:40; 8:20

†**THAT HAMILTON WOMAN** (1941)
Laurence Olivier, Vivien Leigh, Gladys Cooper, Sara Allgood
Lord Nelson's love for Emma Hamilton causes a national scandal.
DIRECTED by ALEXANDER KORDA.
2:25; 6:05; 9:40

---

**Tues., Nov. 25–Wed., Nov. 26**

†*** CLOUDS OVER EUROPE** (1938)
Laurence Olivier, Ralph Richardson, Valerie Hobson
Following the disappearance of four bombers, an eccentric investigator from British Secret Service is called in to solve the mystery.
DIRECTED by TIM WHALEN.
12:00; 3:00; 6:00; 9:00

†*** THE SPY IN BLACK** (1939)
Conrad Veidt, Valerie Hobson, Sebastian Shaw, June Duprez
A World War I episode in which three conspirators plot to sink the British fleet.
DIRECTED by MICHAEL POWELL.
1:30; 4:30; 7:30; 10:30

■ ■ ■

**Thurs., Nov. 27–Sat., Nov. 29**
**(THANKSGIVING)**

†**THE SCARLET PIMPERNEL** (1934)
Leslie Howard, Merle Oberon, Raymond Massey, Nigel Bruce
An English dandy leads a double life as he defies the zealots of the French Revolution.
DIRECTED by HAROLD YOUNG.
12:00; 3:10; 6:30; 9:45

†**THE GHOST GOES WEST** (1936)
Robert Donat, Jean Parker, Eugene Pallette, Morton Selten
When a Scottish castle is moved to Florida, the resident ghost makes the trip as well.
DIRECTED by RENE CLAIR.
1:40; 4:55; 8:15

program continued...

**ALL FILMS IN 35MM.**
Series Card—5 Shows for $18.00

**REGENCY**
BROADWAY & 67th • 724-3700

---

Regency glossy schedule.

Show" with Alexander Jodorowsky's surreal 1970 cult film *El Topo*. It ran for six months until John Lennon and Yoko Ono purchased the rights and pulled it from the theater. They tried to open it on Broadway but it didn't click in that location. Other midnight shows included John Water's *Pink Flamingos* (1972). These were not mainstream pictures so the late night screenings were a separate demographic from the daily shows.

The midnight venue expanded into other theaters both rep and first run with revivals of *Night of the Living Dead* (1968), *Eraserhead* (1978) and the notorious *Rocky Horror Picture Show* (1975) where the audience came dressed in costumes and participated in the performance by throwing rice at the screen. Tom Cooper played it in his theater for many years. I booked my cult Technicolor film, *Space Avenger*, at the Bleecker Street Cinema for a midnight run before in closed in 1991.

Smaller rep houses included the Thalia, Theater 80 St. Marks, the Art, Hollywood Twin and above mentioned Bleecker Street Cinema which had a film bookstore inside the theater. A later entry was the Film Forum which still survives as an art house. Other locations included the Parkway and Music Box in Chicago, the River Oaks in Houston, the Temple Theater in Michigan, the Neptune, Varsity and Egyptian in Seattle, Times Cinema in Milwaukee and many others. Programmers included Eric Levin (Times Cinema), Bruce Goldstein (the Film Forum) and the late Richard Schwartz (the Thalia).

I participated in several Repertory programs over the years. In 1989, I assisted Robert A. Frischmuth in securing original dye transfer prints for a Technicolor Festival at the Paramount Center of the Arts in Peekskill. Among the pictures that were screened were *The Alamo, Spartacus, West Side Story, The Music Man, It's a Mad, Mad, Mad, Mad World* and *The Wizard of Oz*. We booked the studio copies which were in poor condition and played mint prints that were borrowed from local film collectors. Audience response was enthusiastic and patrons came dressed in costumes for *Oz* screening. Many young people had never seen a Technicolor print before and remarked how superior they were to current Eastmancolor release copies. Makeup artist Dick Smith attended the *Mad World* screening and discussed his contribution to the film. I introduced the showing of *The Music Man* and explained the Technirama process.

I also helped coordinate the Cleveland Cinematheque Technicolor series in 1991 which featured my own dye transfer production, *Space Avenger*.[2] It was titled, "Fade Away: The Lost Art of I.B. Technicolor" and was part of my campaign to revive the process domestically. In 1997, I worked with Asaf Ashkinazi in programming a Tel Aviv 3-D retrospective which premiered my film, *Run for Cover* in Israel. Other titles included

The author helped coordinate the Tel Aviv 3-D retrospective along with two U.S. Technicolor Festivals.

*House of Wax, Dial M for Murder, The Bubble* and *Comin' at Ya.* I traveled to the country to promote the event which was very successful although we almost lost the booking on *House of Wax* due to political correctness. An executive at Warners tried to cancel it because Phillip Morris was sponsoring the event. Fortunately, Asaf was able to bypass this person. I had a great time because there's nothing I enjoy more than putting on a show. It's how I define cinema.

What differentiated a Repertory theater from a conventional Art house was their showmanship. Cooper persuaded Howard Keel to attend the 3-D revival of *Kiss Me Kate. The Silent Clowns* festival had live organ accompaniment. Gould and Zlatkin invited John Waters and his bizarre troupe to attend screenings of *Pink Flamingos.* Bruce Goldstein programmed a "Gimmickorama" festival at the Film Forum in 1990 which featured the films of William Castle. Seats were rigged with original "Percepto" motors for *The Tingler* (1959) to make them vibrate. The ballyhoo absent from most contemporary releases was integral to these presentations. Audiences sensed which theater managers cared and which ones didn't and responded accordingly.

The print quality in revival theaters was usually excellent compared to what was exhibited in multiplexes. While some post-seventies films were shown, most bookings encompassed the studio era with its lush and vibrant cinematography. Many Technicolor classics were shown including *One Eyed Jacks* (1961), *The Gang's All Here* (1974 dye transfer reissue) and *West Side Story* (1961). The rich contrast of older black and white films was apparent in *Psycho* (1960), Val Lewton horror films and film noir thrillers. Movies printed in Eastmancolor had faded but the distributors and multitude of rep houses made it worth their while to strike new copies. De Luxe titles like *There's No Business Like Show Business* (1954) and *The Seven Year Itch* (1954) were reprinted in CinemaScope. Andrew Sarris reviewed revivals in the *Village Voice* and gave viewers a historical perspective.

On occasion, first run theaters would book theme festivals. The Cinerama theater in New York City played a "Broadway Comes to Broadway" program. Original 70mm prints of *Camelot, My Fair Lady, Paint Your Wagon* and *South Pacific* were shown on their curved screen. Although *South Pacific* was slightly faded, the other prints were in good shape. They were spectacular presentations. The theater returned to first run after the engagement.

Sadly, Repertory cinema began to die off in the mid-eighties. The popularity of home video and cable reduced the size of the audience. Greedy distributors raised the price of print rentals when they saw how

"Those 1950's Gimmicks Are Back!" ad.

popular their classics were in these venues. They ended up losing the extra revenue since the programmers couldn't afford to book them anymore. Print sources dried up as the exchanges folded and distributors destroyed release copies rather than pay storage costs. Most of the houses had relied on old prints for bookings. Even National Screen Service was gone by the nineties. As the revival theaters closed, it was no longer cost efficient for studios to strike new prints for limited bookings. Famous venues like the Bleecker Street Cinema and the Thalia shut their doors. The Regency was purchased by Cineplex Odeon and returned to first run through 1999 when it was converted to a Victoria's Secret store.

Tom Cooper left the business as did a number of festival coordinators. Frank Rowley moved to the Biograph Cinema on 57th Street and Broadway in New York City but it too switched to first run and was renamed the Angelika 57. I booked my 3-D feature, *Run for Cover*, and installed a silver screen before it shut down. It was a tremendous loss to film buffs and students since screening a film on video was not the same experience as watching them projected on screen. The impact of movies like *2001: A Space Odyssey* and *Kiss Me Kate* in 3-D was lost on television monitors. Viewing *Duck Soup* at home could not compare to seeing it in a theater with an appreciative audience. It was impossible to remain silent as the auditorium exploded with infectious laughter during the song, "Freedonia's Going to War." A different effect occurred during the *Psycho* shower scene. You could feel the collective terror as the curtain opened to reveal Norman Bates with a knife. There was something magical about watching a movie on a large screen with a group of complete strangers that were sharing the exact same emotions together. You would never see these people again and yet for two hours you were connected.

While a few revival houses like New York's Film Forum, Milwaukee's Times Cinema, Chicago's Music Box and California's Standard Theater and Ken Cinema survive, the "Golden Age of Repertory" was over. Of all the losses suffered during the medium's decline, I miss them the most. I used to make schedules to coordinate my travel time from theater to theater so I wouldn't miss rare screenings at the Bleecker Street Cinema, Elgin, Thalia and Regency. These theaters were a time capsule of cinema's glorious past.

## Full Restorations

Another forum to see classic motion pictures was theatrical restorations. It's important to make the distinction between revivals and restoration. Revivals referred to the exhibition of old prints and restorations involved extensive manipulation of deteriorated negatives to manufacture new prints that replicated the quality of the originals. It also involved preservation of the restored negative so that future generations could enjoy the film.

Among the noted archivists in this area were Kevin Brownlow, Bob Gitt and Robert A. Harris. Brownlow spent years cobbling together the complete version of Abel Gance's silent epic, *Napoleon*. It was reissued by Robert A. Harris and Universal with the triptych climax accompanied by a live orchestra under the direction of Carmine Coppola. I saw it at the Radio City Music Hall and it was quite an event.

Robert A. Harris is the best known archivist due to his high profile restorations of *Lawrence of Arabia* (1989), *Spartacus* (1991), *Vertigo* (1993) and *My Fair Lady* (1995). Each project took years to complete but he was able to resurrect the severely faded and damaged negatives to their original quality. I attended 70mm screening of these features and they were some of the best shows I'd ever seen. At the premiere of *Lawrence of Arabia* at New York's Ziegfeld, David Lean introduced the film. He pointed to the enormous screen and said, "this is what movies are all about." The superior quality of the cinematography, screenplay and large format illustrated what was lacking in contemporary cinema. By the late nineties many theaters had abandoned 70mm which will make screening these restorations difficult in the future.

In 2000, Harris restored Hitchcock's *Rear Window* in the new dye transfer process at Technicolor. The quality was superb but the distributor didn't give the film the promotion it deserved. Bookings were limited, often to art houses.

## Limited Restorations

A limited restoration was one that replicated the original quality and experience of seeing the film but did not preserve the original printing elements. Eric Spilker persuaded 20th Century–Fox to reprint Busby Berkeley's 1943 musical, *The Gang's All Here* in the dye transfer process at Technicolor in 1973 prior to their shutdown. The quality was impressive and the vibrant primaries of Carmen Miranda's production numbers so saturated they were almost surrealistic. The prints played the revival circuit for many years. Unfortunately, the negative was not preserved. Fox had De Luxe make CRIs of the nitrate three strip Technicolor films then discarded the originals. The CRIs were unstable and began to fade.

The late Ron Haver, author of *David O. Selznick's Hollywood*, supervised the semi-restored presentation of *A Star Is Born* (1954) at Radio City Music Hall in 1981. Haver found an original 35mm dye transfer short version of the film in the Warner vaults. He also located the complete four track magnetic stereo mix and alternate takes of many scenes cut after its premiere. Still montages were used to fill in the gaps. New prints were made of the extra scenes and spliced into the Technicolor print. It was interlocked with the fullcoat and exhibited at the Radio City Music Hall. Liza Minelli and James Mason attended. Sadly, director George Cukor died shortly before the screening. While the presentation was impressive, the negative was not restored. Warners made new Eastmancolor prints of the longer version but the color was poor due to dye coupler fading.

In 1982, the Samuel Goldwyn company purchased the rights to *Oklahoma!* (1955) and *South Pacific* (1958). New 35mm Eastmancolor prints were made on both titles and made the rounds of the revival houses. The quality was fairly good considering the age of the negatives. They also made a new 70mm Todd-AO print of *Oklahoma!* which was photographed simultaneously with the 35mm CinemaScope version. Despite some fading in the exteriors, the studio sets looked superb with razor sharp focus, rich color and fine grain resolution when projected at 30 frames per second. Unfortunately, the distributor failed to promote the 70mm print and attendance was poor.

Film collector John Harvey resurrected the three panel Cinerama process in 1997 at Ohio's New Neon Cinema. The Cinerama corporation had abandoned the three panel process in 1963 and ceased operations in the seventies. Over the subsequent decades, Harvey pieced together multiple panels of *This Is Cinerama* (1952) and *How the West Was Won* (1962), both in the dye transfer process. He secured appropriate projectors with seven channel magnetic dubbers and installed a curved louvered screen inside his house. Exhibitor Larry Smith attended a private screening and proposed setting up his cinema for the process.

A new Cinerama screen was installed at the theater along with Harvey's projectors. Celebrities like Janet Leigh and Leonard Maltin attended. I saw both films in 1997 and the illusion of peripheral vision was spectacular with its unlimited depth of field. The magnetic stereo soundtracks had an expanded range but were very hissy due to deterioration. The Technicolor photography was superb. The hype and ballyhoo made the experience more enjoyable although there was no getting around the inherent flaws in the process. Join lines were often apparent even though they were blurred by projection gate "jiggolos." They were more noticeable in the travelogue than in the Western where a great deal of effort was made to disguise them in the compositions.

Cinerama (New Neon Movies) postcard ad.

The opening of *This Is Cinerama* contained one of the great moments of motion picture showmanship when the black and white image of Lowell Thomas exclaiming, "Ladies and Gentlemen, This is Cinerama" expanded to the three panel panoramic shot of the roller coaster in Technicolor. The curved screen made the audience dizzy as if they were on the ride. This was the most expensive movie I'd ever attended when the costs of travel and hotel were included but it was worth it since it will be difficult to see the process again.

## Performing Arts Centers

While the bulk of the movie palaces were torn down, a select few survived as performing arts centers. In many cases, the city declared the buildings cultural landmarks and restored them to their former glory. These locations offered the classic movie going experience on a limited basis. Most centers programmed live shows and musical performances along with occasional motion picture presentations. In general, showmanship was good. For example, Poughkeepsie, New York's Bardavon hired an organist to play pop tunes on the Mighty Wurlitzer prior to the shows. This theater had a large forty foot wide screen with curtains and a 520 seat capacity with a balcony. I attended a screening of a brand new 35mm print of Hitchcock's *Strangers on a Train* there. Since it was a Halloween event, a plastic skeleton was lowered on strings to sit at the organ. The Hitchcock television theme was played. The sellout crowd was very enthusiastic about the show and applauded at the end. I cannot recall any multiplex or megaplex screening that received applause.

Other movie palace art centers included the Paramount Center of the Arts in Peekskill, New York, the Union County Arts Center and Loews in New Jersey and on the West Coast, the Samuel Goldwyn Theater and El Capitan. The Roxy in Pennsylvania was a palace that played contemporary films and the Music Box in Chicago an atmospheric theater that played revivals. I highly recommend attending these showings which in many cases are less expensive than Mall cinemas.

## Imax

Imax remains one of the few places to see large screen images outside of performing arts centers. The format was introduced at Expo '70 in Osaka. The process utilizes a 70mm print exhibited horizontally with a 15 perf image and a $3 \times 4$ ratio. It is actually a variation of the 35mm VistaVision process of the fifties which used an 8 sprocket horizontal image and $1.85 \times 1$ ratio. Imax is similar to Cinerama in that it contains a separate soundtrack that is not on the print and requires a special projector. While multiple discrete magnetic tracks were originally used, they were replaced with a Digital Disc Playback (DDP) with patented Samplelock which gives eight channel playback via ample-accurate phase synchronization. The enormous projector uses a rolling loop to advance the film. Film travels at the rate of 336 ft. per minute. Imax films can only be played in their theaters and are not compatible with other formats in 70mm or 35mm although a few titles have been released in home video formats.

Imax prints are all made off the original camera negatives with razor sharp first generation imagery derived from a frame ten times the size of conventional 35mm. The screens are up to eight stories high with Omnimax Dome presentations 99 feet high. The screen is flat but has a slight compound curvature. Depending on the quality of the cinematography, the format can be quite impressive and generate motion sickness when the camera is airborne. However, it does not simulate the illusion of peripheral vision that three panel Cinerama and early Todd-AO productions did since it is not a wide-screen process nor does it encompass the field of vision of these two formats. In addition, some Imax productions have had sub-standard photography with under-exposed shots that defeat the purpose of the large frame resolution. *Behold Hawaii* (1983), for example, had some murky looking sequences. Cinerama and Todd-AO films all had superb cinematography.

In 1997, Imax added 3-D to their process which utilized uncomfortable electronic liquid crystal shutter glasses. *T-Rex* (1999) was one of the better subjects and had excellent CG dinosaur effects and a clever animated introduction. However, some of the live action portion of the film was photographed with a shallow depth of field which was inappropriate for 3-D.

Omnimax and Imax simulator rides were other formats used in museums and theme parks which also offered entertaining experiences differ-

IMAX Palisades Center cardboard ad/flyer.

## PALISADES CENTER

**IMAX®** . . . A film experience like no other! IMAX, the original large format technology brings to life images on our screen over six stories high, enhanced by a wrap around, 12,000 watt, electrifying IMAX® Digital Sound System. Treat your senses to the most powerful and involving film experience yet discovered.

**IMAX® 3D.** . . Put on your 3D headset as entertainment takes on a whole new dimension at the IMAX Theatre at Palisades Center. 3D images feel so incredibly real, you'll have to resist the urge to reach out and grab them.

## EXTREME

**No rules. No limits. No boundaries.**
One minute you are hanging on for dear life, next you could be praying for it. For the world-class athletes of *EXTREME,* danger is a given. Only respect and pure ability keep it at bay. And only *EXTREME,* An IMAX® Experience™, takes you to the edge of human achievement in some of the most intense natural realms imaginable. Ski in Alaska. Climb in Utah. Surf 60-foot waves in Hawaii. It's your chance to see how the other .002% lives.

## T-REX
*BACK TO THE CRETACEOUS*     IMAX 3D

Prepare to take a pre-historic adventure as *T-REX: Back To The Cretaceous* slices through the mysteries and the millenia to bring dinosaurs to life with ground-breaking detail, unparalleled realism and the awesome size and thrilling feeling of IMAX® 3D. *T-REX: Back To The Cretaceous* melds time travel with the latest in computer-generated IMAX® 3D imagery to bring the prehistoric past alive like never before.

### SHOW TIMES
For showtimes and information call (914) 358-IMAX (4629)
For Group Sales or Theatre rental, call: (914) 353-5555, ext. 202

### TICKETS
Purchase tickets at the IMAX Theatre Palisades Center box office or advance tickets may be charged by phone at (914) 358-IMAX (4629)

**Visit our website at**
**www.imax.com/palisades**

**WHERE TO FIND US**
Take exit 12 on
NYS Thruway to the
**IMAX® Theatre**
**at Palisades Center,**
4th Floor, "thEATery" level.

4270 Palisades Center Drive,
West Nyack, NY 10994

IMAX® & IMAX®3D are registered trademarks of Imax Corporation, Mississauga, Canada. All rights reserved.
Printed in Canada

ent from the typical multiplex screening. There are 100 Imax theaters in the United States which includes the latter venues. While the process is generally interesting, it has its limitations. The average running time is 45 minutes which is not conducive to narratives. Most Imax films fall into the travelogue or featurette category. While Disney's *Fantasia 2000* length was expanded to 75 minutes,[3] this was still too short to make a viable drama with character development. There are 160 films produced in the process with 50 distributed by the Imax corporation.

Shooting an Imax film is extremely cumbersome. The camera weighs 80 lb. or 300 lb. if a blimp is used. The unit is so noisy, dialogue has to be post-looped which affects performance. Film loads are only 3 minutes long compared to standard 10 minute loads for 35mm. They are only good for a few shots and then have to be reloaded which takes 10 minutes for standard Imax cameras and 20 minutes for the 3-D unit. The first 3-D units were dual camera rigs. Recently, a single body unit was developed that contained a pair of modified lenses. It weighs 265 lb. Huge cranes and dollies with rugged camera heads are needed to withstand the motor vibrations from the camera. Extensive lighting is required to generate the depth of field necessary for the large format presentation. The diffused and desaturated style of the seventies and eighties is not appropriate for this format.

I enjoy this process within its limitations as it offers superior quality to megaplex showings. However, the 70mm format generated a more natural field of vision and was better suited to narrative filmmaking.

## Film Collecting and Home Movie Theaters

Circa 1993, I walked into the screening room and took a seat that was close to the twenty foot wide screen. The film began and I watched *Airport* in Technicolor with four channels of discrete magnetic sound blasting from the speakers. This wasn't a rep house or multiplex but a private collector's theater built in the basement of his house. There was even a concession stand and antique pinball machines.

Another collector set up a large theater in his neighborhood dwelling with a curved screen and 70mm projection. If one was in the mood to see dual projection 3-D, there were two set ups in suburbia. In Washington, DC, a film buff had a wide curtain that appeared to be a living room window but actually hid a motion picture screen. The projector was in his den and the light was shown through a window in the wall that was covered by a picture. Collectors set up screens in their back yards with old Simplex drive-in speakers to simulate the ozoner experience during the summer complete with cartoons and intermission clocks.

In the past, many celebrities had private screening rooms and prints including Roddy McDowall, William Holden, Errol Flynn, Clark Gable and Norman Taurog to name a few. Stars like Charlie Chaplin and Harold Lloyd produced their own films and preserved the negatives. Chaplin even saved his out-takes which was the subject of a documentary by Kevin Brownlow entitled, *Unknown Chaplin* (1980). Few people were aware of the number of collectors who had set-ups that were superior to industry insiders. Who were these obscure film fanatics? They were college professors and students, retired television programmers, computer technicians and people from every income bracket and profession. The late film historian and teacher, William K. Everson, had one of the largest private collections in the world which he used for his lectures while I attended NYU. He showed rare British Technicolor prints of Michael Powell features like *A Matter of Life and Death* (1946) and lost silent classics.

While 16mm was the most popular format, there were also 35mm and 70mm collectors. Some specialized in one genre, actor or director. I met an elderly individual who saved copies of lost Yiddish films from the thirties and forties. TV buffs saved kinescopes of shows junked by the station which were the only record of the broadcast. John Harvey was well known for his preservation of the Cinerama process. He remodeled his house to accommodate the projectors and curved louvered screen. Others preferred tinkering with antique projectors and prints in defunct systems like 22mm, 8mm, 9.5mm and Super 8mm.

Film collecting was an expensive hobby. The hottest collectibles were Technicolor prints since they didn't fade and the color was superior. For example, Fox's 35mm CinemaScope films were printed at De Luxe and both negatives and release copies faded. Fortunately, 16mm anamorphic Technicolor prints were made and survive in private archives. Black and white movies were also sought depending on the title. Pre-1983 Eastmancolor titles were the least desirable since the color lacked the richness of Technicolor and faded over time. Post-1983 copies were on low fade stock (LPP) although the color never matched the quality of a dye transfer print. 70mm looked and sounded great but was not an archival process. The iron and binder in the magnetic stripes served as a catalyst for the hydrolysis reaction commonly known as "vinegar syndrome." There were a few large format collectors that rewound their reels to air them out and keep them stable for a longer period of time. "Rejuvenated" chemically treated film were also subject to deterioration as was all tri-acetate in bad storage. Some collectors built temperature and humidity controlled vaults to

Reel Images Super 8 and 16mm catalogue cover.

extend the life of their collection. A number of individuals have the best surviving copies of classic features that remain stable after forty or fifty years. Despite the potential of vinegar syndrome, tri-acetate prints in decent storage have held up better than other audio-visual data.

In the past, prints were modestly priced in the range of $100 to $200 but over the years they increased in value. The "holy grail" for collectors was Clark Gable's personal 16mm Technicolor print of *Gone with the Wind* which was auctioned off for $10,000. 35mm dye transfer prints of *The Wizard of Oz* cost upwards of $3,000. Why would anyone spend this kind of money and go through the trouble of building a home theater just to see pictures which were available on cable and home video formats? The reason was, it was the only way to see them projected in their original format. No videotape, laserdisc or DVD could reproduce the three dimensional vibrancy of a dye transfer print of *Singin' in the Rain* with its primary colors glowing from the screen or the rich B&W contrast of *Abbott and Costello Meet Frankenstein*. Like stamp collectors and antique dealers, they liked owning a piece of Americana while preserving our cultural history. Many were "baby boomers" who were trying to recapture the cinematic memories of their youth. Others were passionate movie buffs with a love of certain films that they want to experience, study and preserve for the future the way as an art aficionado would cherish a Rembrandt painting. Distributors treated release prints as disposable plastic whereas collectors considered them works of art.

Despite the publicity surrounding recent restorations, studios were negligent about preserving their assets. Most films shot in early Eastmancolor had deteriorated. Some nitrate negatives also displayed decomposition prior to their transfer to safety film, especially from the silent era. Film archives were subject to nitrate fires. In August of 1977, the National Archive lost a great deal of footage from the *March of Time* series as a result although some reels may still exist in private collections. Even if the negative survived, there was no guarantee prints were available or intact. If you wanted to watch the Roadshow version of *Around the World in 80 Days*, Warner Bros. was the last place you'd look. While the studio was restoring *A Star Is Born* they were butchering Mike Todd's Oscar winning epic. The negative was cut from 175 minutes to 140 minutes. Fortunately, a number of individuals saved complete Technicolor prints in their vaults. The color negative of Abbott and Costello's *Jack and the Beanstalk* was lost. A 1952 35mm Super Cinecolor preview copy was preserved by a fan of the team that contained extra songs and scenes missing from the standard theatrical release. The video distributor borrowed it and released it on laserdisc. Studios removed footage of dual strip 3-D negatives to make repairs throwing them out of synch. Film buffs preserved complete dual prints on many fifties dimensional pictures.

One of Disney's better features was *Song of the South* (1946). The current management of Buena Vista withdrew it from release in a typical example of political correctness. Some of Disney's South American pictures were censored for the same reason. The only way to see them intact was in private screening rooms. The same applied to Goldwyn's *Porgy and Bess* (1959). If movie buffs, historians and archivists could be assured that distributors saved every title in their library and made top quality prints available for exhibition, film collecting would be unnecessary. It's obvious they haven't so the hobby should be considered a part of preservation and film scholarship.

Film collecting has a checkered history. Over the decades, distributors either encouraged or condemned the hobby. As early as 1931, 16mm was a popular format for home exhibition. The October 1931 issue of *American Cinematographer* noted, "Fully 300,000 projectors or motion picture machines of the 16mm. class have been sold in the U.S.... Pictures are now offered on the 16mm. market by leading producers, including Paramount, Universal, Pathé, Columbia, Fitzpatrick and others."[4] Silent and sound films were available on diacetate film. While non-flammable, this early safety stock tended to shrink rapidly and was replaced by tri-acetate safety film in 1948. Estar stock replaced tri-acetate in the nineties which did not shrink but scratched easier.

16mm silent features printed on amber tinted stock were available for sale and known as "kodascopes." The quality was excellent since they were reduction printed directly from the 35mm nitrate negatives. In many cases, the only surviving materials on the film were these copies. Sound films were also available including short subjects and cartoons. In the pre-television era, negatives were considered useless inventory after theatrical exhibition. Distributors squeezed extra revenue from their libraries in the non-theatrical market.

There were earlier home movie formats that came and went, all of which used safety film. In 1910, Kodak offered their first acetate safety film on 22mm stock. Pathé introduced 28mm the same year and 9.5mm in 1922. By 1938, 9.5mm sound prints were available. The sprockets were contained between the frames rather than on the sides of the film. Another obscure process was the Movette 17.5mm. In 1932, Kodak introduced 8mm film which survived for forty years. Super 8 was developed in 1965 which had a 50 percent larger image area due to the smaller sprockets. In 1973, magnetic sound stripes were added so that Super 8 sound prints of features and shorts could be exhibited in living rooms.

One of the leading distributors of films for home use was Blackhawk. The company was established in 1927 by Kent D. Eastin who was a specialist in distributing institutional product to schools, businesses and churches. He became a liquidator of dormant or defunct 16mm libraries. For example, early "soundies" negatives were purchased and prints marketed to consumers. Soundies were musical shorts made for 16mm coin operated jukebox machines in the forties. The prints played on rear projection screens contained in the unit. In 1952, Blackhawk licensed the Hal Roach library and sold prints of Laurel and Hardy and Our Gang films. They also duped off a number of "lost" silent films from surviving 35mm nitrate prints. They eventually had a customer base of 125,000.

In the fifties Castle films (later called Universal 8) released scenes from Universal classics like *Abbott and Costello Meet Frankenstein* along with live action short subjects. Around the same time, film studies programs were offered in many colleges. 16mm features were available for purchase by these institutions from the studios. Technicolor prints of *The Adventures of Robin Hood* (1937) and other classics were sold for classroom use. The heyday of 16mm and 8mm collecting was the late sixties through late seventies. A number of companies offered a wide selection of features, shorts and cartoons for home use. Studios like Disney, Paramount, MGM, Hal Roach and offered 8mm and Super 8 films (silent and sound) for sale through outlets like "Famous Films of Florida." The Chaplin estate released many of his titles with a strange contract that came with the purchase. Consumers had to agree to return the prints or destroy them after a fixed period of time. Naturally, collectors ignored this unenforceable edict.

Twenty minute digest versions of features were also popular. Many were cut by editor Bill Compton. He was a friend of screenwriter Haskell Wexler, who used his name for one of the lead characters in *Joe* (1970). Collectors could buy a reel containing sequences from *Creature of the Black Lagoon* in anaglyph 3-D complete with red and blue glasses. By the late seventies, feature length classics were available in Super 8 sound from the studios including MGM's *Gone with the Wind* and Paramount's *Once Upon a Time in the West*. Technicolor even made Super 8 dye transfer prints.

Other companies like Reel Images, Festival Films and Canterbury Films sold both 8mm and 16mm public domain titles including *Gulliver's Travels* (1939) and *Night of the Living Dead* (1968). Some pushed their luck by releasing films of questionable P.D. status. Canterbury discovered some episodes of the *Star Trek* TV show did not contain a copyright in the credits and released dupes to collectors. There was also a handful of shady dealers who actually fell into the category of "film pirates" when they illegally duped off copyrighted films. The trouble with all 8mm and 16mm color films sold to the public was that they were on Eastmancolor stock which faded over time.

I had an extensive Super 8 feature collection while I was in high school and used to arrange outdoor screenings in the summer of *Night of the Living Dead* along with Buster Keaton silents with a roughly synchronized music score played on a cassette. I always enjoyed putting on shows for friends and family. I disposed of them in 1985 when they started to deteriorate. The colors faded on the Eastmancolor prints and magnetic sound degaussed on the tracks. Fortunately, Kodachrome stock used in home movie cameras has held its colors nicely. I saved my Super 8 amateur productions which are still in good shape and have outlasted the various video formats I invested in over the years.

There were also copies of features for sale that were not officially licensed by the owners. Syndicated television stations aired 16mm prints through the eighties. Some deals were "for the life of the print" and station personnel sold copies to collectors when they were considered too old for broadcast. 16mm rental companies began to fold when videocassettes gained in popularity and collectors scavenged the garbage cans and retrieved the prints. Many film buffs purchased multiple reels of the same movie to piece together a near mint print. The extra reels were swapped to others who used them to upgrade their copy.

The mid-eighties through early nineties was the heyday for 35mm film collecting. This coincided with the decline of Repertory cinema and collapse of the exchange system. Film buffs salvaged prints left forgotten in storage facilities. Many joined the hobby since it was easier and cheaper to secure copies in that format due to the glut in the marketplace. A mint 35mm Technicolor print of *Mary Poppins* could be purchased for $250 in 1985. By 1995, this had reversed itself and the 35mm copies were more expensive than 16mm. The same copy would cost over a $1,000 now.

Discarded prints could be found in many places. Distributors left reels in the basements of theaters and projectionists took them home. As the exchanges folded, whole warehouses of prints were retrieved. Many labs went bust during this era which was another source as were bankrupt independent distributors. Prior to the days of computer editing, used features were sold as "sound fill" for track work during mixing. Some people pieced together the movie and saved it rather than use them for the blank footage between sound effects. I had one assistant who used to do that while I was editing low budget features. He ended up with a complete print of *Rambo* which was screened on the Steenbeck editing machine after hours. Since all of these copies were slated for destruction, distributors were not losing potential revenue. *The Big Reel, Classic Film Collector* and other monthly publications enabled collectors to swap and purchase titles. There were also conventions held in various locations around the country. More recently, a number of websites are devoted to the subject. I owe a debt of gratitude to collectors who assisted me with my book, *Technicolor Movies* in 1993, and in the festivals I helped coordinate. They generously gave me access to rare films for my research and for screenings. In the case of the festivals, we booked the distributor's faded and worn Eastmancolor prints but played the collector's mint Technicolor copies.

In the mid-seventies, the hobby ran into serious opposition from Jack Valenti and the MPAA. In 1974, the FBI raided the Hollywood home of Roddy McDowall and seized his large collection. Many of the films were given to him by the studios he worked for since it was not uncommon for the participants in a picture to request and receive a copy for personal use. Movies like *Sunset Boulevard* and *Words and Music* contained sequences or references of celebrity home theaters. Obviously, they were making an example of him. Under pressure and threats, McDowall named his sources and disclosed the identity of other collectors in a July 22, 1975 U.S. Government Memorandum.

The prosecutions and harassment continued throughout the late seventies when video piracy became an issue. Distributors were losing money when bootleg tapes of their libraries were being sold. Jack Valenti called for a crackdown on film collecting which he called "a cancer in the belly of the industry." While unauthorized duplication was a serious problem, he made no distinction between someone who privately screened a 16mm print of *Gone with the Wind* and a real pirate who made video copies and distributed them. He ignored the fact that distributors had been selling copies to consumers in various gauges since the twenties. The MPAA's position was that no one should have any prints, period. The hobby was driven underground for a few years.

One of the most notorious cases was when the Burbank district attorney seized the collection of Merle Ray Harlin. Among the reels was the negative of the missing musical number, "Lose That Long Face," from *A Star Is Born*. Jack Warner had ordered the film cut in 1954 and the removed scenes discarded. Since it was pre-print, they had a good case in claiming it stolen. As a distributor myself, I cannot condone removing material from the studio yet the reason this sequence existed was because Harlin saved it from Warner's destruction. Archivists faced a moral dilemma.

Attorney John Zinewicz made an interesting argument on behalf of collectors, "The copyright registration that protects the economic interest of the copyright holder must also protect the continued existence and availability of that work of art for all men and for all time.... Thus, unless some obscure collector had somehow managed to possess a forbidden print, that great film, or all great films, could be lost for all time."[5] Fifty percent of pre–1950 films are considered "lost" and eighty percent of the silent era. All of the pre–1983 color negatives have faded although many were printed in the Technicolor process from 1952–1974. Some of these titles survive in private hands.

The FBI failed to prosecute in many cases because it was impossible to prove the print the collector had in his possession was contraband. He could've purchased it from a TV station that secured it in a "life of the print" deal, pieced it together from sound fill, found it in a garbage can or closed theater and exchange. Copyright infringement or unauthorized exhibition was difficult to claim when the same title was available in Super 8 sound from the distributor. Fortunately, a more enlightened attitude was adopted by some studios and home entertainment companies in the eighties when missing scenes, censored pieces and stereo tracks were borrowed from private collections to restore titles like *Frankenstein* (1931), *King Kong* (1933) and *The Brave One* (1956) on tape and disc. The industry stopped the persecution of film collectors in general and focused on the real villains who were video pirates. The exceptions were Universal and Disney, the litigants in the 1974 home entertainment lawsuit against Sony. Jack Valenti continued to condemn the hobby.

Film collecting remains popular for industry insiders, film buffs, historians and college professors. If digital technology replaces film, collectors may be the final curators of the art form. I believe everything should be saved, even bad pictures and exploitation. They're all part of our cultural history and worthy of study. I own the negatives of my features and have saved everything from the mixing elements to out-takes. I also have vault prints of every title. I hope collectors have saved at least one copy of most classics since we cannot trust the owners to preserve their legacy.

# 9. Digital Cinema

In 1999, George Lucas' *Star Wars: The Phantom Menace* was released. Conventional high speed general release prints were shown in most multiplexes. However, in four select theaters in New Jersey and Los Angeles the movie was exhibited with electronic projectors from Texas Instruments and Hughes-JVC. Lucas was an advocate of this technology, which eliminated release prints entirely. As the owner of Industrial Light and Magic (ILM) which did digital effects for feature films, he had a financial stake in its success. The viability of the format was uncertain so a 35mm copy was run on a platter simultaneously. In the event of a system breakdown, the presentation would switch to film projection. Since the source of this picture was a digital master, the color and sharpness were better than a typical high speed third generation release print.

However, after a hundred years of cinema audiences had become accustomed to the motion picture image. The grain structure, depth of field and lighting design generated the illusion of reality that allowed viewers to suspend their disbelief. Digital cinema altered this perception. The way grain is structured in color pixels affects the sense of depth and the persistence of vision is different than film. Despite its sharpness and color rendition, digital imagery often has a flat, artificial appearance like a computer monitor. When an analogue film image is converted to digital, a compression formula must be used. Digital technology relies on "sampling" any input of visual information whereas film printing copies it continuously across the visual spectrum. Digital sampling often results in flaws due to missing computer data. Movement can be marred by a jitteriness known as "crawl." For example, some of the digitally enhanced fight scenes in *Gladiator* exhibited this type of distortion which was very disorienting. Computer generated imagery also suffered from an inability to reflect light convincingly.

Film stock resolution is not easily converted to zeros and ones. The subtle nuance of emulsion grain and how it's different in each frame is essential to the film look. When negative film is exposed in the camera and processed, each frame contains billions of silver halide crystals with each one uniquely shaped and scattered randomly in the emulsion. Digital imagery is fixed by the number of pixels. As Thomas G. Wallis of Kodak notes, "It is physically impossible for them (video devices) to capture all the image that we expect to see on film. The shortfall shows up primarily in color resolution.... In the captured image, this shows up as a lack of texture.[1] "Of course, a person had to be familiar with the film look at its peak to make these arguments. Assuming the best case scenario, film did generate a specific response in the viewer as Wallis continued, "They are part of a silent language, which evokes emotional responses. You can both see and feel the difference in emotional content."[2] This eloquent defense of the medium did not stop Kodak from developing their own digital projection system.

*Star Wars: The Phantom Menace* probably looked good to uncritical viewers in this test engagement. It was a fantasy and Lucas' goal was not to simulate reality like a conventional drama. I thought the movie resembled a cross between an animated feature and a video game rather than a live action story. The computer generated (CG) effects lacked the realism of the optical effects photographed in VistaVision in 1977. The 70mm versions of the first three pictures were superior presentations and had a greater impact. Since I'm a fan of the series, I was disappointed with the changes utilized in the latest edition. Miramax screened *An Ideal Husband* shortly after the Lucas film and just missed being the first company to introduce electronic cinema. Other movies that were given limited digital presentations included Disney's *Toy Story 2, Bicentennial Man, Mission to Mars* and *Dinosaur* in 1999. Warner Bros. exhibited *The Perfect Storm* and *Space Cowboys* in London's Leicester Square cinemas via DLP projectors in 2000 to try and establish the format overseas. Fox released *Titan A.E.* via Internet Protocol IP system over Qwest's secure virtual private network (VPN) cable to the SuperComm trade show in Atlanta as a demonstration. In 2000, Miramax screened *Shakespeare in Love* and *Life is Beautiful* via JVC's ILA e-cinema technology and premiered *Bounce* digitally in New York with satellite delivery from Boeing.

## Electronic Projection History

"Electronic Cinema" dated back to the beginning of the television medium. The concept of exhibiting a video image began in 1950. By 1951 there were approximately 65 theaters set up for large-screen television transmission in various systems. The Swiss Ediphor video projection machine was installed at the Roxy Theater in New York City at the cost of $30,000. It used its own carbon arc lamphouse to broadcast an enlarged standard NTSC bandwidth of 525 lines of resolution. RCA installed a color system at the Colonial Theater in New York which used three color lens barrels that were synchronized and superimposed in a 9 foot by 12 foot image but it was only used for demonstration purposes. The company had previously set up their black and white PT-100 video projection machine at Fabian's Brooklyn-Fox Theater. It utilized a 16 by 20 ft. image with the unit placed 62 ft. in front of the screen. The cost of the machine was $15,650. The Trad was a competing company that provided a 15 by 20 ft. picture from 65 feet in front of the screen but was also adaptable for rear projection 30 feet behind the screen. A built-in ventilating system guarded against heating the component parts. It was manufactured by Motiograph which also made 35mm projectors. The projection tubes were advertised as highly efficient at low cost and required a maximum of only 30,000 volts. Theater-View by Telecoin Corp. provided a 14 by 11 foot picture from 25 feet in front of the screen or could be used as a rear screen system. Ultrasonic, developed by Skiatron, was a rear-screen operation with a 15 by 10 foot picture and arc lamp projection.

Paramount developed a bizarre variation which was sold by Century Projector corporation. A 35mm B&W kinescope was filmed off a television screen on reversal stock. Inside the film booth was a high speed processing machine which enabled the 35mm image to be projected as a delayed "live broadcast." The manufacturers claimed that the delay between kinescope recording and processed film image was only one minute. The cost was $25,000.

"Videofilm" was a similar format developed by General Precision Laboratory in 1950. It used 16mm film rather than 35mm but was more expensive at $33,000. The same company also offered a video projector with a precision corrector lens for balanced light distribution over the entire screen. The speed of the lens was f./0.67 with a diaphragm provided for reducing off-axis aberrations at the edges. It had a recirculation system for cooling the optical barrel and keeping it dust proof. It was constructed by Simplex, another film equipment manufacturer with a throw distance of 65 feet and a 20 by 15 ft. image.

These units were not designed to compete with standard feature film fare. The concept was to broadcast alternate programming as a supplement. Among the subjects aired on video projectors in selected theaters in 1951 was President Truman's State of the Union message in ten theaters, the first exclusive theater telecast of a college basketball game by the Fabian Palace in Albany and other sporting events. An organization called Theater Network Television was created with Nathan L. Halpern as the head. One of the few successful theater broadcasts was the Rocky Marciano vs. Jersey Joe Walcott fight. It grossed $400,000 in 50 theaters in 30 cities. 120,000 people attended. Another popular program shown on video projectors in 31 theaters in 21 cities was The Metropolitan Opera House broadcast of *Carmen*. It attracted 50,000 viewers and grossed $125,000. However, these were exceptions. Although there were 65 theaters with TV equipment in 23 states by the mid-fifties, most cinemas lost money on the deal. Detailed below is a list of theaters that contained video projection in the fifties in each state.

**California**
Fresno
Huntington Park
Downtown
Orpheum
Paramount (Los Angeles)
Ritz
Paramount (San Francisco)
Telenews

**Colorado**
Paramount

**District of Columbia**
Capitol
Keith's

**Florida**
Florida
Capitol
Carib

**Illinois**
Crown
Marbro
State Lake
Loop
Tivoli
Uptown

**Indiana**
Indiana

**Iowa**
Paramount

**Louisiana**
Saenger

**Maryland**
Century
Metropolitan
Stanley
State

**Massachusetts**
Pilgrim
State

**Michigan**
Eastown
Michigan
Palms State

**Minnesota**
Paramount

**Missouri**
State

**Nebraska**
Orpheum

**New Jersey**
Asbury Park
Camden

**New York**
Albany
Binghamton
Buffalo

**New York City**
Fordham (Bronx)
Fox (Brooklyn)

Marine (Brooklyn)
Guild (Manhattan)
Victoria (Manhattan)
Prospect (Flushing)

**North Carolina**
Carolina

**Ohio**
Albee
Allen
Hippodrome
State
Keith's
Rivoli

**Pennsylvania**
Stanley (Chester)
Warner
Stanley (Philadelphia)
J.P. Harris
Penn
Stanley (Pittsburgh)

**Utah**
Utah

**Virginia**
Byrd
National

**Washington**
Orpheum

**Wisconsin**
Riverside
Warner

According to *Film Daily*, 1955 was considered "The Year of Replacement" for theater owners. New equipment had to be installed for CinemaScope, VistaVision, Todd-AO and magnetic or Perspecta stereophonic sound. Owners had to decide which units to acquire and balance the cost and profit potential of these new formats. Projection television machines were the least desirable since they didn't bring in enough consistent customers to warrant the expense compared to CinemaScope Fox features which were very popular. The FCC was also slow and cautious in granting licenses for alternate forms of broadcasting. The equipment remained in some of the above mentioned theaters through the early sixties although it in many cases it was rarely used.

Based on industry reviews of the time, the quality of theater television was poor since the NTSC signal with 525 lines of resolution was not able to withstand the enlargement on theater screens. As the screens got bigger, they looked worse. Other than the novelty of watching a live event, they were no competition for the motion pictures. In 1952, Cinerama and 3-D were introduced followed by CinemaScope in 1953, VistaVision in 1954 and Todd-AO in 1955. The improved image quality of film made the inferiority of projected video signals combined with the expense of the equipment unmarketable. These systems were gradually phased out. New York had the largest number of TV projectors with ten in operation including The Paramount, Guild Newsreel and Victoria theaters in Manhattan. Within a few years the equipment was considered obsolete.

The concept was revived overseas in 1980. EMI installed four video projectors in provincial sites in England. In each case, the "videotheatres" were created out of auditoriums that were former disused restaurant areas which could not accommodate 35mm. Advent projectors were mounted on the ceiling, close to the screens. While they were somewhat better than early U.S. broadcasts due to the higher PAL bandwidth of 625 lines of resolution, the machines produced an image that was only 8 ft. in width. The cost of the unit was $10,000 which was considerably more expensive than film projectors at the time. Response was not good nor were industry reviews. As Simon Perry reported in *Variety*, "Economics aside, there are still problems over image-definition and picture-brightness. Latter can be intensified by using a special high-reflectivity screen, but the benefit is directional — viewed from side-seats it doesn't work."[1]

## D-Cinema

Two decades later, the advent of digital technology inspired the industry attempt it again. The media referred to it as D-Cinema. Since it premiered in 1999, three major digital systems were introduced with many others in the wings. Texas Instruments' DLP (Digital Light Processing) Cinema Projector became the leader because of their association with Lucasfilm. The projector is small and weighs approximately 75 lb. without the lens, lamphouse and power supply. The manufacturer's claimed brightness was 10,000 ANSI lumens maximum with a 5,000 watt lamphouse and TI custom retro-reflector. It utilizes the Digital Light Processing (DLP) chip and ultrahigh-bandwidth digital videotape as the source. In industry tests, the anamorphic lens broke up the colors around pixel edges. The cost of the unit is approximately $100,000.

BarcoGraphics' 9300 DLC is another projector. This unit weighs 207 lb. without the lens. It uses a 3-panel, flat-mirror dichroic system with optical integrator. The lamp is 1800 watts with the manufacturer's claimed brightness at 6800 lumens. In industry tests, the color and brightness weren't as uniform as the Texas Instruments' unit. The cost is approximately $80,000 and the lens $6,000.

NEC HiVid 6500 is the third system which weighs 238 lb. without the lens. It uses a 3-chip cube-based dichroic system with optical integrator. It has a manual zoom, motorized-focus lens and lens shift. The lamp is a 1,600 watt xenon with a manufacturer's claimed brightness at 6500 ANSI lumens. According to industry tests, NEC images were "softer" than the other projectors. The cost is approximately $90,000 and the lens $10,000. All three systems are currently being tested and upgraded.

Other participants included the QuVIS corporation which designed and manufactured the QuBit video server that provides three essential functions including in-theater storage, compression and control of digital motion pictures. Williams Communications Vyvx Services provide secure fiber-optic transmission for digital motion pictures through its network operations center and satellite uplink support.

Kodak has also developed a proprietary system that uses digital imaging chips from JVC, Inc. which they claim offer twice the resolution of competing chips. Technicolor formed a joint venture with Qualcomm, a developer of mobile-phone network standards, to distribute feature films to theaters through satellite transmissions with an ABSolute TM image compression technology with reduced storage requirements. Christie, a "platter" manufacturer, has a digital projector in partnership with Texas Instruments with the trade name, Digipro SLH-D. The Boeing Company teamed with Creative Artists Agency to offer a satellite delivered system they called "Boeing Digital Cinema." At least on the surface it appears that the industry has abandoned film for the future.

The multiple systems being offered to theaters are incompatible and may lead to a format war. Cinemas who invest in equipment that doesn't survive will suffer financial loss as those did who subsidized earlier video formats. This contrasts sharply with 35mm film which has been standardized for most of its history. Most experts believe that 4K (12 million pixels) is needed to "simulate" 35mm resolution and 8K (24 million pixels) for 70mm. Current DLP-Cinema digital projection systems have a fixed resolution on the chip of 1280 × 1024 which is analogous to 2K (6 million pixels) and falls short of the 4K minimum. Digital advocates claim that it's good enough. The question is, good enough for what? The 20 foot screens in smaller multiplexes may be acceptable but not the newer 50 foot wall to wall megaplex screens. Since the audience sits closer to the screen, the pixels would be noticeable in the front rows.

Electronic cinema could be summarized as a high end video projector that exhibits color pixels instead of film's photographic emulsion. Cineplexes that utilize this technology could more accurately be described as "videoplexes." While featuring sharp images with high resolution color, it isn't "Glorious Technicolor" or 70mm. It is also inferior to a first generation camera negative print from a fully exposed negative with classic studio cinematography. It may be better in terms of color rendition than the high-speed third generation sub-standard prints currently shown in multiplexes derived from underexposed negatives with bland photography. Cynically put, D-Cinema may be superior to the motion picture medium in decline but no match for the quality of film at its peak.

If one or more of these digital formats replace motion picture film in theaters, there are important considerations. Color negatives will continue to be used for a while because of their superior resolution. Digital by its very nature approximates the film source regardless of how many bits and pixels are used to create the image. Its primary advantage is the ability to reproduce data over and over without a loss of quality but the digital master will be a conversion of the negative's emulsion. Depending on the type of compression the formats utilize, aliasing and other artifacts may be apparent on screen. Will the industry be willing to toss out one hundred years of advancements in motion pictures to replace them with untested and unstable electronic technology?

Digital companies advertise that switching to electronic cinema will eliminate the platter scratches and bad projection common over the last three decades. This is a ridiculous argument since the same inept managers and operators will be running the videoplexes. Current digital systems still require good focus on the Xenon lamp. If many outlets can't run 35mm correctly, what makes them think they can handle the maintenance of complicated electronic technology? Considering the cost differences, if theaters wanted to improve their presentations they could hire a professional to run the projectors rather than switch formats.

Another option would be to use digital videotape (or other digital source materials) for principal photography. Lucas shot *Star Wars Episode II* digitally. Another advocate is James Cameron, who used computer generated effects throughout *Titanic* (1997). While the digital release copies will be an exact replication of the master, will cinematographers be able to utilize the subtle lighting effects possible on today's emulsion stock? Digital formats have the ability to change the color, locations and backgrounds of each shot. They can also "morph" the characters with CG effects (e.g. *Terminator 2*). Will future movies contain actors or computer animated people? Will viewers suspend their disbelief and become emotionally involved in the story when the sets, locations, stunts and performers are artificial? Will cinema continue to be a medium that photographs actual events that occur in physical space or will everything on screen be electronically altered? Will movies be permanently fixed in their cultural context or digitally enhanced in a succession of "special editions?" It will be a brave new world indeed.

As it stands now, exhibitors have little motive to switch to electronic projection. The equipment costs are astronomical and no one knows what type of problems will arise. Electronics are more affected by heat and humidity than motion picture projectors. There are also hidden costs in the incompatible formats. The Texas Instruments system requires a 5,000 watt Xenon lamphouse. Few cinemas utilize that size bulb which are expensive to replace. There are surviving large screen cinemas and drive-ins and this new technology may not be practical for their use. What will DLP images look like on a 60 foot or 100 foot wide screen? Digital advocates might not care but those theater owners do. Audiences may be more willing to accept film grain than color pixels the size of basketballs.

## Archival Considerations

There are archival problems with electronic cinema. One of the reasons a lot of films have survived is because there were so many hard copies. Camera negatives, interpositives, internegatives, black and white separations, fine grain masters, dupe negatives and numerous release prints were manufactured on motion pictures for both domestic and foreign release. Film collectors saved cut footage and censored scenes which is how they were restored. The missing footage of *Dr. Jekyll and Mr. Hyde* (1932) came from foreign sources. Robert A. Harris used various materials to restore

*Lawrence of Arabia* and *My Fair Lady* including camera negatives, separations and out-takes.

New low fade estar base stock is estimated to have a 75 to 100 year life expectancy. Black and white film and dye transfer prints may last longer. Martin Scorsese's color fading campaign of the eighties persuaded many distributors to upgrade their storage facilities to extend the life of their negatives. Studios like Universal now have state of the art vaults.

In future digital formats, there will be fewer hard copies. Digital masters and copies will be on magnetic tape or digital data discs. Some may use a computer hard drive. Others will beam the digital signal from a satellite which increases the threat of piracy. None of these systems are archival. The U.S. National Media lab stated that the best case scenario for the survival of magnetic media is approximately 20 years. Most videotapes from the sixties have deteriorated due to their polyurethane binder. Magnetic media is subject to magnetization loss, edge oxidation and tape wear. Compact Discs have problems too and the stability of Digital Video Discs is unknown. As technology changes, it may be difficult to recover the data from obsolete processes. Early video formats that were used professionally and abandoned include two inch and one inch videotape. There may be no way of restoring "lost" digital masters.

The other question is the preservation of original film elements. Will the studios continue to pay for expensive, temperature controlled storage vaults for their negatives or will they transfer them to digital formats and destroy the masters? This has happened in the past. Universal discarded all of their silent film negatives in 1947 which were considered obsolete. Fox did the same with their three strip B&W Technicolor negatives after they were transferred to CRI in the seventies as previously mentioned. Will there be another archival crisis twenty years later when digital masters have lost their data and the camera negatives they were derived from no longer exist? I hope that some of these concerns are addressed before it's too late.

# 10. The Fate of Film

The moviegoing experience as it existed prior to 1968 appears to be gone in most areas with the exception of select venues. The demise of the Production Code and Seal combined with changes in content resulted in a drop in weekly attendance. New Hollywood directors and exploitation distributors abandoned whole segments of the audience and geared their product to a targeted youth crowd. Exhibitors twinned their theaters and built small screen multiplexes to compensate. In the late seventies there was an attempt to restore the lost general audience but cable and video-cassette competition undermined their gains in the eighties. The quality of home entertainment improved as the theatrical experience declined. Technicolor, 70mm and other superior processes were phased out over the years. In the nineties, there was a movement within the industry to replace cinema megaplexes with digital videoplexes and put the final nail in the coffin of the motion picture art form.

## *Survival of the Medium*

The trouble with defending film is it's been so degraded over the past three decades by poor cinematography, sub-standard release prints, inferior projection, small screens and shoddy showmanship. Fortunately, all of the elements still exist to restore the medium. Detailed below is a list of suggestions. Platter projection and Xenon illumination have become universal so the goal would be to make them work effectively. Operators should take crash courses in professional film handling and learn the craft so SMPTE standards are adhered to. The person who shows the film should be a vital part of the presentation even if they're running multiple machines. They must constantly monitor each screen to check focus, light levels and run appropriate Dolby and digital test loops for each new feature that's booked. Prints should be cleaned with media rollers and Film Guard as needed. Projectionists should be paid well since minimum wage workers have no motivation to do a good job. Inept or cynical theater managers should be replaced by people who want to put on a good show for paying customers.

In terms of theater design, simple modifications like installing wall to wall screens with curtains should be implemented in places that lack them. No screen should be smaller than 30 foot wide with 40 or 50 ft. ideal for big budget presentations. The curtains could be automated with cue tape functions so they open as the trailers begin. Even with limited space, the house could be decorated with promotional materials supplied by the distributor. Standees could be placed outside the door of each cinema. Program books could be printed by distributors and sold at the concession stands as souvenirs. A little bit of showmanship would go a long way in restoring the concept of moviegoing as an event. It's also a great deal of fun for the participants. At least one theater per complex should be set aside for independent films, foreign features and classic revivals. This would give audiences real choice instead of two screens within a complex playing the same Hollywood blockbuster.

I would also like to propose an Internet database of every theater in the country with viewer participation. Patrons could rate each screen in terms of performance of the film they were exhibiting. This would encourage competition among the theaters and inspire them to improve quality. Theater managers could log on to verify viewer complaints had been remedied. Consumers could also indicate the type of pictures they preferred to see including classic revivals and reissues of popular recent films.

Cinematography also needs to be improved to match the quality that was standard thirty years ago. Advanced T-grain emulsion, 70mm and the revived dye transfer process are available and should be utilized. Fully exposed negatives with dramatic compositions and use of color will be enhanced by this technology. Theatrical motion pictures should not resemble made for television programs. Both large format and dye transfer presentations should be advertised as they were in the past when "color by Technicolor" was prominently featured on the posters and in the newspaper ads. Contemporary directors of photography should study the work of Freddie Young, Robert Burks and other brilliant craftsmen. While there have been some recent films like *Pearl Harbor* that simulate the classic studio look, most productions have a long way to go in replicating the breathtaking visuals of *Lawrence of Arabia* or *Vertigo* much less surpassing them.

The studios, financiers and filmmakers should limit the number of

R rated films and keep most pictures in the PG/PG-13 category to expand the movie going demographic. This is not post-production censorship but pre-production coordination between distributors and exhibitors. Ticket prices should be lowered so a night at the movies doesn't cost a fortune. Ideally, they should be no more expensive than a videocassette rental. Many people would probably enjoy cartoons before the feature. There are hundreds of classics in the vaults and it might create a new generation of short subject filmmakers. For example, some of Rowan Atkinson's hilarious *Mr. Bean* shows were remade on film. Prints were struck but never booked. A while ago new *Roger Rabbit* cartoons were made. Including this type of programming with the feature would give audiences their money's worth. As home entertainment continues to improve, cinemas must offer something unique to retain consumer interest. Cutting corners is not the way to go.

Finally, the industry needs a new president of the MPAA who acts as a mediator to all factions of the business including exhibitors, independent producers and moviegoers. Booking terms have to be reasonable so the theaters can profit along with the distributors. It serves no one's interest if they all go bankrupt. Production budgets must be controlled since they have an impact on the consumer with inflated ticket prices and concessions costs. The way films are currently financed, produced, distributed and exhibited is fiscally unsound as evidenced by the number of theater chains in Chapter 11. The fact that some are profiting is unacceptable if others in the industry are suffering including exhibitors and cinema customers.

On the other hand, generations have gone by that define cinema and the moviegoing experience in different terms than I do. Whether motion pictures as a medium will survive or be merged with other technologies will be determined in the near future.

# Appendix A:
# Surviving Movie Palaces

The following theaters still offer the classic "moviegoing experience" as described in Chapter 1. Of course, the success of the presentation will be limited by the quality of the release copy sent by the distributor. Most are restored movie palaces and performing arts centers that offer live performances as well as films. Some are surviving single screen cinemas although given the precarious nature of exhibition, a number might have closed in the interim. I've omitted the palaces that no longer exhibit movies or those that have been twinned. Others are currently undergoing restoration but are not in operation. Ideally, classics look the best in these large screen houses since the style of cinematography leant itself to this kind of presentation. Those who attend a performance in one of these cinemas might have a difficult time returning to multiplexes.

## Alabama

*The Alabama Theatre*
Located in Binghamton, Alabama. This cinema was built in 1927 by Paramount-Publix and has Moorish architecture and 2,200 seats. It was restored in 1998 as a performing arts center that occasionally shows films.

*The Bama Theatre*
Located in Tuscaloosa, Alabama. This cinema opened in 1938 and was an Atmospheric house with Art Deco architecture and 800 seats. It shows classic, foreign and art films.

*Capri Theatre*
Located in Montgomery, Alabama. This cinema was built in 1941 and was originally called the Clover. It's currently operated by the Capri Community Film Society.

*Saenger Theater*
Located in Mobile, Alabama. This cinema has Italian Renaissance architecture and has recently been restored.

*The Strand Theater*
Located in Atmore, Alabama. This is one of the few surviving single screen houses that plays new first run films.

## Arkansas

*The UA Cinema 150*
Located in Little Rock, Arkansas. This cinema has a dome roof, similar to the Cinerama dome in California and an enormous 120 degree curved screen installed for the Dimension 150 70mm process in 1966.

## California

*The Aero*
Located in Santa Monica, California. This art deco theater was built in 1939 and saved by Robert Redford. It operates for the benefit of his Sundance Channel.

*The Alex Theatre*
Located in Glendale, California. This 1,460 seat theater was modeled after the *Egyptian*. The Alex Film Society programs occasional festivals there.

*The Arlington Theater*
Located in Santa Barbara, California. This 2,025 seat palace was constructed in the Mission Revival style and is an atmospheric. It gives the illusion that viewer is watching the film in an outside courtyard.

*Balboa Theatre*
Located in San Francisco, California. This Art Deco palace was built in 1926 and continues to operate as a second-run theater for contemporary films.

*Bridge Theatre*
Located in San Francisco, California. This Art Deco palace exhibits independent and foreign films. It was named after the Golden Gate Bridge.

*Century 21*
Located in San Jose, California. This theater was built in 1964 as a Cinerama theater. The curved unit was replaced by a flat one but it remains a large screen venue in the area.

*Cinerama Dome*
Located in Hollywood, California. One of the few remaining Cinerama palaces, it opened in 1963 to premiere *It's a Mad, Mad, Mad, Mad World* in the 70mm process. It's currently being redesigned to exhibit three panel Cinerama for future engagements. Its dome like structure is one of the icons of sixties showmanship.

*Cove Theatre*
Located in La Jolla, California. This theater was built in 1948 in the Art Moderne/

Streamline style of architecture. It remains in business exhibiting independent and foreign films.

*Crest Theatre*
Located in Los Angeles, California. This art deco theater features shooting stars on the ceiling as the beginning of each show. It books contemporary films.

*The Crest Theatre*
Located in Sacramento, California. This 975 seat Art Deco theater was recently restored.

*Egyptian Theatre*
Located in Hollywood, California. This is the famous movie palace with Egyptian architecture that was originally a single screen house. It is now a twin with a large screen upstairs with 733 seats and a smaller screen downstairs with 650 seats. Although not as impressive as it was in its heyday, it's worth visiting for the unique design.

*El Capitan Theatre*
Located in Hollywood, California. This theater was originally the *Paramount Theater*. It was restored and reopened by the Disney company and Pacific Theaters which uses it to premiere the features from that studio. It's across the street from Mann's *Chinese Theatre*.

*Fox Theatre*
Located in Redwood City, California. This 1,400 seat Art Deco palace is an atmospheric that was placed on the National Register of Historic Places. It's now a performing arts center that plays movies, concerts and special events.

*Grenada Theater*
Located in Santa Barbara, California. This 950 seat palace has Spanish architecture and is a performing arts center that shows movies and concerts.

*Grauman's Chinese Theatre*
Located in Hollywood, California. Although this Art Deco palace with the famous Chinese front was originally a single screen house, it's now a seven theater multiplex. I include it on the list because of its famous cement prints of the stars outside the entrance.

*The Guild*
Located in Menlo Park, California. This 300 seat palace still features a huge screen with two golden wings on either side and Art Deco architecture. It now shows foreign films.

*Ken Cinema*
Located in San Diego, California. This Art Moderne theater was built in 1946 and now exhibits foreign films and restored classics. It still uses reel to reel projection with carbon arc illumination which makes it worth attending for those attributes alone.

*Lido Cinema*
Located in Newport Beach, California. This palace is an atmospheric cinema that plays contemporary films.

*Mann Bruin*
Located in Los Angeles, California. This Art Moderne cinema was designed by S. Charles Lee and plays contemporary films.

*Mann Festival Theater*
Located in Los Angeles, California. This is a smaller 560 seat palace with Spanish architecture that plays contemporary films.

*Mann National Theatre*
Located in Los Angeles, California. This 1,112 seat theater was built in the sixties and is more of a large screen venue than a movie palace. It plays contemporary films.

*Mann Regent Theater*
Located in Los Angeles, California. This 400 seat theater is one of the surviving single screen houses rather than a palace. It plays contemporary films.

*Mann Village Theater*
Located in Los Angeles, California. This 1,400 seat palace features Mission Revival architecture and an exterior tower. It's often used for movie premieres.

*Mt. Burney Theatre*
Located in Burney, California. This is a smaller 252 seat Art Deco palace that has a 33 ft. wide screen and neon lighting on its front facade. It plays contemporary films.

*Park Theatre*
Located in Menlo Park, California. This 688 palace was designed in Art Moderne architecture in 1947. It plays independent films and foreign language movies.

*Rialto Theater*
Located in South Pasadena, California. This single screen palace features a gargoyle that sits on top of the proscenium. It plays contemporary films.

*The Silent Movie Theatre*
Located in Hollywood, California. This 224 seat theater has Art Deco architecture by John Hampton. It exhibits movies and special events.

*The Stanford Theatre*
Located in Palo Alto, California. This 1,175 palace has Greek Revival architecture by A.B. Heinsbergen. It's one of the few surviving Repertory houses in the country.

*Tower Theater*
Located in Fresno, California. This 900 seat palace has Art Deco architecture designed by S. Charles Lee. It features live performances and movies.

*The Vine*
Located in Hollywood, California. This is a 400 seat single screen theater that plays contemporary films on a sub-run basis.

*Visalia Fox Theater*
Located in Visalia, California. This 1,285 seat palace has Mission Revival architecture and is a Performing Arts Center that plays movies.

*Vista Theater*
Los Angeles, California. This is a mini-palace that still shows movies but is located in a decaying section of the city.

*Vogue Theater*
Located in Hollywood, California. This 500 seat palace was designed by S. Charles Lee in 1934. It's now a Conference Center that also shows movies.

*Warner Grand Theater*
Located in San Pedro, California. This Art Deco theater hosts live performances and movies.

*WGA Theatre*
Located in Beverly Hills, California. This 540 seat single screen house is restricted to members of the Writer's Guild of America and restricts the general public unless they are invited as guests.

## Colorado

*Bluebird*
Located in Denver, Colorado. This is a restored 600 seat Art Deco palace that books concerts and movies.

*Rialto Theater*
Located in Loveland, Colorado. This 1,040 seat Art Nouveau palace was designed by Robert K. Fuller in 1920. It's now a performing arts center that plays concerts and books silent films.

## Connecticut

*Cinestudio*
Located in Hartford, Connecticut. This neo–Vintage single screen house plays second-run, classics and art house product.

*County Cinema*
Located in Watertown, Connecticut. This single screen house has Colonial Revival architecture and plays second-run films.

*Garde Art Center*
Located in New London, Connecticut. This 1,488 seat house has Moorish architecture and is a performing arts center that still plays occasional classics.

*State Theater*
Located in Stanford, Connecticut. This large screen single house plays second-run features.

## Delaware

*Clayton Theatre*
Located in Dagsboro, Delaware. This small 150 seat theater features Art Deco architecture and continues to play movies.

# District of Columbia

*The Cinema*
Located in Washington, D.C. This 800 seat large screen single house was renovated in 1997 and continues to play movies.

*Uptown Theater*
Located in Washington, D.C. This 840 seat Art Deco palace is one of the few single screen theaters that still has a deeply curved Cinerama screen that is 32 feet x
70 feet. It plays contemporary films and classics.

# Florida

*Florida Theatre*
Located in Jacksonville, Florida. This 1,978 seat theater palace features Moorish
architecture. It's a performing arts center that plays movies.

*San Marco Theater*
Located in Jacksonville, Florida. This single screen theater has Art Deco architecture and continues to show movies.

*Tampa Theatre*
Located in Tampa, Florida. This 1,446 seat palace is an Atmospheric theater and
is a performing arts center today that plays classics.

# Georgia

*Rylander Theater*
Located in Americus, Georgia. This 600 seat palace opened in 1921 and was restored
in 1999. It plays second-run films and classics.

*Zebulon Theatre*
Located in Cairo, Georgia. This 650 seat theater opened in 1936. It was restored
in 1990 and is still an Adams style building with a reduced seating capacity of 350
that plays sub-run G and PG films.

# Hawaii

*Palace Theatre*
Located in Hilo, Hawaii. This Neo-Classical style palace opened in 1925 and is
built out of redwood. It was restored in 1991 as a performing arts center that plays
movies.

# Idaho

*Burley Theatre*
Located in Burley, Idaho. This 500 seat palace has Italian Renaissance architecture. It was restored in 1991 and continues to play movies.

*Egyptian Theater*
Located in Boise, Idaho. This Egyptian style palace has recently been restored. It
plays classics from the twenties and thirties.

# Illinois

*Adelphi Theater*
Located in Chicago, Illinois. This 900 seat Art Moderne still exists but only plays East Indian movies.

*Avon Theatre*
Located in Decatur, Illinois. This Art Nouveau theater opened in 1916 and was restored in 1999. It currently plays art house and foreign films.

*Egyptian Theatre*
Located in Dekalb, Illinois. This palace features Egyptian architecture and was opened in 1929. It's now a performing arts center that plays movies.

*Gateway Theater/Copernicus Cultural & Civic Center*
Located in Chicago, Illinois. This 2,045 seat Atmospheric palace designed by Mason Rapp. Today it's a performing arts center that plays silent films with musical accompaniment on a Mighty Wurlitzer organ.

*Heart Theater*
Located in Effingham, Illinois. This 500 seat Art Deco theater was designed by Carl T. Meyer. It originally contained 720 seats but was modified in the seventies. It continues to show movies.

*Lincoln Square Theatre*
Located in Decatur, Illinois. This 1,200 seat palace was built in 1916. Today it features live performances and movies.

*Music Box Theatre*
Located in Chicago, Illinois. This 850 seat Atmospheric palace was designed by Louis A. Simon. Although a smaller 100 seat screen was added in 1991, the main screen remains a venue for independent and art house films. I booked my Technicolor feature, *Space Avenger*, there in 1991.

*New Art Theatre*
Located in Champaign, Illinois. This palace was originally known as the Park Theatre and opened in 1913. It remains a single screen house that plays independent films.

*Normal Theater*
Located in Normal, Illinois. This 395 seat Art Moderne theater plays independent films and classics.

*Patio Theater*
Located in Chicago, Illinois. This 1,500 seat palace continues to show movies.

*The Princess*
Located in Rushville, Illinois. This Art Deco theater continues to show movies.

*Tivoli Theatre*
Located in Downers Grove, Illinois. This 1,928 seat palace was built with French Renaissance architecture and is now a performing arts center that plays classics.

*Vic Theatre*
Located in Chicago, Illinois. This 1,000 seat Art Nouveau theater was designed by

John E. Pridmore in 1912 and shows cult, art house movies and revival theater product. It has three bars and sells alcohol to patrons.

## Indiana

*Eagles Theatre*
Located in Wabash, Indiana. This 700 seat Art Deco palace continues to show movies.

*Paramount Theatre Center and Ballroom*
Located in Anderson, Indiana. This 1,475 seat Art Deco Atmospheric was designed by John Eberson in 1929. It's now a performing arts center that plays movies.

*State Theatre*
Located in Anderson, Indiana. This movie palace is undergoing restoration. It continues to show movies after 70 years of operation.

*Town Theatre*
Located in Highland, Indiana. This 425 seat theater was designed in Medieval style architecture. It opened in 1946 and plays foreign films now.

## Iowa

*Hardacre Theatre*
Located in Tipton, Iowa. This 375 seat Art Deco theater was renovated in 1991 and now shows second-run films.

*Merle Hay Mall Cinema*
Located in Des Moines, Iowa. This 808 single screen house has the largest screen in Des Moines and continues to play movies.

*Story Theatre/Grand Opera House*
Located in Story City, Iowa. This 388 seat theater was built in 1913 as a Vaudeville house. It continues to show movies.

## Kansas

*Augusta Historical Theatre*
Located in Augusta, Kansas. This Art Deco theater was designed by Karl and Robert Boller in 1935. It continues to show movies.

*Chief Theatre*
Located in Coldwater, Kansas. This 300 seat Art Deco theater continues to play new movies.

*Doric Theatre*
Located in Elkhart, Kansas. This theatre, which is currently being restored, shows silent films and stage shows.

*Dream Cinemas*
Located in Russell, Kansas. This 220 seat Art Deco theatre plays movies on weekends.

*Isis Theatre*
Located in Lucas, Kansas. This theatre was renovated in 1999 and features live performances and movies.

*Mainstreet Theatre*
Located in Beloit, Kansas. This 200 seat theatre was built in 1928. It is currently being renovated and plays movies.

*Orpheum Theater*
Located in Wichita, Kansas. This 1,300 Art Moderne was designed by John Eberson in 1922. It's now a performing arts center that plays movies.

*Sherman Theater*
Located in Goodland, Kansas. This single screen theatre is a performing arts center that plays movies.

*Ute Theater*
Located in Mankato, Kansas. This single screen house plays movies on Friday, Saturdays and Sundays.

# Kentucky

*Kentucky Theater*
Located in Lexington, Kentucky. This 1,276 seat palace has Italian Renaissance architecture. It plays concerts and movies.

# Maine

*Alamo Theatre*
Located in Bucksport, Maine. This theater was renovated and rebuilt in 1992 and is currently a performing arts center that plays classic and contemporary movies. The second floor contains a film library and study center.

*The Criterion*
Located in Bar Harbor, Maine. This 869 seat Art Deco theatre was opened in 1932 and plays concerts and movies.

*The Leavitt Fine Arts Theatre*
Located in Ogunquit, Maine. This 636 seat large screen house opened in 1923 and continues to play first run movies.

# Maryland

*Old Greenbelt Theatre*
Located in Greenbelt, Maryland. This 500 seat theatre features a 40 ft. wide screen and continues to play movies.

*The Senator Theatre*
Located in Baltimore, Maryland. This 900 seat Art Deco theatre was designed by John Zink in 1939. It continues to play first run movies.

# Michigan

*Fox Theatre*
Located in Detroit, Michigan. This 5,000 seat palace was designed by C. Howard Crane. It was recently restored and is now a performing arts center that occasionally plays classic movies.

*Landmark Main Art Theatre*
Located in Royal Oak, Michigan. This single screen theatre continues to show independent, foreign and classic films.

*Pines Theatre*
Located in Houton Lake, Michigan. This 450 seat theatre is designed like a log cabin chalet and continues to show movies.

*Pix Theatre*
Located in Lapeer, Michigan. This 306 seat Art Deco theatre is a community arts center that shows second-run movies.

*The Redford Theatre*
Located in Detroit, Michigan. This 1,661 seat Atmospheric cinema opened in 1928 and continues to be used for movies and special events.

*State Theatre*
Located in Detroit, Michigan. This 2,200 seat palace was designed in Renaissance architecture by C. Howard Crane. It's used for concerts and shows classic movies during the summer.

*Temple Theatre*
Located in Saginaw, Michigan. This 2,300 seat Art Deco palace has a theatre organ and plays classic movies.

## Minnesota

*Norshor Theater*
Located in Duluth, Minnesota. This Art Deco palace plays concerts and movies. It is also being restored.

*Riverview Theater*
Located in Minneapolis, Minnesota. This 700 seat Art Deco palace features stadium seating and plays movies.

*Suburban World*
Located in Minneapolis, Minnesota. This 800 seat Atmospheric plays classic movies.

*Uptown Theater*
Located in Minneapolis, Minnesota. This 800 seat Art Deco palace functions as a Art house and also plays foreign films.

## Missouri

*Englewood Theater*
Located in Englewood, Missouri. This Art Deco theatre opened in 1949 and continues to play movies.

*Fox Theater*
Located in St. Louis, Missouri. This 4,500 seat Atmospheric was built by C. Howard Crane in 1929. It's now a performing arts center that continues to play movies.

*Hi-Point Theater*
Located in St. Louis, Missouri. This single screen house continues to operate as an Art theatre.

*Orpheum Theater*
Located in St. Louis, Missouri. This single screen house is a performing arts center that shows movies.

*Princess Theater*
Located in Aurora, Missouri. This Art Deco theatre was built by Carl and Robert Boller. It continues to show movies.

*The Trail*
Located in St. Joseph, Missouri. This 300 seat single screen house plays second run movies.

## Montana

*The Ellen Theater*
Located in Bozeman, Montana. This single screen house was built by Fred Willson and continues to play movies.

*Roxy Theatre*
Located in Forsyth, Montana. This 214 seat house features Spanish architecture by Charles Wood. It continues to show movies.

## Nebraska

*The Grand*
Located in Grand Island, Nebraska. This single screen house was built in the thirties and featured stadium style seating which was unusual. It continues to play movies.

*Joyo Theatre*
Located in Lincoln, Nebraska. This 300 seat Art Deco theatre shows old and new movies.

*Midwest Theatre*
Located in Scottsbluff, Nebraska. This 700 seat Art Moderne was built in 1946. It shows second run movies now.

*Omaha Orpheum Theater*
Located in Omaha, Nebraska. This 2,500 seat Baroque palace plays movies on reel to reel projectors with carbon arc lamphouses.

*Rococo Theater*
Located in Lincoln, Nebraska. This 1,800 seat palace features Renaissance architecture. It shows concerts and classic movies now.

## Nevada

*Gem Theatre*
Located in Pioche, Nevada. This single screen house continues to play second run movies.

# New Hampshire

*The Colonial Theatre*
Located in Keene, New Hampshire. This 886 seat Art Deco theatre plays concerts, stage shows and movies.

## *New Jersey*

*Broadway Theatre*
Located in Pitman, New Jersey. This 1,036 seat theater opened in 1926 and featured French Renaissance architecture. It continues to show movies.

*Loews Jersey Theatre*
Located in Jersey City, New Jersey. This 3,300 seat Baroque theatre was built by the Rapps. While under restoration, it plays classic movies and is set up for dual projector 3-D and Perspecta sound.

*Union County Arts Center*
Located in Rahway, New Jersey. This palace is now a performing arts center that occasionally shows movies. The house also has a Mighty Wurlitzer organ.

# New Mexico

*El Cortez Theater*
Located in Truth or Consequences, New Mexico. This single screen house was built in 1941 in Mission Revival architecture. In plays first run movies.

*El Sol Theatre*
Located in Silver City, New Mexico. This 200 seat theatre was built in Pueblo Deco architecture and continues to play first run movies.

*Gila Theatre*
Located in Silver City, New Mexico. This 520 seat Art Moderne theatre was designed by August A. Neuner. It continues to play first run movies.

# New York

*59th Street East Cinema*
Located in New York, New York. This single screen house is part of the "Block cinemas" on the east side of the city that plays Art house movies.

*Astor Plaza*
Located in New York, New York. This large single screen house is built underground and is one of the few theaters that's still set up to play 70mm. In the past it was a top cinema for event movies. However, it's declined somewhat in terms of presentation with platter projectors and management running the machines rather than professionals. It was one of my favorite cinemas until the nineties.

*The Bardavon*
Located in Poughkeepsie, New York. This 944 seat building was originally an opera house which was built in 1869. It's currently a performing arts center with a large 40 foot screen and Wurlitzer organ. It plays classic movies. I've attended some screenings and the presentations are impressive.

*Beekman Theatre*
Located in New York, New York. This single screen Art Moderne cinema plays first run movies and still has curtains.

*Glen Theater*
Located in Watkins Glen, New York. This single screen house is a sub-run theatre.

*The Palace Theater*
Located in Lake Placid, New York. This palace was built in 1926 and continues to operate by showing stage shows and silent movies.

*The Paramount Center of the Arts*
Located in Peekskill, New York. This 1,025 seat Art Deco palace was built in 1929 by the Rapp brothers. It became a grind-house in the seventies then folded. It was restored and reopened as a performing arts center in 1988 with Robert Frischmuth as the programmer. It plays foreign films and classics. The projection booth contains two Norelco 70mm projectors. I premiered my feature, *Space Avenger*, there in 1989 and co-sponsored a Technicolor Festival in 1988.

*Paris Theatre*
Located in New York, New York. This single screen art house plays foreign films focusing on French cinema.

*Proctor's Theatre*
Located in Schenectady, New York. This 2,700 seat Atmospheric was designed by Thomas Lamb. Today it's a performing arts center that plays movies.

*The Riviera*
Located in North Tonawanda, New York. This single screen theatre plays second run movies.

*Star Theatre*
Located in Dansville, New York. This 279 seat Art Deco cinema was built in 1921. I plays first run movies.

*The Strand*
Located in Brockport, New York. This single screen theater was designed in the Neo-Vintage style and plays movies.

*The Ziegfeld*
Located in New York, New York. This 1,131 seat large screen cinema has curtains and is one of the few premiere theatres left in the city. It played *Close Encounters of the Third Kind* in 1977 and the *Lawrence of Arabia* restoration in 1989. It continues to show first run features.

# North Carolina

*The Rialto*
Located in Raleigh, North Carolina. This single screen theatre continues to play movies.

*Stevens Center*
Located in Winston-Salem, North Carolina. This 1,380 seat theatre is a performing arts center that plays movies.

# North Dakota

*The Fargo Theatre*
Located in Fargo, North Dakota. This 800 seat Art Moderne theatre opened in 1926 and is now a performing arts center that plays movies.

# Ohio

*Akron Civic Theatre*
Located in Akron, Ohio. This 2,672 seat Atmospheric was designed by John Eberson. It now shows concerts and movies.

*Canton Place Theatre*
Located in Canton, Ohio. This 1,509 seat Atmospheric was designed by John Eberson. It plays movies and stage shows.

*Cla-Zel Theatre*
Located in Bowling Green, Ohio. This 501 seat single screen house is a performing arts center that plays movies and is undergoing restoration.

*The Highland Theater*
Located in Akron, Ohio. This 1,100 Art Deco theatre was built in 1936. It now books concerts and serves as an Art house.

*The Mariemont*
Located in Cincinnati, Ohio. This single screen cinema was renovated and serves as an Art house now.

*Ohio Theatre*
Located in Columbus, Ohio. This 200 seat Baroque palace was designed by Thomas W. Lamb in 1928. It's a performing arts center now that plays movies.

*Palace Theater*
Located in Marion, Ohio. This 1434 seat Atmospheric was designed by John Eberson and features a Wurlitzer organ. It's a Performing Arts Center now that plays movies.

*St. Marys Theater/Grand Opera House*
Located in St. Marys, Ohio. This 465 seat theater is 106 years old. It plays classic movies.

*The Studio 35 Camera*
Located in Columbus, Ohio. The 400 seat single screen house opened in 1938. It shows second run features and serves beer.

*Towne & Country Theater*
Located in Nowalk, Ohio. This 924 seat Art Deco theatre was designed by John Eberson. It now shows live concerts and movies.

# Oregon

*Alger Theatre*
Located in Lakeview, Oregon. This Art Deco theatre continues to show first run movies.

*Bagdad Theatre*
Located in Portland, Oregon. This 700 seat palace opened in 1927 has Middle Eastern architecture. It is a second run theater that sells beer at its concessions.

*Bijou Theatre*
Located in Lincoln City, Oregon. This 174 seat single screen house opened in 1937. It functions as an Art house and is used for film festivals.

*Cameo Theatre*
Located in Newberg, Oregon. This Art Deco theater plays first run movies.

*CineMagic*
Located in Portland, Oregon. This single screen theater plays Indian films.

*Columbia Theatre*
Located in Saint Helens, Oregon. This single screen theatre plays first run films.

*The Grenada Theatre*
Located in The Dalles, Oregon. This theater opened in 1929 and featured Moorish architecture. Today it shows live performances and movies.

*The Guild Theatre*
Located in Portland, Oregon. This single screen house is now used for film festivals.

*The Harbor Theatre*
Located in Forence, Oregon. This 220 seat Art Deco theatre plays first run movies.

*The Rio Theatre*
Located in Sweet Home, Oregon. This small, single screen house is known for it's large marquee and continues to play movies.

*Valley Theater*
Located in Raleigh, Oregon. This single screen theater has murals on the wall and plays second run films.

## Pennsylvania

*The Campus Theatre*
Located in Lewisburg, Pennsylvania. This 600 seat Art Deco theatre was built in 1940. It plays first run independent and art house movies today.

*Coudersport Theatre*
Located in Coudersport, Pennsylvania. This 500 seat single screen theatre plays second run movies.

*Elks Theatre*
Located in Middletown, Pennsylvania. This 469 seat Art Deco theatre still has a balcony and continues to show movies.

*The Glen Theatre*
Located in Glen Rock, Pennsylvania. This 180 seat theatre features Colonial Revival architecture and plays second run movies.

*Marietta Theatre*
Located in Marietta, Pennsylvania. This single screen house was built in 1914 and plays classic movies.

*Prince Music Theater*
Located in Philadelphia, Pennsylvania. This 1,066 seat theatre opened in 1921. It books stage shows and plays movies today.

*Roxy Theater*
Located in Northhampton, Pennsylvania. This 558 seat theatre was built in 1921 and features Art Deco architecture by David Supowitz. Today it books stages shows and movies.

*Watson Theatre*
Located in Watsontown, Pennsylvania. This 490 seat single screen house was built in 1940. It continues to show movies.

## Rhode Island

*Avon Cinemas*
Located in Providence, Rhode Island. This single screen Art Deco house continues to play movies.

*Providence Performing Arts Center*
Located in Providence, Rhode Island. This 3,200 seat palace is now a performing arts center that shows classic movies.

*Stadium Theatre*
Located in Woonsocket, Rhode Island. This single screen Art Nouveau theater was built in 1926. It's now a performing arts center that plays classic movies.

## South Carolina

*American Theater*
Located in Charleston, South Carolina. This single screen Art Moderne cinema is a theater restaurant which offers dining and a movie.

## Texas

*The Cliftex Theatre*
Located in Clifton, Texas. This 199 seat single screen theatre plays movies part of the week.

*The Lakewood Theater*
Located in Dallas, Texas. This 900 seat Art Deco cinema was designed by H.F. Pettigrew in 1938. It now plays concerts and movies.

*Majestic Theatre*
Located in Eastland, Texas. This single screen Art Moderne cinema plays first run and classics as well as concerts.

*Paramount Theatre*
Located in Austin, Texas. This 1,300 seat palace was built in 1915. Today it books stage shows and classic movies.

*Paramount Theatre*
Located in Abilene, Texas. This 1,300 seat palace features Spanish Moorish architecture. It's now a performing arts center that shows classic movies.

*Perot Theater*
Located in Texarkana, Texas. This single screen house was built in 1924. It contains a statue dedicated to Ross Perot's brother who died at age 3. The theatre continues to play movies.

*Texan Theater*
Located in Cleveland, Texas. This single screen theatre was built in 1939. It shows second run films today.

## Utah

*Huish Theatre*
Located in Richfield, Utah. This 650 seat Art Moderne with a large balcony was built in 1938 and continues to show movies.

*Peery's Egyptian Theater*
Located in Ogden, Utah. This 822 seat palace was built in 1924 and features Egyptian architecture. It's now used for live performances and movies.

*The Tower*
Located in Salt Lake City, Utah. This single screen cinema was built in 1926 but no longer has its tower facade. It currently used as an art house.

*Villa Theatre*
Located at Salt Lake City, Utah. This 975 Art Moderne cinema was designed by Alton B. Paulson and features an enormous 93 ft. wide, deeply curved Cinerama screen. It continues to play movies.

## Virginia

*Arlington Theater*
Located in Arlington, Virginia. This Art Deco palace is now a restaurant cinema which serves beer.

*Byrd Theatre*
Located in Richmond, Virginia. This 1,394 seat palace features French Renaissance architecture by Fred A. Bishop. It plays second run movies now.

*Commodore Theatre*
Located in Portsmouth, Virginia. This 506 seat Art Deco cinema was designed by John Zink in 1945. It continues to show first run movies.

*Lyric Theatre*
Located in Blacksburg, Virginia. This 487 seat Art Deco theater was designed by Louis Phillipe Smithey. It plays concerts, stage shows and movies.

*State Theater*
Located in Lexington, Virginia. This single screen house continues to show movies.

## Washington

*Capitol Theatre*
Located in Olympia, Washington. This 800 seat theatre functions as an art house and shows foreign, independent and classic movies. It also books concerts.

*Egyptian Theatre*
Located in Seattle, Washington. This single screen house is run by the Seattle International Film Festival and plays independent, classic and foreign movies.

*The G Theatre*
Located in Mossyrock, Washington. This 350 seat Art Deco theater continues to play movies.

*The Kiggins*
Located in Vancouver, Washington. This 600 seat Art Deco theatre was designed by Day Hilborn. It shows classic movies and film festivals.

*Liberty Theatre*
Located in Camas, Washington. This theatre was originally called the Granada and features Moorish architecture. It continues to show movies.

*Lincoln Theatre*
Located in Mount Vernon, Washington. This 500 seat theatre was designed by William Aitken in the Mediterranean Renaissance style. It's now a performing arts center that shows movies.

*McEachern Auditorium*
Located in Seattle, Washington. This 373 single screen location shows movies along with concerts and other live venues.

*The Neptune*
Located in Seattle, Washington. This unique single screen theater features a nautical architecture with tridents and portholes. It continues to show movies.

*Olympic Theatre*
Located in Arlington, Washington. This restored single screen house has digital sound and plays first fun films.

*Raymond Theatre*
Located in Raymond, Washington. This 450 seat Atmospheric is owned by the city and plays movies.

*Rose Theatre*
Located in Port Townsend, Washington. This restored old theater plays Art house movies.

*Roxy Theatre*
Located in Bremerton, Washington. This 900 seat Art Moderne cinema is used for church events and movies.

*Roxy Theatre*
Located in Eatonville, Washington. This 400 seat Art Deco theatre plays first run movies.

*Seattle Cinerama*
Located in Seattle, Washington. This 808 seat theater is one of the few locations still set up to show widescreen movies on a deeply curved screen. It continues to play movies.

*Uptown Theater*
Located in Port Townsend, Washington. This 350 seat theatre is made of wood and plays first run films.

*Vashon Theater*
Located in Vashon, Washington. This 500 seat Art Deco theatre plays first run movies.

## Wisconsin

*Al Ringling Theater*
Located in Baraboo, Wisconsin. This cinema was designed in French Renaissance style in 1915. It shows concerts and movies today.

*Majestic Theater*
Located in Madison, Wisconsin. This single screen house continues to show movies.

*Rosebud Cinema Drafthouse*
Located in Wauwatosa, Wisconsin. This single screen theatre plays first run movies.

*Times Cinema*
Located in Milwaukee, Wisconsin. This single screen house is run by Eric Levin and plays classic movies. Levin booked my feature, *Run for Cover* in 3-D and contributed editorial suggestions to this book.

*America Theatre*
Located in Casper, Wyoming. This single screen house continues to show movies.

*Rialto Theatre*
Located in Casper, Wyoming. This theatre features a large screen and balcony. It continues to show movies.

# Appendix B:
# Surviving Drive-Ins

Detailed below are the surviving drive-ins. Most show first-run contemporary films and many utilize radio sound rather than the portable speakers on a stand. The atmosphere of an ozoner is not what it used to be when cartoons proceeded sub-run double bills and children played on swings below the screen tower. Given the precarious nature of exhibition, some might have folded in the interim. At least the drive-ins all have large screens and there remains some appeal in seeing movies under the stars.

## Alabama

Argo Drive-In Theatre
411 Drive-In Theater
Cheyenne Drive-In
Blue Moon Drive-In Theater
Piedmont Drive-In Theatre
Roanoke Drive-In
King Drive-In Theatre

## Arizona

Apache Drive-In Theater
Glendale 9 Drive-In
Scottsdale Six Drive-In
De Anza Drive-In Theatres

## Arkansas

112 Drive-In
Stone Drive-In Theatre
Kenda Drive-In Theatre

## California

Skyline Drive-In Theatre
South Bay Six Drive-In Theatre
Ceres Drive-In Theatre
Solano Drive-In
Red's Crescent Drive-In
Woodward Park 4 Drive-In
Kings Drive-In Theatre
Motor Vu Twin Drive-In
LakePort Auto Movies
Vineland Drive-In Theatre
Madera Drive-In Theatre
Marysville Drive-In Theatre
Mission Drive-In Theatre
Harbor Drive-In Theatre
Pottersville Drive-In Theatre
Rubidoux Drive-In Theatre
Van Buren Drive-In Theatre
Forty-niner 6 Drive-In Theatre
Sacramento On-Six Drive-In
Sunrise Drive-In Theater

South Bay Drive-In
Capitol Drive-In Theatre
Sunset Drive-In Theatre
Skyview Drive-In Theatre
Hi-Way Drive-In Theatre
Santee Drive-In Theatre
Valley 99 Drive-In Theatre
Smith's Ranch Drive-In
Mooney Auto Theatre

## Colorado

88 Drive-In Theatre
Tru Vu Drive-In Theatre
Commanche Drive-In
Big Sky Drive-In
Rocket Drive-In Theatre
Cinderella Twin Drive-In
Holiday Twin Drive-In Theatre
Best Western Movie Manor
Star Drive-In
Star Drive-In Theatre
Mesa Drive-In Theatre
Kar-Vu Drive-In Theatre
Starlite Drive-In Theatre

## Connecticut

Mansfield Drive-In Theatre
Southington Drive-In
Pleasant Valley Drive-In

## Delaware

Diamond State Drive-In Movies

## Florida

Joy-Lan Drive-In and Swapshop
Thunderbird Drive-In Theatre
    (Swap/Show)
Northside Drive-In Theatre
Playtime Triple Family Drive-In
Silver Moon Drive-In Theatre
Trail Drive-In Theater
Naples Drive-In Theater
Ocala Drive-In Theatre
Ruskin Drive-In Theatre
Fun Lan Drive-In Theatre

## Georgia

Starlight Six Drive-In Theatre
Swan Drive-In
Commence Drive-In Theatre
Jesup Drive-In Theatre

## Idaho

Terrace Drive-In Theatre
Spud Drive-In Theatre
Sunset Audo Vue Theatre
Motor Vu Drive-In
Sky Vu Theatre
Perma Motor Vue Drive-In
Sunset Drive-In Theatre
Teton View Drive-In
Teton View Drive-In
Idan-Ho Drive-In
Grande-W Drive-In Theater
Motor-Vu Drive-In Theater

## Illinois

Hi-Lite 30 Drive-In Theatre
Bal Skyview Drive-In
Placke's Drive-In
Bel-Air Drive-In
Midway Drive-In Theatre
34 Drive-In Theatre
Harvest Moon Drive-In Theatre
Cascade Drive-In Theater
Hilltop Drive-In Theatre
Skyview Drive-In
McHenry Indoor and Outdoor
Cicero Outdoor Theatre
Fairview Drive-In Theatre
Green Meadows Drive-In
Clark Drive-In Theatre

## Indiana

Starlite Drive-In Theatre
Auburn Garritt Drive-In
Georgetown Drive-In Theatre
Huntington Drive-In Theatre
CTS Outdoor Theatre
Clermont Deluxe Outdoor Theaters
Mel's Drive-In

Melody Drive-In Theatre
Linton Drive-In Theatre
Skyline Drive-In Theatre
Holiday Drive-In
Monticello Drive-In Theatre
Center Brook Drive-In
Ski-Hi Drive-In Theater
Ski-Vue Drive-In Theatre
Tri-Way Drive-In Theatre
Holiday Drive-In Theatre
Cinema 67 Drive-In
Skyline Drive-In
Back to the 50s Drive-In
49'er Drive-In Theatre
Bel-Air Drive-In
13-24 Drive-In Theater
Shannon's Airline Auto

## Iowa

Concil Bluff's Drive-In
61 Drive-In Theatre
Valle Drive-In

## Kansas

Star-Vue Drive-In Theatre
South Drive-In Theatre
Star-Vu Drive-In Theater
54 Drive-In Theatre
Twin Drive-In Theatre
Kanopolis Drive-In Theatre
Pageant Drive-In Theatre
I-70 Drive-In Theatre
Boulevard Drive-In Theatre
Star Drive-In
Mid-Way Drive-In Theatre
Chisholm Trail Drive-In
Starlite Drive-In Theatre

## Kentucky

Tri City Drive-In
Moonlite Drive-In Theatre
Calvert Drive-In
Corbin Drive-In Theatre
Franklin Drive-In Theatre
Starlite Drive-In
Irvington Drive-In
Jeremiah Drive-In

Kenwood Drive-In Theatre
Judy Drive-In Theatre
Knox Drive-In
27 Drive-In Theatre
Bourbon Drive-In Theatre
Stanford Drive-In Theatre
Mountain View Drive-In Theatre
Sky View Drive-In
Pixie Drive-In Theater
Shy-Vue Drive-In Theatre

## Maine

Bridgton Drive-In
Skylite Drive-In
Saco Drive-In
Skowhegan Drive-In Theatre
Pride's Corner Drive-In

## Massachusetts

Leicester Drive-In Theater
The Mendon Twin Drive-In
Mohawk Drive-In
Tri-Town Drive-In Theater
Northfield Drive-In Theater
Wellfleet Drive-In Theatre

## Maryland

Bengies Drive-In Theatre
Bel Air Drive-In Theatre

## Michigan

Miracle Twin Drive-In Theatre
Hi-Way Drive-In Theatre
Capri Drive-In Theater
Michigan Drive-In
Ford-Wyoming Drive-In Theatre
Five-Mill Drive-In Theatre
US 23 Twin Drive-In Theatre
Sunset Auto Theatre
Cherry Bowl Drive-In
Cinema 2 US-2 Drive-In
Getty 4 Screen Drive-In

## Minnesota

Cottage View Drive-In

75 Hi Drive-In Theater
Vali-Hi Drive-In Theatre
Verne Drive-In Theater
Starlite Drive-In Theatre
Long Drive-In
65 Hi Drive-In Theatre
Sky Vu Drive-In Theater

## Montana

Silver Bow Twin Drive-In
Midway Drive-In Theatre
Midway Drive-In Theatre
Westernaire Drive-In
Libby Drive-In Theatre
Sunset Drive-In
Prairie Drive-In Theatre

## Nebraska

Sands Hill Drive-In
Kearney Drive-In Theatre
Starlite Drive-In Theatre

## Nevada

Century Las Vegas 6 Drive-In Theatre
El Rancho Drive-In Theatre

## New Hampshire

Northfield Drive-In Theatre
Weirs Drive-In Theatre
Milford Drive-In Theatre
Theater Meadows Drive-In

## New Mexico

Fiesta Drive-In Theatre
Apache Drive-In
Fort Union Drive-In
85 Drive-In

## New York

Bay Drive-In Theatre
Allegany Drive-In
Grandview Drive-In
Hollywood Drive-In Theater
Fingerlakes Drive-In

East Avon Vintage Drive-In
Malta Drive-In Theatre
Bath Drive-In Theater
Buffalo Drive-In Theater
Hi-Way Drive-In Theatre
Delavan Drive-In Theatre
Elmira Drive-In Theatre
Glen Drive-In Theatre
Greenville Drive-In Theatre
Mountain Drive-In Theatre
Hyde Park Drive-In Theater
Valley Brook Drive-In
Transit Drive-In Theatre
Fifty-Six Auto Theatre
Sunset Drive-In
Fair Oaks Drive-In Theater
Hathaway's Drive-In Theatre
Midway Drive-In Theatre
El Rancho Drive-In
Silver Lake Drive-In
Portsville Drive-In
Overlook Drive-In Theatre
West Rome Drive-In Theater
Jericho Drive-In Theatre
Unadilla Drive-In Theatre
Warwick Drive-In Theatre
Lin-Ray Drive-In Incorporated

## North Carolina

Badin Road Drive-In Theatre
Belmont Drive-In Theatre
Starlite Drive-In Theater
Eden Drive-In
Fort Drive-In Theatre 1, 2 & 3
Tri-City Drive-In Theatre
Raleigh Road Outdoor Theatre
Bessemer City Drive-In Theatre
Bright Leaf Drive-In Theatre
Sunset Drive-In
Waynesville Drive-In Theatre

## North Dakota

Lake Park Drive-In Theatre

## Ohio

Starlite Drive-In Theatre
Pymatuning Lake Drive-In

Magic City Drive-In
Melody 49 Drive-In Theatre
Lake Drive-In Theatre
Mayfield Road Drive-In Theatre
Oakley Drive-In Theater
Memphis Drive-In Theatre
South Drive-In Theatre
Kingman Drive-In Theatre
Aut-O-Rama Outdoor Theatre
Skyborn Drive-In Theatre
Kanuga Drive-In Theatre
Ranch Drive-In Theatre
Holiday Auto Theatre
Stardust Drive-In
Hi Road Drive-In
Skyview Cruise-In Theater
Scioto Breeze Drive-In
Springmill Drive-In Theatre
Sunset Drive-In Theatre
Starlight Drive-In Theatre
Park Layne Drive-In Theatre
Van-Del Drive-In
Star View Drive-In
Midway Drive-In Theatre
40 East Auto Theatre
East Bend Drive-In
Lynn Auto Theatre
Sandusky Drive-In Theatre
Auto Vue Drive-In Theatre
Melody Cruise Drive-In
Springfield Drive-In
Ridgeway Drive-In Theatre
Winter Drive-In Theatre
Tiffin Drive-In Theatre
Sundance Kid Drive-In Theatre
Dixie Drive-In Theatre
Blue Sky Drive-In Theater
Skyway Drive-In Theatre
Elroad Twin Drive-In Theatre
Wilmington Drive-In

## Oklahoma

Chief Drive-In Theatre
Beacon Drive-In Theatre
Cinema 69 Theatres
Winchester Drive-In
Airline Drive-In
Poteau Theatres/Tower Drive-In

Tee Pee Drive-In
Tahlequah Drive-In Theatre
Admiral Twin Drive-In
66 West Twin Drive-In

## Oregon

Frontier Drive-In
Motor-Vu Drive-In Dallas
Hermiston Drive-In Theatre
Trail Twin Indoor Outdoor
Wilderness Outdoor Theatre
Starlite Indoor & Outdoor
Mototvu Drive-In Theatre
K & D Drive-In Theatre
M & F Drive-In Theatre
Ninety-Nine West Drive-In
Woodburn Drive-In Theater

## Pennsylvania

Kane Rd Drive-In
Moonlite Drive-In Theatre
Malden Drive-In
Brownsville Drive-In Multi
    Theaters
Pioneer Drive-In
Skyview Twin Drive-In
Carroll Town Drive-In
Super 322 Drive-In
Columbia Drive-In
The Comet Drive-In
Dependable Drive-In
Corry Drive-In Theatre
Point Drive-In Theatre
Haar's Drive-In
Garden Drive-In Theatre
Peninsula Drive-In Theatres
Sky Vu Drive-In
Laurel Drive-In
Maple Drive-In Theatre
Silver Drive-In
Palace Garden Drive-In
Family Drive-In
Hi-Way Drive-In Theatre
Mahoning Valley Drive-In
Port Drive-In Theater
Tri-States Drive-In Theater
Midway Drive-In Theater

Pike Drive-In Theatre
Evergreen Drive-In Theater
Motor Vu Drive-In Theatre
Cumberland Drive-In Theatre
Galaxy Drive-In Theatre
Shankwieler's Drive-In Theatre
Bar Ann Drive-In Theater
Circle Drive-In Theatre & Fair
Starlite Drive-In Theatre
Reynolds Drive-In
Becky's Drive-In Theatre Incorporated
Sunset Drive-In Theatre
Wysox Drive-In Theatre

## Rhode Island

Rustic Tri-View
Drive-In Theatre

## South Carolina

Plaza 21 Drive-In Theatre
Auto Drive-In
Big Mo. Drive-In Theatre

## South Dakota

Midway Drive-In
Starlite Outdoor Theatre
Pheasant Drive-In
Siskota Drive-In Theatre
Pix Drive-In Theatre
Winner Drive-In Theatre

## Tennessee

Midway Drive-In Theatre
Twin City Drive-In Theatre
Pink Cadillac Drive-In
Broadway Drive-In Theatre
Dunlap Drive-In Theater
State Line Drive-In Theatre
Sky-Vue Drive-In
Midtown Drive-In Theatre
Macon Drive-In Theater
Highway Fifty Drive-In
Parkway Drive-In
Southwest Twin Drive-In

Summer Quartet Drive-In
Valley Drive-In Theatre

## Texas

Town and Country Drive-In
Tascosa Drive-In
Fiesta Drive-In Theatre
The Last Drive-In Picture Show
Graham Drive-In Theatre
Brazos Drive-In
Zocalo Theater & Performance Art Co.
Sky-Vue Drive-In Theatre
Valley Drive-In Theatre
Wes-Mer Drive-In
Midway Drive-In
Mission Drive-In Theatre
Crossroads Drive-In Theater
Apache Drive-In

## Utah

Basin Drive-In Theatre
Motor Vue Drive-In Theatre
North Star Drive-In Theater
Timp Drive-In Theatre
Pioneer Twin Drive-In Theatre
Echo Drive-In Theatre
Redwood Drive-In Theatre
Valley Vu Drive-In Theatre
Art City Drive-In
Motor Vue Theatre

## Vermont

Randall Drive-In
Sunset Drive-In
Fairlee Drive-In
St. Albans Drive-In

## Virginia

Moonlite Theatre
Starlite Drive-In Theatre
Fort Union Drive-In Theatre
Keysville Drive-In
Hull's Drive-In Theatre
Park Palace Drive-In
Central Drive-In Theatre
Hiland Drive-In Theatre
Family Drive-In Theatre

## Washington

Valley 6 Outdoor Theaters
Samish Twin Drive-In
Auto Vue Theatre
Dayton Drive-In Theatre
Puget Park Drive-In
Your Drive-In Theatre
Rodeo Tri Drive-In Theatre
Blue Fox Drive-In Theater
River-Vue Drive-In
Skyline Drive-In Theatre
Wheel-In Motor Movie
Vue Dale Drive-In Theatre
Country Drive-In Theatre

## West Virginia

Pipestem Drive-In Theatre
Hilltop Drive-In Theatre
Warner Drive-In Theater
Glendale Drive-In Theatre
Grafton Drive-In
Meadow Bridge Drive-In
Mt. Zion Drive-In

Jungle Drive-In Theatre
Pineville Drive-In Theatre
Sunset Drive-In Theatre
Moonlite Drive-In Theatre

## Wisconsin

Gemini Drive-In Theatre
Forty-One Twins Outdoor Theatre
Starlite Drive-In Theater
18 Outdoor Theatre
Keno Outdoor Theater
Sky-Vu Drive-In Theatre
Moonlight Outdoor Theatre
Skyway Drive-In Theater
Sky-Vue Drive-In
Big Sky Drive-In Theatre

## Wyoming

Park Drive-In Theater
Sky-Hi Drive-In Theatres
Lusk Drive-In
Vali Drive-In Theatre
Skyline Drive-In Theatre

# Appendix C: Classic Studio Style Cinematographers

Detailed below is a list of major cinematographers that photographed films in the "classic studio style" during the zenith of motion picture exhibition 1952–1968. I consider them the finest in the history of the medium and I've listed all of their features including those shot in black and white. Many of the titles were photographed in large format negatives and printed in the Technicolor dye transfer process. Some are available on VHS and DVD. Unfortunately, no video format can replicate the quality of the original release prints that were derived from fully camera negatives with dramatic lighting and compositions.

An asterisk (*) indicates the movie had exceptional color cinematography based on my opinion of what good camerawork should be.

## Robert Burks

Robert Burks was born in 1909. He began his career as a special effects technician on films like *Marked Woman* (1937), *Kings Row* (1942) and *Night and Day* (1946). He also did the montages in *Brother Orchid* and *They Drive by Night* in 1940. His first two features as a cinematographer were the B movies *Make Your Own Bed* and *Jammin' the Blues* in 1944. His first major film was *The Fountainhead* in 1949 but it was *Strangers on a Train* two years later that began an association with Alfred Hitchcock that defined his style. He won the Oscar for best B&W photography for that film. His collaboration with the director was among the most notable ones in the cinema history. Burks' camerawork and lighting design on pictures like *Rear Window* (1954) and *Vertigo* (1958) were superior in all respects to films of any era. He won another Oscar for the former and a third won for *To Catch a Thief* in 1955 which was shot in VistaVision. In 1954 he filmed

Hitchcock's *Dial M for Murder* in 3-D. Burks' fourth Academy Award was his B&W work in *A Patch of Blue* in 1965. He died in a tragic house fire on May 13, 1968, at age 59.

## FEATURE FILMS

Make Your Own Bed 1944
Jammin' the Blues 1944
Star in the Night 1945
Escape in the Desert 1945
The Verdict 1946
To the Victor 1948
The Fountainhead 1949
Beyond the Forest 1949
A Kiss in the Dark 1949
Task Force 1949
The Glass Managerie 1950
Close to My Heart 1951
Strangers on a Train 1951
The Enforcer 1951
Tomorrow Is Another Day 1951
Come Fill My Cup 1951
Room for One More 1952
Mara Maru 1952
I Confess 1953
Hondo 1953
So This Is Love 1953
The Desert Song 1953
Dial M for Murder 1954

Rear Window 1954*
The Boy from Oklahoma 1954
To Catch a Thief 1955*
The Trouble with Harry 1955*
The Vagabond King 1956
The Wrong Man 1956
The Man Who Knew Too Much
    1956*
The Spirit of St. Louis 1957
Vertigo 1958*
The Black Orchid 1958
North by Northwest 1959*
But Not for Me 1959
The Rat Race 1960
The Great Impostor 1960
The Pleasure of His Company 1961
The Music Man 1962*
The Birds 1963*
Marnie 1964*
Once a Thief 1965
A Patch of Blue 1965
Waterhole #3 1967

## Winton C. Hoch

Winton C. Hoch was born in 1905. He began his career as a 3 strip Technicolor camera operator on *The Vogues of 1937*. Next, he was the associate director of photography on *Dr. Cyclops* (1940) and did the aerial work on *Captain of the Clouds* (1942). He moved up to short subjects and was the cinematographer for the live action scenes in Disney's *The Reluctant Dragon* in 1941. Hoch became one of the top Technicolor cameramen in titles like *Joan of Arc* (1948), *3 Godfathers* (1948), *She Wore a Yellow Ribbon* (1949) and *The Quiet Man* (1952). All of them featured superior color photography. Hoch is best known for his work on *The Searchers* (1956) which was photographed in VistaVision and printed in the dye transfer process. He won Academy Awards for *Joan of Arc*, *She Wore a Yellow Ribbon* and shared the Oscar with Archie Stout for *The Quiet Man*. He died in 1979.

## FEATURE FILMS

The Reluctant Dragon 1941
Dive Bomber 1941
Melody Time 1948
Joan of Arc 1948*
3 Godfathers 1948*
Tap Roots 1948
So Dear to My Heart 1949
Tulsa 1949
She Wore a Yellow Ribbon 1949*
The Sundowners 1950
Halls of Montezuma 1950
Bird of Paradise 1952
The Quiet Man 1952*
The Redhead from Wyoming 1953
Return to Paradise 1953
Mister Roberts 1955

The Searchers 1956*
Jet Pilot 1957
The Missouri Traveler 1958
The Young Land 1959
The Earth Is Mine 1959
Darby O'Gill and the Little People
  1959*
The Big Circus 1959
The Lost World 1960
Voyage to the Bottom of the Sea 1961
Sergeants 3 1962
Five Weeks in a Balloon 1962
Robinson Crusoe on Mars 1963
The Green Berets 1968
Necromancy 1952

## Charles Lang

Charles Lang was born in 1902. He career began in the silent era with *The Night Patrol* (1926) and *Ritzy* (1927). His first Technicolor feature was *The Shepherd of the Hills* (1941). Later features in the process included *Fancy Pants* (1950) and the VistaVision films, *Gunfight at the O.K. Corral* (1957) and *Loving You* (1957). Lang's best color work was in the sixties with titles like *The Magnificent Seven* (1960), *One Eyed Jacks* (1961), *How the West Was Won* (1962), *Charade* (1963) and *Wait Until Dark* (1967). Lang won the Oscar for his B&W work in *A Farewell to Arms* (1932). He died in 1998 of pneumonia.

## FEATURE FILMS

The Night Patrol 1926
Ritzy 1927
The Shopworn Angel 1928
Halfway to Heaven 1929
Innocents of Paris 1929
Behind the Make-up 1930
Seven Days' Leave 1930
Sarah and Son 1930
The Light of Western Stars 1930
Shadow of the Law 1930
For the Defense 1930
Anybody's Woman 1930
Tom Sawyer 1930
The Right to Love 1930

Unfaithful 1931
Vice Squad 1931
Newly Rich 1931
The Magnificent Lie 1931
Caught 1931
Once a Lady 1931
Tomorrow and Tomorrow 1931
No One Man 1932
Thunder Below 1932
A Farewell to Arms 1932
Devil and the Deep 1932
She Done Him Wrong 1933
A Bedtime Story 1933
Gambling Ship 1933

The Way to Love 1933
Cradle Stone 1933
He Learned About Women 1933
Death Takes a Holiday 1934
We're Not Dressing 1934
She Loves Me Not 1934
Mrs. Wiggs of the Cabbage Patch
  1934
The Lives of a Bengal Lancer 1935
Peter Ibbetson 1935
Mississippi 1935
Desire 1936
I Loved a Soldier 1936
Souls at Sea 1937
Angel 1937
Tovarich 1937
Dr. Rhythm 1938
Spawn of the North 1938
You and Me 1938
Zaza 1939
Midnight 1939
The Cat and the Canary 1939
The Gracie Allen Murder Case 1939
Adventure in Diamonds 1940
Women Without Names 1940
Buck Benny Rides Again 1940
The Ghost Breakers 1940
Arise, My Love 1940
Dancing on a Dime 1940
The Shepherd of the Hills 1941
Nothing but the Truth 1941
Sundown 1941
Skylark 1941
The Lady Has Plans 1942
Are Husbands Necessary? 1942
The Forest Rangers 1942
No Time for Love 1943
So Proudly We Hail! 1943
True to Life 1943
Standing Room Only 1944
Frenchman's Creek 1944
The Uninvited 1944
Practically Yours 1944
I Love a Soldier 1944
Here Come the Waves 1944
The Stork Club 1945
Miss Susie Slagle's 1946
Blue Skies 1946
Cross My Heart 1946

The Ghost and Mrs. Muir 1947
Desert Fury 1947
Where There's Life 1947
Miss Tatlock's Millions 1948
My Own True Love 1948
A Foreign Affair 1948
Rope of Sand 1949
The Great Lover 1949
Fancy Pants 1950
September Affair 1950
Copper Canyon 1950
Branded 1950
The Mating Season 1951
The Big Carnival 1951
Peking Express 1951
Red Mountain 1951
The Atomic City 1952
Sudden Fear 1952
Salome 1953
The Big Heat 1953
It Should Happen to You 1954
Phffft! 1954
Sabrina 1954
The Long Gray Line 1955 (un-cred-
  ited)
Female on the Beach 1955
The Man from Laramie 1955*
Queen Bee 1955
Autumn Leaves 1956
Solid Gold Cadillac 1956
The Rainmaker 1956
Gunfight at the O.K. Corral 1957*
Loving You 1957*
Wild Is the wind 1957
Separate Tables 1958
The Matchmaker 1958
Some Like It Hot 1959
Last Train from Gun Hill 1959
Strangers When We Meet 1960
The Facts of Life 1960
The Magnificent Seven 1960
One Eyed Jacks 1961*
Summer and Smoke 1961
Blue Hawaii 1961
How the West Was Won 1961*
Something's Got to Give 1962
A Girl Named Tamiko 1962
Critic's Choice 1963
The Wheeler Dealers 1963

Charade 1963*
Paris—When It Sizzles 1964
Father Goose 1964
Sex and the Single Girl 1964
Inside Daisy Clover 1965
How to Steal a Million 1966
Not with My Wife, You Don't 1966
Hotel 1967
Wait Until Dark 1967*
The Flim-Flam Man 1967

A Flea in Her Ear 1968
The Stalking Moon 1969
How to Commit Marriage 1969
Bob & Carol & Ted & Alice 1969
Cactus Flower 1969
A Walk in the Spring Rain 1970
Doctor's Wives 1971
The Love Machine 1971
Butterflies Are Free 1972
40 Carats 1973

## Lionel Lindon

Lionel Lindon was born in 1905. Like many cinematographers of his era, he began his career in silents acting as the additional camera operator on *Time to Love* in 1927. His first feature as a director of photography was *Let's Face It* in 1943. Other notable B&W titles he shot included *Going My Way* (1944), *Road to Utopia* (1945) and *The Blue Dahlia* (1946). Lindon's first Technicolor feature was *Destination Moon* in 1950. He also filmed *Prehistoric Women* (1950) in Cinecolor and *Drums in the Deep South* (1951) in Super Cinecolor. *Sangaree* (1953) and *Jivaro* (1954) were in Technicolor and 3-D. Lindon's greatest accomplishment was the breathtaking Oscar winning cinematography in Michael Todd's *Around the World in 80 Days* in 1956 which was photographed in 65mm. In later years, Lindon photographed episodes of the TV shows *Alfred Hitchcock Presents*, *Thriller* and *The Munsters* proving that small screen camerawork could be stylish too. Lindon died in 1971.

Feature Films

Let's Face It 1943
Going My Way 1944
Masquerade in Mexico 1945
A Medal for Benny 1945
Duffy's Tavern 1945
Road to Utopia 1945
The Blue Dahlia 1946
O.S.S. 1946
Monsieur Beaucaire 1946
Welcome Stranger 1947
Variety Girl 1947
The Trouble with Women 1947
Tap Roots 1948
The Sainted Sister 1948
Isn't It Romantic? 1948

Top O' the Morning 1949
Alias Nick Beal 1949
The Great Rupert 1950
Quicksand 1950
Without Honor 1950
Prehistoric Women 1950
Destination Moon 1950*
Only the Valiant 1951
The Sun Sets at Dawn 1951
Rhubarb 1951
Hong Kong 1951
Drums in the Deep South 1951
The Turning Point 1952
Japanese War Bride 1952
Caribbean 1952

The Blazing Forest 1952
Sangaree 1953*
Here Come the Girls 1953
The Starts Are Singing 1953
Tropic Zone 1953
Those Redheads from Seattle 1953
The Vanquished 1953
Jamaica Run 1953
Jivaro 1954*
Casanova's Big Night 1954*
The Secret of the Incas 1954
A Man Alone 1955
Hell's Island 1955
Lucy Gallant 1955*
Conquest of Space 1955*
Around the World in 80 Days 1956*
The Scarlet Hour 1956
The Lonely Man 1957
The Black Scorpion 1957

I Want to Live! 1958
Alias Jesse James 1949
The Young Savages 1961
Too Late Blues 1961
All Fall Down 1962
The Manchurian Candidate 1962
The Final Hour 1962
The Devil's Children 1962
The Brazen Bell 1962
McHale's Navy in the Airforce 1965
The Trouble with Angels 1966
Boy, Did I Get a Wrong Number 1966
Grand Prix 1966*
Dead Heat on a Merry Go Round
    1966
Pendulum 1968
Generation 1969
The Extraordinary Seaman 1969

## Ted Moore

British cinematographer Ted Moore was born in 1914 in South Africa. He began his career as a camera operator on the Technicolor features *The African Queen* (1941) and *Genevieve* (1953). His first feature as a director of photography was *April in Portugal* (1954). Moore's greatest work was done on the James Bond features of the sixties. His unique lighting design and rich color cinematography defined the spy genre. Among them were *Dr. No* (1962), *From Russia with Love* (1963), *Goldfinger* (1964), *Thunderball* (1965) and *Diamonds Are Forever* (1971). All of them were printed in the dye transfer process at Technicolor and remain some of the best looking films of the era and among my favorite movies of all time. Other notable color films included *The Trials of Oscar Wilde* (1960) in Technirama and *A Man for All Seasons* (1966). He won an Oscar for his work on the latter. Moore died in 1987.

FEATURE FILMS

April in Portugal 1954
A Prize of Gold 1955
The Cockleshell Heroes 1955
Zarak 1956
Odongo 1956
High Flight 1956
The Gamma People 1956

How to Murder a Rich Uncle 1957
Interpol 1957
No Man Inside 1958
No Time to Die 1958
The Bandit of Zhobe 1959
Killers of Killimanjaro 1959
Idle on Parade 1959

The Trials of Oscar Wilde 1960*
Let's Get Married 1960
Jazz Boat 1960
In the Nick 1960
Johnny Nobody 1961
The Hellions 1061
Dr. No 1962*
Mix Me a Person 1962
The Day of the Triffids 1962
Nine Hours to Rama 1963
Call Me Bwana 1963
From Russia with Love 1963*
Goldfinger 1964*
The Amorous Adventures of Moll
    Flanders 1965
Thunderball 1965*
A Man for All Seasons 1966*

The Last Safari 1967
Prudence and the Pill 1968
Shalako 1968
The Prime of Miss Jean Brodie 1969
The Chairman 1969
Country Dance 1970
Diamonds Are Forever 1971*
She'll Follow You Anywhere 1971
Psychomania 1971
Live and Let Die 1973
The Man with the Golden Gun 1974
Golden Voyage of Sinbad 1974
Orca 1977
Sinbad and the Eye of the Tiger 1977
Dominique 1978
Class of the Titans 1981
Priest of Love 1981

# Robert Surtees

Robert Surtees was born in 1906. He began his career as an assistant cameraman on *Devotion* in 1931 and moved up to camera operator on *A Midsummer Night's Dream* (1935). His first features as the director of photography were *Nursery Rhyme Mysteries, Don't You Believe It, Election Daze, Lost Angel* and *Heavenly Music* in 1943 which was quite an output for one year. His first Technicolor film was *The Unfinished Dance* in 1947. Other notable three strip films were his Oscar winning *King Solomon's Mines* (1950) and *Quo Vadis?* (1951). Surtees' best work was in large format processes in the fifties. He shot *Oklahoma!* (1955) in Todd-AO and *Ben-Hur* (1959) in MGM Camera 65 for which he received his second Academy Award. Other memorable Technicolor features included *Mutiny on the Bounty* (1962), *The Graduate* (1967) and *Sweet Charity* (1969). Surtees's best work featured rich and saturated colors with extraordinary sharpness. In later years he opted more a more subdued style of photography in *Summer of '42* (1971) and *The Sting* (1973). He won Oscars for his photography on *King Solomon's Mines, The Bad and the Beautiful* and *Ben-Hur*. He died in 1985.

## FEATURE FILMS

Nursery Rhyme Mysteries 1943
Don't You Believe It 1943
Election Daze 1943
Lost Angel 1943

Heavenly Music 1943
Two Girls and a Sailor 1944
Thirty Seconds Over Tokyo 1944
Music for Millions 1944

Meet the People 1944
Our Vines Have Tender Grapes 1945
Strange Holiday 1946
Two Sisters from Boston 1946
No Leave, No Love 1946
The Unfinished Dance 1947
A Date with Judy 1948
Tenth Avenue Angel 1948
Big Jack 1949
That Midnight Kiss 1949
The Kissing Bandit 1949
Intruder in the Dust 1949
Act of Violence 1949
King Solomon's Mines 1950*
Quo Vadis? 1951*
The Strip 1951
The Light Touch 1951
The Merry Widow 1952
The Wild North 1952
The Bad and the Beautiful 1952
Ride, Vaquero! 1953
Mogambo 1953*
Escape from Fort Bravo 1953
Valley of the Kings 1954
The Long, Long Trailer 1954
Trial 1955
Oklahoma! 1955*
The Swan
Tribute to a Bad Man 1956
Raintree County 1957*
Les Girls 1957
The Law and Jake Wade 1958

Merry Andrew 1958
Ben-Hur 1959*
It Started in Naples 1960
Cimmaron 1960
Mutiny on the Bounty 1962*
PT 109 1963*
Kisses for My President 1964
The Satan Bug 1965
The Collector 1965
The Hallelujah Trail 1965
The Third Day 1965
The Chase (un-credited) 1966
Lost Command 1966
Doctor Dolittle 1967
The Graduate 1967*
Sweet Charity 1969*
The Arrangement 1969
The Liberation of L.B. Jones 1970
Summer of '42 1971
The Last Picture Show 1971
The Cowboys 1972
The Other 1972
Lost Horizon 1973
Oklahoma Crude 1973
The Sting 1973
The Great Waldo Pepper 1973
The Hindenburg 1975
A Star Is Born 1976
The Turning Point 1977
Bloodbrothers 1978
Same Time, Next Year 1978

## Freddie Young

British cinematographer Freddie Young was born in England in 1902.
He began in the silent era as a second cameraman on films like *The Flag
Lieutenant* (1926) and *The Somme* (1927). He became a director of photography in 1928 with the features *Victory, The Tonic* and *Daydreams*. His
first Technicolor movie was *Caesar and Cleopatra* in 1945. Other notable
three strip color features were *Treasure Island* (1950) and *Ivanhoe* (1952).
Young is best known for his collaboration with director David Lean, which
was the most successful one outside of Hitchcock and Burks. *Lawrence of
Arabia* (1962), *Doctor Zhivago* (1965) and *Ryan's Daughter* (1970) had spectacular color and dramatic widescreen compositions. Other notable color
features included *Lord Jim* (1965) and *You Only Live Twice* (1967). Young's

brilliant sunsets were his trademark. He won Oscars for *Ivanhoe, Lawrence of Arabia, Doctor Zhivago, Ryan's Daughter* and *Nicholas and Alexandra*. He retired in 1985 and became a painter, dying of natural causes in 1998.

FEATURE FILMS

Victory 1928
The Tonic 1928
Daydreams 1928
Blue Bottles 1928
White Cargo 1930
Rookery Nook 1930
A Warm Corner 1930
A Peep Behind the Scenes 1930
The Loves of Robert Burns 1930
Canaries Sometimes Sing 1930
The W Plan 1931
Up for the Cup 1931
Tons of Money 1931
Tilly of Bloomsbury 1931
The Sport of Kings 1931
The Speckled Band 1931
Plunder 1931
A Night Like This 1931
Mischief 1931
The Chance of a Night Time 1931
Carnival 1931
Goodnight Vienna 1932
Yes, Mr. Brown 1932
Thank, Turkey Time 1932
The Mayor's Nest 1932
The Love Contract 1932
Leap Year 1932
The Blue Danube 1932
Up for the Derby 1933
Trouble 1933
That's a Good Girl 1933
Summer Lightning 1933
Night of the Garter 1933
The Little Damozel 1933
The King's Cup 1933
Just My Luck 1933
It's a King 1933
A Cuckoo in the Nest 1933
Bitter Sweet 1933
The Queen's Affair 1934
Nell Gwyn 1934
The King of Paris 1934
Girls Please! 1934

Peg of Old Drufy 1935
Escape Me Never 1935
Come Out of the Pantry 1935
When Knights Were Bold 1936
Two's Company 1936
Three Maxims 1936
This'll Make You Whistle 1936
Limelight 1936
The Frog 1936
Fame 1936
Victoria the Great 1937
Sunset in Vienna 1937
The Rat 1937
Millions 1937
London Melody 1937
Sixty Glorious Years 1938
A Royal Divorce 1938
Goodbye, Mr. Chips 1939
Nurse Edith Cavell 1939
Busman's Honeymoon 1940
Contraband 1940
Forty-Ninth Parallel 1941
The Young Mr. Pitt 1942
Caesar and Cleopatra 1945*
Bedelia 1946
While I Live 1947
So Well Remembered 1947
The Winslow Boy 1948
Escape 1948
Conspirator 1949
Edward My Son 1949
Treasure Island 1950*
Calling Bulldog Drummond 1951
Ivanhoe 1952*
Giselle 1952
Time Bomb 1953
Mogambo 1953*
Knights of the Round Table 1953
Betrayed 1954
Bedeviled 1955
Bhowani Junction 1956
Invitation to the Dance 1956*
Lust for Life 1956

The Barrets of Wimpole Street 1957
The Little Hut 1957
Island in the Sun 1957
Indiscreet 1958
The Inn of Sixth Happiness 1958
I Accuse! 1958
Gideon's Day 1958
Solomon and Sheba 1959*
Hand in Hand 1960
The Greengage Summer 1961
Gorgo 1961
Lawrence of Arabia 1961*
The 7th Dawn 1964
Lord Jim 1965*
Doctor Zhivago 1965*
Rotten to the Core 1965

The Deadly Affair 1967
You Only Live Twice 1967*
Battle of Britain 1969
Ryan's Daughter 1970*
Nicholas and Alexandria 1971*
Luther 1973
The Asphyx 1973
The Tamarind Seed 1974
Permission to Kill 1975
The Blue Bird 1976
Stevie 1978
Bloodline 1979
Rough Cut 1980
Richard's Things 1981
Sword of the Valiant 1982
Invitation to the Wedding 1985

# Appendix D: Contemporary Style Cinematographers

This is a list of cinematographers and the films they photographed that institutionalized the contemporary style from 1968 to 2001. Some were printed in Technicolor's dye transfer process which disguised the grain and improved contrast in the underexposed negatives. Surviving release prints printed in Eastmancolor prior to 1983 have faded to pink. Many features are available on VHS and DVD. Since video masters are made from first generation materials, they may look better than the original theatrical release prints derived from CRIs or Internegatives.

An asterisk (*) indicates the movie had good color cinematography based on my opinion of what good camerawork should be.

## John A. Alonzo

John A. Alonzo was born in 1934. He began his career as an actor appearing in *The Magnificent Seven* (1960), *The Long Rope* (1961) and *Invitation to a Gunfighter* (1964). His first assignments as a cinematographer were in National Geographic Specials and the TV films, *The Big Land* (1967) and *Sophia: A Self-Portrait* (1968). Alonzo's first theatrical features were *San Sebastian 1746 in 1968* (1968) and Roger Corman's *Bloody Mama* (1970). He photographed the counterculture picture, *Harold and Maude* in 1971 which was printed in Technicolor. Alonzo's utilized diffusion in *China-town* (1974) which many critics noted in their reviews. Other films of his that featured low key muted colors included *Norma Rae* (1979) and *Tom Horn* (1979). Alonzo died in 2001.

FEATURE FILMS

San Sabastian 1746 in 1968
Bloody Mama 1970
Vanishing Point 1971
Harold and Maude 1971*
Sounder 1972
Pete n' Tillie 1972
Lady Sings the Blues 1972
Get to Know Your Rabbit 1972
The Naked Ape 1973
Wattstax 1973
Hit! 1973
Conrak 1974
Chinatown 1974
Jacqueline Susann's Once Is not
   Enough 1975
Farewell, My Lovely 1975
The Fortune 1975
The Bad News Bears 1976
I Will, I Will … for Now 1976
Black Sunday 1977
Which Way Is Up? 1977
Beyond Reason 1977
The Cheap Detective 1978
Casey's Shadow 1978
Norma Rae 1979
Tom Horn 1979

Zorro, the Gay Blade 1981
Back Roads 1981
Blue Thunder 1983
Scarface 1983
Cross Creek 1983
Terror in the Aisles 1984
Runway 1985
Out of Control 1985
Nothing in Common 1986
Jo Jo Dancer, Your Life Is Calling You
   1986
Real Men 1987
Physical Evidence 1989
Steel Magnolias 1989
Internal Affairs 1990
The Guardian 1990
Navy Seals 1990
House Sitter 1992
Cool World 1992
Meteor Man 1993
Clifford 1994
Star Trek: Generations 1994
The Grass Harp 1995
Letter from a Killer 1998
The Dancing Cow 1998
The Prime Gig 2000

## Andrzej Bartkowiak

Andrzej Bartkowiak was born in Poland in 1950. His first feature was *Deadly Hero* in 1976. He is best known for his dark cinematography in films like *Prince of the City* (1981), *The Verdict* (1982) and *Daniel* (1983) where characters often appear in silhouette. Director Sidney Lumet used him for many of his dramas and he is popular with other filmmakers who like this style of low key photography. Barkowiak's last feature was *Thirteen Days* (2000).

FEATURE FILMS

Deadly Hero 1976
Prince of the City 1981
Deathtrap 1982
The Verdict 1982
Terms of Endearment 1983
Daniel 1983

Garbo Talks 1984
Prizzi's Honor 1985
The Morning After 1986
Power 1986
Nuts 1987
Twins 1988

Family Business 1989
Q & A 1990
Hard Promises 1991
A Stranger Among Us 1992
Falling Down 1993
Guilty as Sin 1993
Speed 1994
A Good Man in Africa 1994
Losing Isaiah 1995
Species 1995

Jade 1995
The Mirror Has Two Faces 1996
Dante's Peak 1997
The Devil's Advocate 1997
U.S. Marshals 1998
Lethal Weapon 4 1998
Turkey Cake 1999
Gossip 2000
Thirteen Days 2000

## Michael Chapman

Michael Chapman was born in 1935. He began his career as a camera operator for Gordon Willis in the films, *The Landlord* (1970) and *The Godfather* (1972). Chapman's first feature as a director of photography was *The Last Detail* (1973). Like his mentor, his camerawork and lighting design tends to be dark with muted colors. His work includes *The White Dawn* (1974), *Taxi Driver* (1976) and *The Fugitive* (1993). His latest film was *Evolution* in 2001.

### Feature Films

The Last Detail 1974
White Dawn 1974
Taxi Driver 1976
The Front 1976
The Next Man 1976
The Last Waltz 1978
Fingers 1978
Invasion of the Body Snatchers 1978
American Boy 1978
Hard Core 1978
The Wanderers 1979
Raging Bull 1980
Personal Best 1982
Dead Men Don't Wear Plaid 1982
The Man with Two Brains 1983
The Lost Boys 1987
Bad 1987

Scrooged 1988
Shoot to Kill 1988
Ghostbusters II 1989
Quick Change 1990
Kindergarten Cop 1990
Doc Hollywood 1991
Whispers in the Dark 1992
Rising Sun 1993
The Fugitive 1993
Primal Fear 1996
Space Jam 1996
Six Days Seven Nights 1998
The Story of Us 1999
The White River Kid 1999
The Watcher 2000
Evolution 2001

## William A. Fraker

William A. Fraker was born in 1923. Fraker was a graduate of the USC School of Cinema-Television in 1950. He began his career as a camera operator on *The Adventures of Ossie and Harriet* sitcom in 1952. His first theatrical films were *Forbid Them Not* (1961) and *The President's Analyst* (1967). Although the latter had saturated Technicolor, Fraker was better know for his later work which featured soft-focus and diffused lighting. Among them were *Paint Your Wagon* (1969) and *Heaven Can Wait* (1978). Author Todd McCarthy called him the "Dean of the New Breed cinematographers." Fraker also directed several features including *Monte Walsh* (1970), *A Reflection of Fear* (1973) and *The Legend of the Lone Ranger* (1981). His latest feature as cinematographer is *Waking up in Reno* (2002).

FEATURE FILMS

| | |
|---|---|
| Forbid Them Not 1961 | The Best Little Whorehouse in Texas |
| The President's Analyst 1967* | 1982 |
| Games 1967 | Wargames 1983 |
| The Fox 1968 | Irreconcilable Differences 1984 |
| Rosemary's Baby 1968* | Protocol 1984 |
| Bullitt 1968 | Murphy's Romance 1985 |
| Paint Your Wagon 1969 | Fever Pitch 1985 |
| Dusty and Sweets McGee 1971 | Space Camp 1987 |
| The Day of the Dolphin 1973 | Baby Boom 1987 |
| Coonskin 1974 | Burglar 1987 |
| Rancho Deluxe 1975 | Chances Are 1989 |
| Aloha, Bobby and Rose 1975 | An Innocent Man 1989 |
| Gator 1976 | The Freshman 1990 |
| The Killer Inside Me 1976 | Memoirs of an Invisible Man 1992 |
| Looking for Mr. Goodbar 1977 | Honeymoon in Vegas 1992 |
| Close Encounters of the Third Kind | Tombstone 1993 |
| 1977 | There Goes My Baby 1993 |
| The Exorcist II: The Heretic 1977 | Street Fighter 1994 |
| American Hot Wax 1978 | Father of the Bride II 1995 |
| Heaven Can Wait 1978 | Island of Dr. Moreau 1996 |
| 1941 1979 | National Lampoon's Vegas Vacation |
| Old Boyfriends 1979 | 1997 |
| The Hollywood Knights 1980 | Rules of Engagement 2000 |
| Divine Madness! 1980 | Town and Country 2001 |
| Sharkey's Machine 1981 | Waking Up in Reno 2002 |

## Conrad L. Hall

Conrad L. Hall was born in Tahiti in 1926. He's the son of James Norman Hall who wrote the book, *Mutiny on the Bounty*. Like Fraker, he studied filmmaking at USC. Hall began his career making commercials and industrial films. His first feature as a director of photography was *Edge of Fury* in 1958. His early color films were photographed in the classic studio style including *The Professionals* (1966) and *Divorce, American Style*

(1967). However, beginning with *Cool Hand Luke* (1978) he began to experiment with new techniques. He incorporated lens flares from the sunlight in that picture and photographed images reflected in sunglasses. His desaturated photography in *Butch Cassidy and the Sundance Kid* (1969) won him an Oscar. He adopted a similar look in later pictures like *Fat City* (1972) and *Marathon Man* (1976). He won a second Academy Award for *American Beauty* in 1999. His latest feature is *Road to Perdition* (2002).

FEATURE FILMS

Edge of Fury 1958
Wild Seed 1965
Morituri 1965
Incubus 1965
Harper 1966
The Professionals 1966*
Divorce, American Style 1967
Cool Hand Luke 1967*
In Cold Blood 1967
Rogue's Gallery 1968
Hell in the Pacific 1968
Butch Cassidy and the Sundance Kid 1969
Trilogy 1969
Tell Them Willie Boy Is Here 1969
The Happy Ending 1969

Fat City 1972
Electra Glide in Blue 1974
Catch My Soul 1974
Day of the Locust 1975
Smile 1975
Marathon Man 1976
Black Widow 1986
Tequila Sunrise 1968
Class Action 1991
Jennifer Eight 1992
Searching for Bobby Fischer 1993
Love Affair 1994
Without Limits 1998
A Civil Action 1998
American Beauty 1999
Road to Perdition 2002

## Victor J. Kemper

Victor J. Kemper was born in 1927. His first feature film job as a photographer was as camera operator on *Alice's Restaurant* in 1969. He was the director of photography on *The Magic Garden of Stanley Sweetheart* (1970), *Who Is Harry Kellerman and Why Is He Saying Those Terrible Things About Me?* (1971) and other counterculture films. Later films like *Dog Day Afternoon* (1975) and *Slap Shot* (1977) had a gritty realistic look that many directors adopted in the era. Kemper did shoot with a more conventional studio look in films like *National Lampoon's Vacation* in 1983. His last theatrical film was *Jingle All the Way* in 1996 although he's shot some television pictures recently.

FEATURE FILMS

The Magic Garden of Stanley Sweetheart 1970
Husbands 1970

Who Is Harry Kellerman and Why Is He Saying Those Terrible Things About Me? 1971

They Might Be Giants 1971
The Candidate 1972
Last of the Red Hot Lovers 1972
Shamus 1973
Gordon's War 1973
From the Mixed-up Files of Mrs.
  Basil E. Frankweiler 1973
The Friends of Eddie Coyle 1973
The Gamblers 1974
Dog Day Afternoon 1975
The Reincarnation of Peter Proud
  1975
Stay Hungry 1976
Mickey and Nicky 1976
The Last Tycoon 1976
Slap Shot 1977
Audrey Rose 1977
Oh God! 1977
Coma 1978
The One and Only 1978
The Eyes of Laura Mars 1978
Magic 1978
…And Justice for All 1979
The Jerk 1979
The Final Countdown 1980

Xanadu 1980
Night of the Juggler 1980
The Four Seasons 1981
Chu Chu and the Philly Flash 1981
Partners 1982
Author! Author! 1982
Mr. Mom 1983
National Lampoon's Vacation 1983
The Lonely Guy 1984
Cloak and Dagger 1984
Pee-Wee's Big Adventure 1985
Clue 1985
Secret Admirer 1985
Walk Like a Man 1987
Hot to Trot 1988
See No Evil, Hear No Evil 1989
Cohen and Tate 1989
Crazy People 1990
F/X 2 1991
Another You 1991
Married to It 1991
Beethoven 1992
Tommy Boy 1995
Eddie 1996
Jingle All the Way 1996

## Arthur J. Ornitz

Arthur J. Ornitz was born in 1916. He was the son of "Hollywood Ten" screenwriter, Samuel Ornitz. His first job as cinematographer was in the documentary, *Power and the Land* (1940). After shooting some Scandinavian films in the early fifties, he photographed a number of B&W studio pictures including *The Goddess* (1958), *The Young Doctors* (1961) and *Requiem for a Heavyweight* (1962). His first color film was *Without Each Other* (1962) followed by *The World of Henry Orient* (1964) which had conventional studio camerawork with saturated flash-tones and color. Ornitz was known for his illusion of "source lighting" in later films like *Serpico* (1973) and *Death Wish* (1974). His last theatrical feature was *Hanky Panky* in 1982. Ornitz died in 1985.

### FEATURE FILMS

Power and the Land 1940
Vester Housdrenge 1950
Kranes Konditori 1951
Vi Arme Sydere 1952

The Goddess 1958
Kiss Her Goodbye 1959
The Pusher 1960
The Young Doctors 1961

The Connection 1961
Requiem for a Heavyweight 1962
Without Each Other 1962
Jack Town 1962
Act One 1963
The World of Henry Orient 1964
A Thousand Clowns 1965
A Midsummer Nights' Dream 1966
The Tiger Makes Out 1967
Charly 1968
Change of Mine 1969
Me, Natalie 1969
The Boys in the Band 1970
The House of Dark Shadows 1970
The Anderson Tapes 1971

Minnie and Moskowitz 1971
The Possession of Joel Delaney 1972
Badge 373 1973
Serpico 1973
Black Snake! 1973
Death Wish 1974
Law and Disorder 1974
Forever Young, Forever Free 1976
Next Stop, Greenwich Village 1976
Thieves 1977
An Unmarried Woman 1978
Oliver's Story 1978
Tattoo 1981
The Chosen 1982
Hanky Panky 1982

# Bruce Surtees

Bruce Surtees was born in 1937. He was the son of Robert Surtees, one of the top cameramen who established the "studio look" in large format films. Bruce Surtees began his career as a camera operator on *The Lost Command* (1966) which was photographed by his father. His first features as a director of photography were the Clint Eastwood films *The Beguiled*, *Play Misty for Me* and *Dirty Harry* in 1971. Eastwood utilized him as his cameraman again in *High Plains Drifter* (1972), *The Outlaw Josey Wales* (1976) and *Pale Rider* (1985) among others. Like Conrad Hall, Surtees adopted a diffused, de-saturated look for his Westerns which distinguished them from earlier ones by John Ford, Howard Hawks or Henry Hathaway. Surtees' last film was *Joshua* in 2001.

FEATURE FILMS

Beguiled 1971
Play Misty for Me 1971
Dirty Harry 1971
The Great Northfield Minnesota Raid 1972
Conquest of the Planet of the Apes 1972
Joe Kidd 1972
High Plains Drifter 1972
Blume in Love 1973
The Outfit 1974
Lenny 1974
Night Moves 1975
The Outlaw Josey Wales 1976

Sparkle 1976
The Shootist 1976
Leadbelly 1976
Three Warriors 1977
Movie Movie 1978
Big Wednesday 1978
Escape from Alcatraz 1979
Dreamer 1979
Inchon 1981
Ladies and Gentlemen, the Fabulous Stains 1981
Firefox 1982
Tightrope 1984
Beverly Hills Cop 1984

Pale Rider 1985
Psycho III 1986
Out of Bounds 1986
Ratboy 1986
Back to the Beach 1987
License to Drive 1988
Men Don't Leave 1990
Run 1991

The Super 1991
The Night 1992
The Crush 1993
Corrina, Corrina 1994
The Stars Fell on Henrietta 1995
The Substitute 1996
Just a Little Harmless Sex 1999
Joshua 2001

## Vilmos Szigmond

Vilmos Szigmond was born in 1930 in Hungary. *Hajnal Elott* was his first feature, which was made in that country in 1955. He fled the country with Lasko Kovacs in 1956 and eventually settled in Hollywood where he shot some low budget pictures like *The Sadist* and *The Incredibly Strange Creatures Who Stopped Living and Became Mixed Up Zombies* both in 1963. He made his mark with *McCabe and Mrs. Miller* in 1971 which was one of the movies that established the diffused and de-saturated look. *Heaven's Gate* (1980) was an extreme example of this style. Most of Szigmond's features had dark interiors and low key lighting. He won the Oscar for his work in *Close Encounters of the Third Kind* in 1978 although William A. Fraker and Douglas Slocombe photographed some sequences and Douglas Trumbulls' special effects contributed to the visuals. His last feature was *Bank Ban* in 2001. Szigmond's style of cinematography is an acquired taste I'm not partial to but there's no denying his impact on the medium.

### FEATURE FILMS

Hajna elott 1955
What's Up Front 1963
Summer Children 1963
The Sadist 1963
Living Between Two Worlds 1963
Incredibly Strange Creatures Who Stopped
Living and Became Mixed-up Zombies 1963
The Time Travelers 1964
The Nasty Rabbit 1964
Deadwood '76 1965
Rat Fink 1965
Tales of a Salesman 1965
Psycho a Go-Go 1965
The Name of the Game Is Kill 1968
The Picasso Summer 1969

The Monitors 1969
Futz! 1969
Horror of the Blood Monsters 1970
Five Bloody Graves 1970
The Hired Hand 1971
McCabe and Mrs. Miller 1971
The Ski Bum 1971
Red Sky at Morning 1971
Images 1972
Deliverance 1972
The Blood of Ghastly Horror 1972
Scarecrow 1973
The Long Goodbye 1973
Cinderella Liberty 1973
The Sugerland Express 1974
The Girl from Petrovka 1974
Obsession 1976

Death Riders 1976
Close Encounters of the Third Kind
   1977
Sweet Revenge 1977
The Last Waltz 1978
The Deer Hunter 1978
Winter Kills 1979
The Rose 1979
Heaven's Gate 1980
Blow Out 1981
Jinxed! 1982
Table for Five 1983
The River 1984
No Small Affair 1985
Real Genius 1985
The Witches of Eastwick 1987
Journey to Spirit Island 1988

Fat Man and Little Boy 1989
The Two Jakes 1990
The Bonfire of the Vanities 1990
Silver 1993
Maverick 1994
Intersection 1994
The Crossing Guard 1995
Assassins 1995
The Ghost and the Darkness 1996
Playing by Heart 1998
Illegal Music 1998
The Argument 1999
The Body 2000
Mr. Hughes 2000
Life as a House 2001
Waterlooi Gyozelem 2001
Bank Ban 2001

## Geoffry Unsworth

British cinematographer Geoffry Unsworth was born in London in1914. He began his career as a three strip camera operator on Michael Powell's Technicolor classics, *The Life and Death of Colonel Blimp* (1943) and *A Matter of Life and Death* (1946). His first film as cinematographer was the B&W documentary, *The People's Land* in 1943. His early Technicolor features were *The Laughing Lady* (1946), *The Man Within* (1946) and *Scott of the Arctic* (1948). He was the director of photography of a number of notable films including *Becket* (1964) and *2001: A Space Odyssey* (1968) which featured saturated colors and dramatic composition. Unsworth might be considered one of the "classic studio" cinematographers if it wasn't for his change of look in the seventies. Films like *Cabaret* (1972), *Superman* (1978) and *Tess* (1979) established the diffused style of photography in the medium. Unsworth won Oscars for *Cabaret* and *Tess* although he died during the production and the Academy Award was shared with Ghislain Cloquet.

FEATURE FILMS

The People's Land 1943
The Laughing Lady 1946
The Man Within 1947
Jassy 1947
Blanche Fury 1947
Scott of the Antarctic 1948
The Blue Lagoon 1949

The Spider and the Fly 1949
Fools Rush In 1949
Trio 1950
Double Confession 1950
The Clouded Yellow 1951
Ivory Hunter 1951
Outpost in Malaya 1952

Penny Princess 1952
Made in Heaven 1952
Turn the Key Softly 1953
The Sword and the Rose 1953
The Million Pound Note 1953
The Purple Plain 1954
Land of Fury 1954
Simba 1955
Value for Money 1955
Passage Home 1955
A Town Like Alice 1956
Tiger in the Smoke 1956
Jacqueline 1956
Hell Drivers 1957
Dangerous Exile 1957
A Night to Remember 1958
Whirlpool 1959
Flame Over India 1959
The World of Suzie Wong 1960
On the Double 1961
Why Bother to Knock 1961
The 300 Spartans 1962
Playboy of the Western World 1962
The Main Attraction 1962
An Evening with the Royal Ballet
   1963
Becket 1964*
Tamahine 1964
Genghis Kahn 1965
You Must Be Joking! 1965
Go Go Mania 1965
Othello 1965
Oh Dad, Poor Dad, Mama's Hung
   You in the Closet and I'm Feeling
   So Sad 1967

Half a Sixpence 1967
2001: A Space Odyssey 1968*
Dance of Death 1968
The Bliss of Mrs. Blossom 1968
The Assassination Bureau 1969
The Magic Christian 1969*
The Reckoning 1969
Cromwell 1970
Three Sisters 1970
Goodbye Gemini 1970
Unman, Wittering and Zigo 1971
Say Hello to Yesterday 1971
Cabaret 1972
Love, Pain and the Whole Damn
   Thing 1972
Alice's Adventures in Wonderland
   1972
Voices 1973
Don Quixote 1973
Baxter 1973
The Internecine Project 1974
Abdication 1974
Murder on the Orient Express 1974
Zardoz 1974
The Return of the Pink Panther 1974
Royal Flash 1975
Lucky Lady 1975
A Matter of Time 1976
A Bridge Too Far 1977
Superman 1978
The Great Train Robbery 1979
Tess 1979
Superman II 1980

## Gordon Willis

Gordon Willis was born in 1931. He began his career as a cinematographer by filming the counterculture pictures, *The Landlord* (1970),
*The People Next Door* (1970) and *Little Murders* (1971). Willis established
his reputation as the "Prince of Darkness" with Coppola's *Godfather* films
in 1972 and 1974. Both featured dark, underexposed negatives with portions of the composition in blackness. The colors were warm and primaries were avoided. Woody Allen became enamored with this look and
used Willis for his films, *Annie Hall* (1977), *Interiors* (1978) and *The Pur-*

*ple Rose of Cairo* (1985). His black and white photography in *Manhattan* (1979) received critical acclaim and while there were some nice establishing shots of New York City, the interiors remained dark. Like Vilmos Szigmond's photography, this style is an acquired taste and is not suited for all subjects although in the case of Coppola's gangster classics it did enhance the underworld theme. Willis directed and photographed the film, *Windows* in 1980. He most recent film was *The Devil's Own* in 1997.

## FEATURE FILMS

End of the Road 1970
The People Next Door 1970
Loving 1970
The Landlord 1970
Klute 1971
Little Murders 1971
The Godfather 1972*
Up the Sandbox 1972
Bad Company 1972
The Paper Chase 1973
The Parallax View 1974
The Godfather Part II 1974*
The Drowning Pool 1974
All the President's Men 1976
Annie Hall 1976
Interiors 1978
September 30, 1955 1978
Comes a Horseman 1978

Manhattan 1979
Stardust Memories 1980
Windows 1980
Pennies from Heaven 1981
A Midsummer Night's Sex Comedy
   1982
Zelig 1983
Broadway Danny Rose 1984
The Purple Rose of Cairo 1985
Perfect 1985
The Money Pit 1986
The Pick-up Artist 1987
Bright Lights, Big City 1988
Presumed Innocent 1990
The Godfather Part III 1990
Malice 1993
The Devil's Own 1997

# Notes

## Introduction

1. Maggie Valentine, *The Show Starts on the Sidewalk*, Yale University Press, 1994, page xii.

## Chapter 1

1. *The Film Daily Yearbook 1968*, Wids Films and Film Folk, Inc., pages 104–08.
2. James Morris, "Platitude Challenged," *The Film Daily Yearbook 1958*, page 807.

## Chapter 2

1. Leonard J. Leff and Jerold L. Simmons, *Dame in the Kimono*, Preface xiii, Doubleday, 1991.
2. Arbuckle was later exonerated but his career as an actor was ruined.
3. The Supreme Court later ruled it unconstitutional. The "NRA" seal appears in the credits of some early Warner Bros. musicals.
4. Eric Schaefer, *A History of Exploitation Films 1919–1950*, Duke University Press, 1999, page 37.
5. Brian Crozier, *The Rise and Fall of the Soviet Empire*, Forum 1999, page 74.
6. Deb Riechmann, "Communists tried to slant film scripts, panel told," Associated Press, *The Journal News*, Aug. 25, 2001, page 4A.
7. Victor S. Navasky, *Naming Names*, Viking Press, 1980, page 69
8. Stalin announced the dissolution of the Comintern in 1943 to appease Western allies. It turned out to be one of his misinformation ploys because he replaced it with the Cominform in 1947 which served the same purpose.
9. "The Motion Picture Code and Rating Program," *The Film Daily Year Book of Motion Pictures 1969*, pp. 625–26.
10. The grosses are estimates based on *Variety* listings of initial bookings and do not include sub-run or reissues.
11. Irwin and Debi Unger, *Turning Point:1968*, Scribner's, 1988, page 344.

12. *Independent Film Journal Booking and Buying Guide*, Vol. 65, No. 6, February 18, 1970, Section Two, page 1196.

13. Addison Verrill, "Porno Public's Static Size; 1971 Year of Thrust & Bust; A Few Makers Build B.O. 'Rep,'" Wednesday, January 5, 1972, Sixty-Sixth *Variety* Anniversary, page 7.

14. Earlier pictures were Francis Ford Coppola's *Playboy and the Playgirl* in 1962 and *Swing Tail* in 1969. Condon's StereoVision lenses were later upgraded and used on my mainstream 3-D film, *Run for Cover*, in 1995.

15. Abel Green, "Negro Talent, Riots & Video," Sixty-second *Variety* Anniversary, Wednesday, January 3, 1968, page 4

16. Warner Bros., *The Devils* (1971) also had graphic gore but was rated X.

17. Pauline Kael, *Pauline Kael Reeling*, Atlantic–Little, Brown, 1976, page 249.

18. Lee Beaupre, "Debate Over Brutality," Sixty-Seventh *Variety* Anniversary, Wednesday, January 3, 1973, page 16.

19. Robert J. Landry, "Sex as a Spectator Sport: Liberal Professors Shrug; Incest, Bestiality Treated," Sixty-Ninth *Variety* Anniversary, Wednesday, January 8, 1975, page 10.

20. "Valenti Takes on the Film Critics Vs. Public Taste" (no author listed), Sixty-Fifth *Variety* Anniversary, Wednesday, January 6, 1971, page 34.

21. John Hinckley claimed he was obsessed with the film *Taxi Driver* (1976) and actress Jodie Foster when he shot President Reagan in 1981.

22. Information derived from MPAA website and *The Independent Film Journal Booking and Buying Guides*.

23. Eugene Picker, "Use Research for Number One Job of Recapturing the Lost Family Folk and Older Patrons," Sixty-Fifth *Variety* Anniversary, Wednesday, January 6, 1971, Variety Inc., page 7.

24. *Ibid.*

25. Estimates derived from *Film Daily* Yearbooks and *Variety* Anniversary Editions.

26. Jack Valenti, "Portrait of U.S. Moviegoers Demographics Cue Upped B.O.," Sixty-Seventh *Variety* Anniversary, Wednesday, January 3, 1973, Variety Inc., page 13.

27. Al Alan Friedberg, "The Good News: Hit Films; The Bad News: Rental Terms; Ohio Law Admitted Crucial," Seventy-Third *Variety* Anniversary, Wednesday, January 3, 1979, page 7.

## Chapter 3

1. Jerry Lewis, "Children, Too Have Film Rights," Sixty-Sixth *Variety* Anniversary, Wednesday, January 5, 1972, page 32.

## Chapter 4

1. Dov V. Koepel, editor and coordinator, *Motion Picture Projection and Theatre Presentation Manual* 1969, Society of Motion Picture and Television Engineers, Inc., page 16.

2. Merlin Lewis, "Automation Has Its Place," 1969 *Film Daily Yearbook of Motion Pictures*, page 510.

3. *Ibid.*

## Chapter 5

1. For further technical and historical information about the Technicolor process covered in this chapter, please refer to my book *Technicolor Movies: The History of Dye Transfer Printing* published by McFarland & Company, Inc., 1993.

2. Roger Ebert, *Roger Ebert's Movie Home Companion*, Andrews, McMeel & Parker, 1985, page 165.

3. My first two features contributed to the decline. They looked so awful on large screens that I decided to improve the quality on subsequent productions. I hired topnotch independent cameramen to simulate the classic studio look and even utilized dye transfer and 3-D on two of them.

4. Technical information derived from correspondence with Richard J. Goldberg.

## Chapter 6

1. Syd Silverman, "Show Biz Never the Same Again: New Technologies Change Old Way," *Variety* 76th Anniversary Edition, Wednesday, January 13, 1982, page 1.

2. Paul Klein, "The Network's Incredible Shrinking Pie," Seventy-Sixth *Variety* Anniversary Wednesday, Jan. 13, 1982, page 158.

3. Donald La Badie, "Television: Hollywood's Year," *Film Daily Yearbook 1956*, page 643.

4. Simon Garfinkel, "The DVD Rebellion," *Technology Review* July/August 2001, page 25.

## Chapter 7

1. "NATO Is Silent on Industry-Wide Summit Meet: Next Stop Congress?" (no author), *The Independent Film Journal*, March 31, 1976, pages 5, 27.

## Chapter 8

1. Ralph E. Donnelly, "Special Situations, Supply Discovery, Oddity Repertory," Wed. January 8, 1975, Sixty-ninth *Variety* Anniversary, page 54.

2. The Technicolor process was not available in the U.S. at the time so I had to travel to China to make the prints. The Beijing lab had purchased the dye transfer equipment from England. The facility shut down in 1993. I showed the film at the American Film Institute and donated a print to the Eastmanhouse archive. Leonard Maltin did a segment on the movie and the Chinese facility on *Entertainment Tonight*.

3. The extra running time was needed to incorporate "The Sorcerer's Apprentice" sequence from the original *Fantasia* (1940). The optically enlarged image looked terrible in the Imax format.

4. "300,000 Projectors Sold in the United States," *American Cinematographer*, October 1931, page 42.

5. John Zinewicz, "The Case for Film Piracy," *Classic Film Collector, 1976*, page 33.

## Chapter 9

1. Thomas G. Wallis, Technical Director and Vice President of Entertainment Imaging for Kodak, "Film vs. Video," *Filmwaves* Issue 8, Summer 1999.

2. Ibid.

3. Simon Perry, "Film Trade Ponders Video Projection EMI Experiment Under Scrutiny," Seventy-Fourth *Variety* Anniversary, Wednesday, January 9, 1980, pages 101, 141.

# Bibliography

The documentation of this book was derived from my film archive and library which includes many technical manuals and scrapbooks of articles, magazines and interviews I've compiled over the years. Throughout my career, I've talked with technicians and distributors in all areas of the industry and made notes of their comments on aspects of the business that related to them. For example, I used to discuss film processing and color stability with Frank Houser of Guffanti Film Lab, Jack Rizzo of Metropolis Film Labs and indie distribution with Terry Levine of Aquarius. Prior to forming my own company, I worked for Troma, Inc., for six years and got firsthand experience in the exploitation and sexploitation genres. I spent countless hours in revival theaters in the seventies watching every type of picture from counterculture to midnight cult films. I also went to many roadshow houses in New York including the Cinerama, Rivoli and the National. I saw *Crossed Swords* at the Radio City Music Hall, which was their last feature run as an exhibitor. I even attended grindhouse presentations on 42nd Street before these theaters were torn down. Screenings of original prints in 35mm and 16mm was coordinated with the film collector contacts I used as a source for this book.

## General Reference Materials

The below general reference sources were invaluable in researching box-office information, ratings classification, industry litigation and technical data.

*Film Daily Yearbook of Motion Pictures* 1950–1970, volumes 32–52.
*The Film Daily* (Wid's Films and Film Folk, Inc.).
*The Independent Film Journal Booking and Buying Guide*, 1968–1980, published biweekly by Pubsun Corp.
*Variety* anniversary editions, 1955–2000, Variety, Inc.
*WideGauge Film and Video Newsletter* (Monthly), issues September 1995 — Special Edition 1999 published by Marshall Multimedia.

## General Reference Websites

These websites are a source for some of the subjects covered in this manuscript. I had correspondence with a number of individuals in specific fields.

cinematreasures.com.
film-tech.com.
Jerry Lewis web site.
presentations.com.

technicolor.com.
35mmforum.com.
16mmfilms.com.
widescreenmuseum.com.

## Interviews

While people in all areas of the business were interviewed or questioned over the years, these individuals were quoted or referred to specifically in chapters.

Jeff Brodrick, coordinator of the Jerry Lewis website, correspondence, July 18, 2001.
Bret Charipper, assistant manager of Loews Paradise in Brooklyn, 1953, interview, January 2000.
Tom Cooper, former programmer of the Vagabond Theater, June 22, 2001.
Mitchell Dvoskin, former projectionist in the seventies, August, 2001.
Richard Goldberg, special assistant to the president of Technicolor, correspondence, August 15, 2000.
Robert A. Harris, archivist, correspondence, July 21, 2000.
Martin Hart, of widescreenmuseum.com correspondence, December 16, 2001.
Eric Levin, programmer of Times Cinema, September 20, 2001.

---

Following, chapter by chapter, are reference sources—books, technical manuscripts, periodical articles, and others—that I used for this manuscript.

## Introduction

"Beach Theater Opens August 2" (no author). *The Yorktowner*, Thursday, July 13, 1967.

## 1. Cinema in the Sixties

Cohn, Art. *The Nine Lives of Michael Todd*. Random House, 1958.
Green, Abel, and Laurie, Joe, Jr. *Show Biz, from Vaude to Video*. Henry Holt, 1951.
McGee, Mark Thomas. *Beyond Ballyhoo*. McFarland & Company, Inc., 1989.
Sarris, Andrew. *The American Cinema*. University of Chicago Press, 1968.
Sennet, Robert S. *Hollywood Hoopla*. Watson-Guptill Publishers, 1998.
Todd, Michael, Jr., and McCarthy, Susan. *A Valuable Property: The Life Story of Michael Todd*. Arbor House, 1983.
"Todd's 'World' Anew in Todd Tradition." *Film & TV Daily*, Thursday, January 11, 1968, p. 1.

## 2. Demise of the Production Code

Aspen, Marvin E. "Censorship Just Resting? If MPAA Ratings Fail, Watch Out." *Variety*, Wednesday, January 8, 1969, pp. 5, 7.

Beaupre, Lee. "Debate Over Brutality." *Variety*, Wednesday, January 3, 1973, pp. 16, 32.

Billingsley, Kenneth Lloyd. *Hollywood Party: How Communism Seduced the American Film Industry in the 1930s and 1940s*. Forum, 1998.

Boyd, Malcolm. "The New Morality in Films." *Variety*, Wednesday, January 3, 1968, pp. 5, 32.

Breindel, Eric, and Romerstein, Herbert. *The Venona Secrets*. Basic Books, 1999.

Brode, Douglas. *The Films of the Sixties: From* La Dolce Vita *to* Easy Rider. Citadel Press, 1980.

Brownlow, Kevin. *Behind the Mask of Innocence: Sex, Violence, Prejudice, Crime: The Films of Social Conscience in the Silent Era*. Alfred A. Knopf, 1990.

Brownstein, Ronald. *Power and the Glitter: The Hollywood-Washington Connection*. Pantheon Books, 1990.

Cagin, Seth, and Dray, Phillip. *Hollywood Films of the Seventies: Sex, Drugs, Violence, Rock 'n' Roll and Politics*. Harper & Row, 1984.

Cole, Lester. *Hollywood Red: The Autobiography of Lester Cole*. Ramparts Press, 1981.

Crozier, Brian. *The Rise and Fall of the Soviet Empire*. Forum, 1999.

Friedman, David F. "Wages of Sin David F. Friedman interviewed by Davic Chute." *Film Comment*, Aug. 1986, pp. 32–48.

Ginsberg, Allen. *Howl*. Viking Press, 1987.

Green, Abel. "Show Biz Hurt by Violence Campus & Racist Mobs Mark '68." *Variety*, Wednesday, January 8, 1969, pp. 1, 56.

Hayes, R.M. *3-D Movies: A History and Filmography of Stereoscopic Cinema*. McFarland & Company, Inc., 1998.

Haynes, John Earl. "Hellman and the Hollywood Inquisition." *Film History*, Volume 10, 1998, pp. 408–14.

Hill, Morton A. "To Women Degraded by Porn: Ring the Bell." *Variety*, Wednesday, January 3, 1979, pp. 16, 46.

Hopper, Dennis, Fonda, Peter, and Southern, Terry. *Easy Rider*. Signet, 1969.

Kael, Pauline. *Pauline Kael Reeling*. Atlantic–Little, Brown, 1976.

Karp, Alan. *The Films of Robert Altman*. Scarecrow Press, 1981.

Kerouac, Jack. *On the Road*. Viking Press, 1963.

Kinsey, Alfred C. *Sexual Behavior in the Human Female*. Pondview Books, 1953.

_____. *Sexual Behavior in the Human Male*. Pondview Books, 1953.

Landry Robert J. "Films, Poitier & Race Riots." *Variety*, Wednesday, January 3, 1968, p. 12.

_____. "Sex as a Spectator Sport: Liberal Professors Shrug, Incest, Bestiality Treated." *Variety*, Wednesday January 8, 1975, p. 10.

Leab, Daniel J. *From Sambo to Superspade: The Black Experience in Motion Pictures*. Houghton Mifflin, 1975.

Leff, Leonard J., and Simmons, Jerold L. *The Dame in the Kimono: Hollywood, Censorship and the Production Code*. Doubleday, 1991.

Lorence, James J. "The Suppression of Salt of the Earth in Midwest America." *Film History*, Volume 10, 1998, pp. 346–358.

Marcuse, Herbert. *One Dimensional Man*. Taylor and Francis Books, 1991.

McCarty, John. *Splatter Movies*. Fantaco Pub., 1981.

McDonough, Jimmy. *Sexposed*. Film Comment, Aug. 1986, pp. 53–61.

Medved, Michael. *Hollywood vs. America, Popular Culture and the War on Traditional Values*. Harper Collins, 1992.

Mintz, Marilyn D. *The Martial Arts Films*. A.S. Barnes, 1978.

Navasky, Victor S. *Naming Names*. Viking Press, 1980.

Null, Gary. *Black Hollywood: From 1970 to Today*. Carol Pub. Group, "A Citadel Press Book," 1993.

Randall, Richard S. *Censorship of the Movies: The Social & Political Control of a Mass Medium*. University of Wisconsin Press, 1968.

Reich, Wilhelm. *Beyond Psychology: Letters and Journals 1934–1949*. Farrar, Straus & Giroux, 1994.

_____. *Children of the Future: On the Prevention of Sexual Pathology*. Pondview Books, 1984.

_____. *Cosmic Superimposition: Man's Orgonotic Roots in Nature*. John Gach Books, 1951.

Reisman, Judith A., and Eichel, Edward W. *Kinsey, Sex and Fraud: the Indoctrination of a People: An Investigation Into the Human Sexuality Research of Alfred C. Kinsey, Ward B. Pomeroy, Clyde E. Martin and Paul E. Gebhard*. Pondview Books, 1990.

Riechmann, Deb. "Communists Tried to Slant Film Scripts, Panel Told." Associated Press, *The Journal News*, Saturday, August 25, 2001, p. 4A.

Rotsler, William. *Contemporary Erotic Cinema*. Ballantine, 1973.

Schwartz, Richard A. *Cold War Culture*. Checkmark Books, 2000.

Segrave, Kerry. *Movies at Home: How Hollywood Came to Television*. McFarland & Company, Inc., 1999.

Siomopoulos, Anna. "Entertaining Ethics Technology, Mass Culture and American Intellectuals of the 1930s." *Film History*, Volume 11, 1999, pp. 45–54.

Sorlin, Pierre. "The Cinema: American Weapon for the Cold War." *Film History* Volume 10, 1998, pp. 375–381.

Spiro, Elaine. "Hollywood Strike — October 1945." *Film History*, Volume 10, 1998, pp. 415–418.

Unger, Irwin and Debi. *Turning Point: 1968*. Scribner's, 1988.

"U.S. Rage of Chop-Socky Films: Karate Breaks Out of Chinatown" (no author listed). *Variety*, Wednesday, January 9, 1974, p. 72.

Valenti, Jack. "Now: A 'Great Age' in Films Another Shift in Taste Due?" *Variety*, Wednesday, January 6, 1971, pp. 5, 36.

Wexler, Norman. *Joe, A Screenplay*. Avon Pub., 1970.

## 3. Multiplexes and Twinning

Anderson, Theodore W. "Jury Is Still Out on Videodisks: Mull Chances for Broad Market." *Variety*, Wednesday, January 13, 1982, pp. 1, 38.

Beacher, Robert L. *Multi-plexing Your Theatre? Careful Planning Is a Must*. President, Forest Bay Construction Corp. East Rockaway, N.Y., advertisement.

Foster, Frederick. "Movies on Tape." *American Cinematographer*, June 1956, pp. 352–84.

Frazer, Joe. "Do Customers Care? A Crucial Question for Film Industryites." *Variety*, Wednesday, January 8, 1997, page 85.

Gillette, Don Carle. "Though Losing Patronage, Distribs Ignore Middle-America Situations: Thousand of Managers 'Uncourted.'" *Variety*, Wednesday, January 5, 1972, p. 32.

Golding, David. "Scared Showmen's Plot to Kill Film Ballyhoo: Where's the Glamour of Old?" *Variety*, Wednesday, January 6, 1971, p. 5.

Lewis, Jerry. "Children, Too Have Film Rights." *Variety*, Wednesday, January 5, 1972, p. 32.

Michie, Larry. "Showmen Await 'Carnal' Appeal; Failure of National Criterion Clouds 1st Amendment Issue." *Variety*, Wednesday, January 8, 1974, pp. 1, 50.

Milick, Jim. "Seeing Films in the Theater: Jim Milick Talks to Richard Vetter." *The Perfect Vision*, Volume 3 issue Number 12, Winter 1991–1992, pp. 54–61.

Mitchell, Jack. "Get Back to Showmanship: Or Advice to Film Exhibs." *Variety*, Wednesday, January 8, 1975, page 36.

Nicholson, James H., and Arkoff, Samuel Z. "How to Offset Drop from 50–75,000,000 to Today's 25-Mil Weekly Admissions." *Variety*, pp. 7, 20.

Picker, Eugene. "Use Research for Number One Job of Recapturing the Lost Family Folk and Older Patrons." *Variety*, Wednesday, January 6, 1971, pp. 7, 18.

"The Screening Room." *TV Guide Dec. 7–Dec. 13, 1974*, Triangle Publications, page A-5.

Stone, Barbara. *America Goes to the Movies: 100 Years of Motion Pictures Exhibition*. National Associate of Theatre Owners, 1993.

Tharp, Paul. "Canadian Cops to Snap Drabinsky." *The New York Post*, Friday July, 6, 2001, p. 29.

Valenti, Jack. "Portrait of U.S. Moviegoers Demographics Cue Upped B.O." *Variety*, Wednesday, January 3, 1973, pp. 13, 62.

Valentine, Maggie. *The Show Starts on the Sidewalk: An Architectural History of the Movie Theatre*. Yale University Press, 1994.

## 4. Projection

Belton, John. *Widescreen Cinema*. Harvard University Press, 1992.

Carr, Robert E., and Hayes, R.M. *Wide Screen Movies*. McFarland & Company, Inc., 1988.

Eastman Kodak. *Cleaning Release Prints*. H-50-10, 1980, Technical manuscript.

_____. *Film Handling*. H-5-2, 1976, Technical manuscript.

_____. *The Kodak Book of Film Care*. Technical manuscript.

_____. *Projection Practices and Techniques*. H-50-3, 1977, Technical manuscript.

_____. *Troubleshooting and Prevention of Damage*. H-50-4, 1977, Technical manuscript.

Fielding, Raymond. *A Technological History of Motion Pictures and Television*. University of California Press, 1974.

Happe, Bernard. *Basic Motion Picture Technology*. Focas Press, Ltd., 1971.

Kloepfel, Don V., editor and coordinator. *Motion Picture Projection and Theater Presentation Manual*. The Society of Motion Picture and Television Engineers, Inc., 1969.

## 5. Cinematography

Coe, Brian. *A History of Movie Photography*. Westfield, NJ: Eastview Editions, 1981.

Eastman Kodak. *Manual for Processing Eastman Color Films Module 8 Effects of Mechanical & Chemical Variations in Process ECN-2*. 1968, Technical Manuscript.

_____. *Manual for Processing Eastman Color Films Module 9 Process ECP-2A and ECP-2B Specifications*. 1988, Technical Manuscript.

_____. *Manual for Processing Eastman Motion Picture Films Module 7 Process ECN-2 Specifications*. H-24-07, 1990, Technical Manuscript.

_____. *Manual for Processing Eastman Motion Picture Films Module 3*. H-24-03, 1991, Technical Manuscript.

Ebert, Roger. *Roger Ebert's Movie Home Companion*. Andrews, McMeel & Parker, 1985.

Higgins, Scott. "Technology and Aesthetics, Technicolor Cinematography and Design in the Late 1930s." *Film History*, Volume 11, 1999, pp. 55–76.

Maltin, Leonard. *The Art of the Cinematographer: Survey and Interviews with Five Masters*. Dover, 1978.

McQueen, Scott. "From the Archives Two-Color Technicolor: The Early Years of Film Color." *The Perfect Vision*, volume 3, issue 10, Spring 1991, pp. 57–61.

Ryan, R.T. *A History of Motion Picture Color Technology*. Focal Press, 1977.

## 6. Home Entertainment Revolution

Daniel, Ralph W. "The View from Fifth Row Center, Who Killed Laserdiscs?" *WideGauge Film and Video Monthly*, November 1997, Volume 2, Number 11, pp. 9–10.

Fischetti, Mark. *The Future of TV*. Technology Review, November 2001, p. 35.

Foster, Frederick. "Movies on Tape." *American Cinematographer*, June 1956, pp. 352–384.

Fremer, Michael. "Inexpensive Combination Laserdisc/CD Players Compared, The Perfect Vision." Volume 3 issue Number 10 Sprint, 1991, pp. 86–88.

Garfinkel, Simon. *The DVD Rebellion*. Technology Review, July/August 2001, p. 25.

Gelman, Morrie. "Cable at Crucial Crossroads: Time to Deliver on Promises." *Variety*, Wednesday, January 13, 1982, pp. 154, 181.

Klein, Paul. "The Network's Incredible Shrinking Pie." *Variety*, Wednesday, January 13, 1982, p. 158.

Tristram, Claire. *Broadband's Coming Attractions*. Technology Review, June 2001, p. 70.

## 7. Distribution Changes in the Seventies, Eighties and Nineties

Bach, Steven. *Final Cut: Dreams and Disasters in the Making of Heaven's Gate*. William Morrow, 1985.

Belton, John. "The Rivoli." *The 70mm Newsletter* Issue 59, December 1999.

McKeon, Elizabeth, and Everett, Linda. *Cinema Under the Stars: America's Love Affair with the Drive-In Movie*. Cumberland House, 1999.

Sanders, Don and Susan. *The American Drive-in Movie Theater*. Motorbooks International, 1997.

_____. *Drive-In Movie Memories*. Carriage House Publishing Company, 2000.

Segrave, Kerry. *Drive-In Theaters*. McFarland & Company, Inc., 1992.

## 8. Alternate Venues

*American Cinematographer*, October 1931.

Auiler, Dan. *Vertigo: The Making of a Classic*. St. Martin's Press, 1998.

Belton, John. "Cinecolor." *Film History*, Vol. 12, Number 4, 2000.

_____. "Getting It Right: Robert Harris on Colour Restoration." *Film History*, Volume 12 Number 4, 2000, pp. 392–409.

Cooper, Duncan. "Who Killed Spartacus." *Cineaste* Vol. XVIII, No. 3, 1991, pp. 18–27.

Davis, Ben. "Children of the Sixties." *Film Quarterly*, Summer 2000.

Donnelly, Ralph E. "Special Situations Supply Discovery, Oddity, Repertory." *Variety*, Wednesday, January 8, 1975, p. 54.

Frumkes, Roy. "Spartacus an Epic Restoration." *The Perfect Vision*, Volume 3, Issue Number 10, Spring 1991, pp. 62–73.

Gebhart, W.W. "Home Movie Theatre Deluxe." *American Cinematographer*, Aug. 1957, pp. 518–530.

Hart, Martin. "The New Neon Experience." *WideGauge Film and Video Monthly*, October 1966, Volume 1, Number 11, pp. 6–7.

Hershenson, Karen. "Arrival of the Media Room." *Gannett Newspapers*, Saturday, May 23, 1998, p. 7.

Higgins, Scott. "Demonstrating Three-Color Technicolor: Early Three-Color Aesthetics and Design." *Film History*, Volume 12, Number 4 2000, pp. 358–383.

Job, Mark Andrew. "Standing Room Only in the Projection Booth: The Audience Demanded to Know Why the Picture Looked So Good." *WideGauge Film and Video Monthly*, December 1997, Volume 2, Number 12, page 11.

Josephson, Marvin. "Imax 3-D Review L5: First City in Space." *WideGauge Film and Video Monthly*, September 1996, Volume 1, Number 10, pp. 1, 4–8.

Kaufman, Dave. "D.A. Probes Burbank Studio Man on 1,200 Recovered Film Reels." *Variety*, Aug. 10, 1983.

Kuiper, John B. "A National Rescue Mission for Film at the Library of Congress in D.C." *Variety*, Wednesday, January 3, 1973, p. 36.

Marshall, Scott. "Dayton!" *WideGauge Film and Video Monthly*, October 1966, Volume 1, Number 11, pp. 1–4.

_____. "Imaxgate." *WideGauge Film and Video Newsletter*, April, 1996, Volume 1, Number 5, pp. 1, 14.

_____. "Interview with Robert A. Harris, Restorer of Large-Format Films." *WideGauge Film and Video Newsletter*, February, 1996, Volume 1, Number 3, pp. 8–13.

Morris, George. "Home Movies Trimming the Classics." *Take One*, Volume 6, Number 2, January 1978.

Rasin, Lawrence, and Morris, Robert L. *Lawrence of Arabia: The 30th Anniversary Pictorial History*. Doubleday, 1992.

Reeves, Hazard. "This Is Cinerama." *Film History*, Volume 11, 1999, pp. 85–97.

Reilly, Jim. "Film Buffs of the World Gather in Salina." *Syracuse-Herald American*, Sunday, March 10, 1991.

Sweeny, Daniel. "Home Theater and Its Double Collecting Original Movies— The Reel Thing." *The Perfect Vision*, Volume 5, Issue 19, Fall 1993, pp. 26–36.

Trace, Maurice. "The British Collecting Scene." *Classic Images Review*, November 1979, p. 12.

Vadeboncoer, Joan. "Cinephiles Gather for Film Orgy." *Syracuse Herald-Journal*, Thursday, March 7, 1991.
Zinewicz, John. "The Case for Film Piracy." *Classic Film Collector*, 1976, p. 33.

## 9. Digital Cinema

Bartley, Rashonda. "Cinematography Panel Tackles New Technology." *Variety*, Aug. 30–Sept. 5, 1999.
Fine, Marshall. "Hollywood Goes Digital." *The Journal News*, Sunday, Dec. 26, 1999.
Lyman, Rick. "New Digital Camera Poised to Jolt World of Filmmaking." *The New York Times*, Friday, Nov. 19, 1999.
Marshall, Scott. "Texas Instrument's 'DLP' Digital Projection." *WideGauge Film and Video Monthly Special Edition 1999*, Volume 4, Number 1, pp. 1, 10–11.
Woods, Mark. "Future Shock: What Images Will Survive the Digital Revolution's Next 25 Years?" International Cinematographers Guild.
Wuntch, Phillip. "Digital Cinema Is Something You'll Want to Take a Look At." *The Dallas Morning News*, Dec. 5, 1999.

# Index

259